CAPITALISM, GOD, AND A GOOD CIGAR

Capitalism, God, and a Good Cigar

CUBA ENTERS THE TWENTY-FIRST CENTURY

edited by Lydia Chávez ∼ *with photographs by Mimi Chakarova*

DUKE UNIVERSITY PRESS   *Durham and London   2005*

© 2005 Duke University Press

All rights reserved

Printed in the United States of

America on acid-free paper

Designed by C. H. Westmoreland

Typeset in Sabon by Tseng Information

Systems, Inc.

Library of Congress Cataloging-in-

Publication Data appear on the last

printed page of this book.

To Cubans for

inventing, surviving, and inspiring.

And to my father, Manuel Chávez,

for the same

Contents

Acknowledgments

I have had the good fortune to work at a wonderful university with colleagues who are deeply committed to training reporters in Latin America. Harley Shaiken, the chair of the Center for Latin American Studies at UC Berkeley, has been especially supportive. Harley is one of few people I know who finds it more difficult than myself to say no, and for that I am grateful. Beatriz Manz, a former chair of the center, has also been tireless in advocating for Latin American projects. Orville Schell, my dean, graciously raised money and encouraged me to spend the time that it took to finish this book.

Amanda Crater, Angelica Jiménez, and Camilo Romero researched many of the articles, but were not attached to any single one. The Freshman Seminar Program run by Alix Schwartz offered generous support.

Vice Provosts Christina Maslach and Jan de Vries and Professor Angelica Stacy have encouraged creative projects. Tom Engelhardt assisted with two of these pieces directly and inspired all of them. Others who helped enormously include Professor Susan Eckstein, Professor María Cristina García, Cynthia Gorney, Paul Grabowitz, Rob Gunnison, Mayra Espina Prieto, Tiffany Mitchell, Richard Nuccio, Susan Rasky, Sandy Tolan, Roberto Guareschi, Carlos Chamorro, Teresa Stojkov, and Carolyn Wakemen.

Valerie Millholland at Duke University Press discovered this book, and Miriam L. Angress helped it along. Kate Lothman and Petra Dreiser were careful, close readers.

Marty Baron, Sandra Salmans, Leslie Wayne, Barbara Wright, Cecilia O'Leary, and Tony Platt have been faithful readers and editors. Mimi Chakarova is not only a wonderful photographer but a diligent reporter. Leslie and Merle Rabine make life better. My siblings Manuel, Andrea, Robert, Susana, and Martin have been close allies through many projects. Professors Penn Kimball and Bernard Taper continue to enrich my teaching.

We are fortunate here to have an incredible staff who make sure we get the finest students and then manage them once they arrive. We especially owe thanks to Gayle Allerson, Roy Baril, Hellen Ettlinger, Mary Anne Glazar, Scott Hacker, Lanita Pace-Hinton, Marcia Parker, and Michele Rabin.

Other students pitched in at the last minute. They include Edward Carpenter, Jonathan Jones, Daniel Moulthrop, Matthew Wheeland, Anna Sussman, Cyrus Farivar, Erin Sweeney, Hillary Briscoe, Melisa Masuda, Tiffany Hsu, Sara Kahlenberg, Molly McLucas, and Colette Hollander.

Felix Varela Sánchez, a Cuban journalist, was invaluable.

Finally, our international reporting program requires an enormous amount of funds, and we are fortunate to have generous friends of the school, including the Center for Latin American Studies, Purnendu Chatterjee, Manuel and Geraldine Chávez and family, Frank and Christine Currie, Gina Despres, Richard Goldman, Peter and Mimi Haas, Peter Halmos, the Koret Foundation, Richard Liu, Nan McEvoy, the McClatchy Papers, Herb McLaughlin, the Open Society Institute, Simone Otus-Coxe, Stephen Silberstein and Anne Lipow, and Nadine Tang and the Tang family.

My husband Mark Rabine is a close reader and a patient sounding board, and he makes all the difference in the world. My daughters, Geraldine and Lola, manage to keep a sense of humor through these projects and inspire with their grit.

Adrift

An Introduction to Contemporary Cuba

∼ LYDIA CHÁVEZ

Is it possible that the secret of Fidel Castro's endurance comes down to standard-issue eyeglasses? Can such a fragile accessory sustain or threaten Latin American governments?

I have been following Cuba for two decades. Twice I led a group of students from the University of California at Berkeley, teaching them how to report on foreign affairs. The first such trip, in 1992, produced a magazine, the *Pacific*. It captured the island's early struggle to survive the end of Soviet subsidies and trade. The second, in 2001, became the basis for this book, portraying Cuba's venture into a sort of never-never land between communism and capitalism. For more than a decade, from the time Castro legalized trading in U.S. dollars in 1993, the island has drifted between two opposing economic systems. Each chapter of this book offers a different glimpse of what it is like to live in a place caught between these two extremes. Even when Castro tried to get rid of the dollar at the end of 2004 and replace it with the convertible peso—known as the *chavito*, or toy money—it was the dollar that continued to reign. *Chavitos* could not be had without dollars, and no amount of economic hocus-pocus could undo that fact.

My own interest in Cuba began in Central America in 1983 when, at the height of U.S. involvement there, I reported on El Salvador for the *New York Times*. No matter how savage the Salvadoran forces—the massacre of thousands of its own citizens, including an archbishop, priests, and labor leaders, or the murder of American nuns and aid workers—the Reagan administration supported the government. It was determined that El Salvador not become another Cuba, a situation that, in Washington's eyes, had already occurred in nearby Nicaragua under the Sandinistas.

The American government spent more than a billion dollars to save El Salvador from this fate, and nearly as much to reverse the Sandinista revolution. Covering Central America and seeing what the U.S. government tried so hard and paid so handsomely to avert, I had to wonder: How bad *was* Cuba?

When I left the *New York Times* and began teaching at Berkeley in 1990, I decided to find out. I was late. By 1992, the Cuban Revolution's golden years—or at least what people there referred to as the consummate revolutionary experience—had long gone. The island's Soviet benefactor no longer existed. It no longer had partners willing to buy its overpriced sugar or its market-priced grapefruit. And those ready to sell Cuba the oil, wheat, and rice the island needed to feed its 11 million residents wanted hard cash.

Hal Klepak, a professor of Latin American history and international relations at the Royal Military College in Kingston, Canada, tallied up the damage in a 2000 report for the Canadian Foundation for the Americas. "In 1988, the USSR imported 63 percent of Cuba's sugar, 73 percent of its nickel, 95 percent of its citrus products and 100 percent of its electrical exports. At the same time, Moscow sold the island 98 percent of its fuel and 90 percent of its machinery and other equipment imports and the Comecon countries accounted overall for 87 percent of Cuba's foreign transactions. By 1992 Havana found these arrangements had gone." So had everything else. Havana in 1992 existed in an odd, becalmed quiet: No gasoline meant no traffic. No trading partners meant no food. No movement or trade meant no trash; the city looked as if it had been picked clean. From the outside, stores appeared closed, but in fact, clerks stood in the dark behind nearly empty counters. Everywhere, Cubans waited— at bus stops, in front of bare government stalls, or in front of Coppelia, the downtown ice cream store that my father and I saw open only once during our week-long visit. Stories circulated about the ways in which Cubans subsisted. A Cuban steak? The fried skin of one of the grapefruits that used to be exported to the Soviet Bloc. Breakfast? A couple of tablespoons of sugar.

Some mornings my father and I would leave our hotel to walk the city, returning at night to see the same people waiting in lines. Few begged in 1992, but it became clear in brief conversations with any Cuban that they could use a good meal. No matter the educational level—and most had studied or were studying for some degree—none were shy about asking for something to eat. The dynamic unsettled. Where had we ever been that well-spoken, literate locals asked for food? Meeting their requests

Rationed goods sold at a government store, Havana, 2001.
Photo by Mimi Chakarova

presented a challenge since few restaurants existed; most tourists went directly from the airport to Varadero's beaches.

In the daily scenes of deprivation, one luxury stood out: eyeglasses. In all my time in Latin America, I had never seen poor children wear glasses. Here in Cuba, someone somewhere was taking care that children with bad eyesight could see. In the context of Latin America, the eyeglasses presented a miracle. I began to think that Castro could not be written off so easily. Conversations with Cubans confirmed this. The fear and visceral hate rampant in El Salvador and Chile in the 1980s simply did not exist in the Cuba of 1992. Castro and Cubans shared something absent elsewhere in Latin America: goodwill. If medicine was no longer available, doctors and nurses stood by to do what they could. Even in crisis, Cuban citizens lived longer and stayed in school more hours than nearly all of their Latin American contemporaries. It seemed unlikely that Cubans would rise up against someone who provided.

And yet, there was something missing that made Cuba feel disappointing. On that same trip, I also met intellectuals and ordinary Cubans who craved information and a connection with the world beyond their island. Cubans had long lived with censored newspapers, magazines, and television programs, and maybe that had worked when they could read or hear about the country's exploits in Central America and Africa or win a trip to one of the Soviet Bloc countries. Those days, however, were gone. Cubans could only look inward: what they saw was a country with Soviet-Bloc drabness and third world scarcities.

Cuba's plight touched off a wave of prophecy by journalists and academics. "It is only a matter of time before Cuban communism collapses," wrote one in *Foreign Affairs*. Another began his piece, in *Newsweek*, with the words, "Fidel Castro is doomed." Walking around Havana, talking to Cubans, I did not see it that way. So when I returned to the island a few months later with my students to produce an issue of the *Pacific* devoted to Cuba, I asked them to focus on what was actually happening on the ground. "If express mail is any barometer, Cuba is alive with business interest," wrote Lee Romney, one of my students. She noted that a new courier service provided by DHL had expanded 300 percent in sales, with "mail going mostly to Mexico, Italy and Spain."

It was not only business that Cuba was trying; the country was ready to attempt anything to stay afloat. Cubans talked of deals with Brazil, Spain, and Mexico. On the island, government workers were sent to the countryside to work in food brigades, scientists practiced new biotechnology techniques at the state-of-the-art Center for Genetic Engineering and Biotechnology, and urban gardens sprang up throughout Havana. We visited workers in the field, scientists in their labs, and Cubans working the soil with small hand shovels. In 1992, these had yet to produce much food or currency—but they were more than empty rhetoric. And at the same time, an earlier gamble was paying off. Nearly 400,000 tourists arrived in 1992 to vacation at the new resorts in Varadero. "Why put a name on it, capitalism, socialism?" Ramón Depromo, a commercial specialist with the government's original tourism organization, asked Michael Arnold in the *Pacific*. "A 'renovated economy,' let's call it."

But in it, goods were scarce. "Everyone smokes in Cuba, but nobody has any matches," joked one security guard. Humor would not sustain even the most dedicated revolutionary for long. Julio Carranzas, a Cuban economist, says that Castro knew well in 1990 that any goodwill would vanish if severe shortages created inflation, panic, and violence. So, to plug inflationary pressure and prevent hoarding, the government froze

Family on wheels, Camagüey, 2001. *Photo by Mimi Chakarova*

prices and imposed rationing; to avoid mass unemployment, it "promised to send money to the government enterprises," so that workers could
keep their jobs even though little could be done without fuel. "Where did
we find the money?" Carranzas asked rhetorically when I visited him in
2004. "We printed it."

The final element of the plan, Carranzas says, was to give Cubans a
sense that they shared the pain equally. The crisis received a name in
early 1990: the Special Period. By the time my students and I arrived
in 1992, freshly painted slogans, "Socialism or Death," were ubiquitous.
That bought Castro time to see if any of his schemes made for signs of life
or panic. At the end of the trip, Mark Nollinger wrote of Castro's demise,
"It hasn't happened yet and there are few signs that it will any time soon.
But life in Cuba today is anything but easy or predictable."

But the Cuban exile community was. In Castro's struggle, they saw the
opportunity to strike, and they played their hand through Representative
Robert Torricelli, a Democrat from New Jersey, a state with one of the
largest concentrations of Cuban Americans. With Castro reaching out to
anyone who might help, Torricelli proposed a bill—the Cuban Democ-

racy Act of 1992—that punished those who dared to do business with the "enemy." Among other restrictions, it forbade the foreign subsidiaries of U.S. corporations to trade with Cuba. "President George Bush fretted that the bill might offend U.S. trading partners," reported *Newsweek* that September. "Then Bill Clinton, on the stump in Florida railed: it's time 'to put the hammer down on Castro.' "

President Bush was right; the country's trading partners were offended. One month after he signed the bill, the United Nations General Assembly voted fifty-nine to three with seventy-nine abstentions in support of a resolution that called on the United States to end the embargo. The gesture might have been symbolic, but what followed was not: The countries that supported the UN resolution continued to do business with Cuba. And why not? With an embargo that excluded Americans from trade, Cuba was a businessman's paradise. "Many small and medium-sized enterprises that would not dare compete against the United States could compete here," said Jorge Mario Sánchez-Egozcue, a researcher at the Center of U.S. Studies at the University of Havana in 2004. And Cuba had an urgent need for everything that could be sold: wheat and rice to feed its citizens and everything from furniture to bottled water to supply the tourist industry.

The scheme averted panic, but in 1992, new problems, including prostitution and inflation, emerged. Cubans could subsist on their pesos for a month, but just barely. And sometimes rations failed to show up at the government stalls. So Cubans went to the black market, but to enter they needed pesos, lots of them. By 1992, the black market exchange had jumped to thirty to one from twelve to one in 1991. By 1993, it was up to one hundred fifty to one, according to Sánchez-Egozcue. A chicken in government stores cost 2 pesos—that was if you could find one. On the black market, they easily went for 120 pesos. "Anything is for sale, a computer or a submarine," one psychologist told my student Hugo Martínez McNaught in 1992. Her journalist husband added: "To sell is the verb in fashion. People conjugate it in every way: I sell, you sell, he sells. . . . If one doesn't sell, one perishes."

In 1990, the slogan "Socialism or Death" might have sounded defiant; by 1993, it merely sounded hopeless. But Castro was not ready to give up. Imagine, if you will, a young, handsome Castro leading a failed attempt in Santiago to overtake the Moncada barracks in 1953. He is arrested and jailed, but becomes a hero after delivering a speech that details his vision and proclaiming "history will absolve me." Now fast-forward forty years to the anniversary of the Moncada attack. Castro is sixty-six years old. His country is bankrupt. The U.S. government hates him. The Miami exile community hates him. But who cares? They have something he wants: dollars. And he is willing to reverse decades of revolutionary rhetoric to get them. Cubans, he announces on the fortieth anniversary of Moncada, can hold, receive, and welcome dollars. If Marx rolled over in his grave, the immediate impact must have absolved Castro of any self-doubt. Remittances from abroad jumped from 43 million dollars in 1992 to 470 million dollars by 1994 and by the end of the decade reached more than 700 million dollars, Lorena Barberia wrote in an MIT working paper.

Castro also began to shed other hallmarks of a communist state: Soviet-style state farms were converted into cooperatives. Farmers' markets, where some products could be sold at market prices, opened, and some areas of self-employment were allowed. New tax laws went on the books. Some of the country's free services such as sporting events and medical prescriptions were eliminated or their subsidies reduced. Finally, in the summer of 1994, came the ultimate concession. With Cubans illegally setting sail for Miami, a skirmish between police and some of the *balseros*—so-called because of the rafts they left on—triggered a riot. After visiting the site, Castro threw up his hands. "What does it matter to us if they want to go?" he asked. With that one question, he signaled a new policy. Within days, thousands more pushed their rafts out to the sea.

Castro's safety valve—letting the unhappy depart—became President Clinton's nightmare. It looked like the 1980 Mariel boatlift that ended with some 125,000 Cuban refugees in Florida. U.S. officials ran to the negotiating table. In exchange for a new immigration deal that permitted 20,000 Cubans a year to enter legally, Castro promised to clamp down on those who tried to float to freedom. By the time that happened in September 1994, 33,000 Cubans, maybe those who most wanted to leave and thereby those most likely to create trouble at home, had gone. But as Archana Pyati found when she spent time with some *balseros*, this wave of Cuban immigrants differed from that which had come earlier. They did not hate Castro. Rather, they resembled Mexican immigrants who travel north to the United States: for many, a job, not politics, lured them into the sea.

On the island, the tension subsided and life there began to improve. From here on, journalists and others stopped predicting the end. Cuba,

Taxi car at the Plaza de la Revolución, Havana, 2004.
Photo by Mimi Chakarova

the most distant of the Soviet satellites, was the only one to survive. This was the country that my class and I visited in 2001. It seemed both remarkably resilient and ineffably sad, not unlike the melodies from the *Buena Vista Social Club* that we heard replayed nearly everywhere we visited on the island. In this book, we seek to describe both the possibilities of Castro's dream and its limits. When I returned to the country in 2004, it was still very much caught between the two.

"This is the land of magical realism," Fernando tells Juliana Barbassa in one of the essays in this book. "Incredible things happen every day so that people can go on. People invent." Invention is necessary because Cubans earn salaries in pesos but depend on dollars from abroad or earned on the island to buy anything more than the basic staples. Inventing often means ignoring the law, but it is hard for the government or the neighborhood committees for the defense of the revolution to keep track. Inventing, says Julian Foley's unofficial tourist guide in his contribution, is the national sport.

And invention pays off. After the economy bottomed out in 1994, all of that earlier activity—sending workers to the countryside to plant beets, planting urban gardens, breaking up the state farms and investing in tourism—began to bear impressive fruits. Some 26,000 urban gardens produced more than half a million tons of organic fruits and vegetables. The number of tourists had quadrupled. New trading partners had been found, and although they did not entirely replace the Soviet Bloc, they did permit some economic growth.

By 2001, Havana looked a changed city. Traffic and entrepreneurs jammed the streets selling cigars, guided tours, or rooms. The restoration of Old Havana and its stunning examples of baroque, neogothic, and neoclassical architecture went on with a vengeance. On Sundays, farmers sold truckloads of produce and thick slices of pork to make and sell sandwiches. At one of dozens of workshops, artists sold their work. "Anything for a dollar," proclaimed one collage.

Anything but pure capitalism, that is. While there are joint ventures with plenty of foreign investors, Cuba remains a tightly centralized economy—albeit one that carefully invests most of its money in sectors that produce foreign exchange. In one of the following essays, Daniela Mohor describes a model collective tobacco farm that she visited. Far from the madness of Havana, cigar rollers in Pilotos live the life of the earlier revolution, but at a capitalist pace. "The government still sets the price of tobacco and furnishes fertilizer and agricultural supplies, but [now] productivity counts," writes Mohor. "The more farmers grow, the more they earn, and part of their income is in dollars." But Cuba's other famous crop, sugarcane, no longer proved cost-effective, so in 2002 and 2003, the government shut down 72 of the country's 156 mills. The workers have been sent back to school or to work in the ever-expanding citrus groves.

And what about those places that do not generate dollars? There, Alicia Roca writes, Cubans struggle mightily to create life out of nothing. "Six years without lunch," one teacher tells Roca. "I am so hungry." While most Cubans live in pursuit of the dollar, the literary and cultural community also pursues art. In her article, Annelise Wunderlich depicts the hip hop scene. "They deserve a very good record deal," a producer tells Wunderlich about two young rappers, Yosmel Sarrias and Maigel Entenza Jaramillo. But, she notes, when their session is over, "they still need to borrow a dollar to catch a bus back home." Trips abroad relieved Entenza's frustrations, but in 2004, when I return for a visit, he is no closer to a record contract. The only change is an additional thirty or so pounds.

A dancer for the Ballet Nacional de Cuba stands next to a photo of founder Alicia Alonso, Havana, 2004. *Photo by Mimi Chakarova*

"I couldn't stop eating once I reached the States," he says as he gets some air in front of El Atelier, a new nightclub where Cubans and tourists go to hear music. If the food was good in New York, however, the nightlife in Venezuela scared Entenza to death. Every time he went outside of his hotel room there, he says, someone was getting killed for a pair of sneakers.

Eduardo Blanco, the young choreographer interviewed by Ana Campoy, still lives in Cuba, but five of the national ballet's dancers defected to the United States in 2003 and another fifteen to twenty left for other countries. Perhaps concerned about Blanco's own commitment, Alicia Alonso, the ballet's director, permitted him to produce a modern ballet in the Gran Teatro in January 2004. Audiences were thrilled. "I would like to work internationally," he says, and he expects that to happen.

Still, artistic freedoms, like economic progress, come at an uneven pace. Raúl Rivero Castañeda, an independent journalist who became part of Ezequiel Minaya's reporting on Cuba's literary community, complained about police harassment in 2001, but managed to work. In March 2003, his life changed dramatically when he and seventy-four independent journalists, librarians, and other alleged dissidents found themselves arrested. Within a month, they were tried and sentenced to jail for up to twenty-seven years. By the end of 2004, Rivero and eleven others had been released. The arrests and the releases were the government's way of reminding Cubans that if it could not keep tabs on the daily infractions, it could come down hard when it wanted to. The prominent writer Antón Arrufat says that with the exception of Rivero's arrest, the censorship of the literary community has actually eased. He is ready to publish a slim new novel that he describes as "softly" critical of the government. And Arrufat predicts that his friend Rivero will be released early. Still, Arrufat himself is reluctant to tempt fate. I can attribute his quotes in a book, he says, but not in a newspaper article.

As in so many dictatorships, the Internet represents an insuperable challenge. The black market in Internet accounts, John Coté tells to us, grew so large that in January 2004, the government announced that it was putting new restrictions on telephone lines. But Cuban hackers will quickly find a way around Castro. On the steps of Havana University, a group of fifth-year math students smile when asked how they make extra money in 2004. The Internet, of course. Private companies hire them to create Web pages, paying them in dollars.

While the peculiarities of carrying out business in never-never land are muted by the country's need for foreign exchange, diplomacy, like art, proves trickier still. Megan Lardner writes about the return of the Spanish investor and the new alliance between Cuba and its old conqueror. That relationship was already strained politically after the conservative prime minister José María Aznar took power in 1996, but it continued to slide, and the Spanish Cultural Center closed in 2003. The March 2003 sweep of dissidents has thrown relations between the European Union and Castro into a standoff. The total number of foreign joint ventures declined by 15 percent in that year, with Spain's interests falling while Canada and Italy increased their shares, according to *Granma*, the Communist Party's daily newspaper. The defeat of Aznar in 2004, however, promised that relations between Cuba and Spain would again warm. In the meantime the United States has emerged as the biggest new player. The U.S. embargo has been partially lifted to favor American products. Cubans cannot sell anything in the United States, but since 2001, U.S. companies have been able to export food and some agricultural products. Agricultural exports reached 256 million dollars for 2003, according to

C. Parr Rosson III, the director of the Center for North American Studies at Texas A&M University.

As they have since 1993, Cubans still live between two worlds, and more than ten years of being adrift have taken their toll. Castro's irrational clampdowns and the race for dollars has produced a collective exhaustion. It is tiring dodging the tax collector, police, or neighborhood spies to earn the dollars needed to live. It is wearing to obey the rules of who can buy a car or travel abroad. And Cubans say it is discouraging to earn pesos that mean less than the dollars of a government for so long portrayed as the enemy. If the burden of the crisis was shared somewhat fairly in 1992, that no longer holds true. Those without dollars can readily see the benefits derived by those who have greenbacks. With their new jeans and stylish jewelry, some Cubans on the island look no different than those shopping in Miami, while others—many of them Afrocubanos—appear to shop only in peso stores.

But even for those with access to dollars, expectations are constantly cut back, and that brings fatigue. "You start out with a plan, and then you make so many compromises that you don't even recognize the idea you started with," says one young man who graduated at the top of his class. A visitor to his family's home—the ceilings crumbling despite the children's best efforts to maintain it—discovers how he survives. He opens a door to reveal shelves of CDs and a guitar. "This is my escape," he says. "They are not going to take away my spirit." Others have turned to religion. "As Cubans again begin to consider God—some for the first time—profound theological and social questions arise," Bret Sigler writes. "Who is God? Who needs him? And whose God are Cubans likely to worship?"

National exhaustion has left Cubans without a lot of hope that their seventy-seven-year-old dictator will be able to take them into the twenty-first century. But still, it is unlikely Cubans will turn him out before he dies. Instead of unrest, there is a kind of paralysis—borne from a mix of loyalty, fear, and indoctrination—as they grudgingly wait for him to die. Castro's government may be the ultimate example of the saying that what comes around goes around. His survival may boil down to those eyeglasses that stood out on my first visit.

Unlike so many elected governments in Latin America, Castro has actually provided his constituents with public services, and he has done so without earning a reputation for corruption. "His leadership also helped Cuba forge a strong sense of peoplehood and solidarity," Jorge I. Domín-

Playing chess, Havana, 2004. *Photo by Mimi Chakarova*

guez, a professor of international affairs at Harvard, wrote in the *New York Times* in 2003. "Cuban schoolchildren are among the world's best performers, with Cuban fourth graders outscoring all Latin American students in mathematics tests. And the rate of infant mortality is lower in Havana than in Washington." All of that is hard to ignore. Even World Bank president James D. Wolfensohn acknowledged in 2001 that Cuba had done a "great job" on education and health care.

Unlike the Eastern Bloc residents who rose up against corrupt political leaders—and some Latin Americans who have done so more recently in Bolivia, Argentina, and Ecuador—Cubans get something from their government. And, unlike other Latin American leaders who live the life of the rich and famous, Cuban officials do not flaunt lavish lifestyles. Among Latin American countries, only Chile and Uruguay rate better than Cuba in Transparency International's corruption index. Antonio Lacayo, a former Nicaraguan official in the democratic government of Violeta Barrios Chamorro, told me that he visited Cuba several years ago and was astonished to see a high government official driving a beat-up Soviet-made Lada. In 2003, the Cuban government began reinvesting some of the tourist dollars to upgrade schools that had deteriorated in the years following the loss of Soviet aid. "Cubans are still endeared by that," says one Canadian resident.

But are eyeglasses enough? I would not want to live in Cuba. Even once daily life improved considerably in the 1990s, the earlier sense of isolation and sensory deprivation remained. But then I am privileged. What would peasants in Nicaragua, El Salvador, or elsewhere in Latin America say? Two in the piece by Olga R. Rodríguez, describe Cuba as, "a paradise, a dream come true, and an example for El Salvador to follow." For these two Salvadorans, one on kidney dialysis, "life here couldn't be better."

The final paradox of Cuba is that life there might look good compared to elsewhere in Latin America, but Cubans rarely compare their home to other Latin American countries. All that education has raised expectations. Cubans talk about Madrid, Paris, New York. Listen to the educated professional with a wife and two children. He takes a breath when he recalls his trip to Spain. "It's hard to explain how I felt when I went there," he says. "It wasn't like another world or another planet. It was like another galaxy." With family in Spain, he could emigrate, but he does not consider the option seriously. "This is where I want to live, but 5 percent of the way things are run has got to change. They blame everything on the embargo. We have a self-imposed embargo. We limit ourselves."

And if the strongest image from my first trip was the child with eyeglasses, the most lasting one from my visit in January 2004 was this: At a rehearsal studio, a young Cuban ballet dancer turns through the air, pivoting as though some invisible power has unfurled him in an arc. Then, without pause, he leaps once, twice, and I gasp at the height of his *grands jetés*, and then gasp again because the room is too small and his pointed toe is heading right for a barre. It's Cuba—a country that dazzles and disappoints, a place where one finds miracles and monsters, but no easy answers.

A closing word on this project. Although the major part of the reporting was done in 2001, where appropriate the articles were updated in 2004. The final essay by Ángel González is a personal piece about his journey to a country that he grew up hearing of. The pieces are placed in order adhering to a certain logic, but readers can flip first to the topic that interests them: religion, cigars, ballet, or the Internet. They can be read individually, but together they offer a fuller picture of what it has been like to live in Cuba during the past ten years.

PART ONE ~ *Inventing*

The New Cuban Capitalist

〜 JULIANA BARBASSA

Heat waves rising from the cracked pavement make the red flower print on a plastic bag shimmer. A bored teenager, the third in line for a public phone, shifts impatiently, her lemon yellow Lycra top glaring bright in the sun. Second in line, a man in a baseball cap checks her out, but settles his glance on the tourist fumbling in her huge American backpack for change, a credit card, or whatever these Cuban phones take.

"Where are you from? Spain?" he asks, without waiting for an answer. "Where are you staying?" When he finds out where, and that I'm paying fifteen dollars a night, he laughs and rolls his eyes. "I can offer you a room for much less. . . . Close by, a block and half, maybe two. Come see."

Welcome to Cuba. The public phone takes only dollars, and the portly, hot dog vendor nearby prefers them too. So do the neighborhood kids, who give a lost tourist directions for a dollar fee, and the cab driver, who won't take Cuban pesos from a foreigner—even as a tip. He wants dollars. So does the Cuban government.

This may still be Castro's Cuba, but the evils the revolution came to vanquish—the dollar, tourism, private enterprise, and inequality—are pushing through. Described by Castro as necessary evils, these small allowances to capitalism are taking root and seeding change at every level of Cuban society. The advent of the dollar and private enterprise means that the worker's paradise now has winners and losers. Staying close to the party line and putting in hours in a state-owned company for a peso salary no longer guarantee a good living. This is a new game, and the one with the most dollars wins, whether the money comes from hard work or relatives abroad.

Surprised Cubans are seeing the other face of government. In addition to providing public service, which in Cuba includes health and education, the government also taxes the entrepreneur and competes against businesses for tourist dollars. Still, even with tight regulations, a little taste of economic freedom goes a long way. "It was like giving an asphyxiating patient a breath of oxygen," says Marta, who rents rooms in her house. "First, he recovers. Then he wants more."

To get more, Cubans everywhere, in legal businesses and in underground markets, tweak the rules and cheat the state. Highly educated Cubans have dumped low-paying professional jobs to work in tourism for dollar tips. In the race for dollars that followed economic reforms in the 1990s, Cubans use what they have: they rent their houses, sell the country's communist appeal (Che berets and T-shirts), and invent a thousand ways to stretch what little income they have.

The Special Period, first introduced in early 1990, had its origins in the November 1989 fall of the Berlin Wall. And it became an enduring concept of economic hardship when the Soviet Union dissolved in 1991. Easy credit and cheap oil were gone. Cuban sugar, which had been sold at artificially high prices, found no buyers, and the island's fragile economy, fed on subsidies and barely standing on its old sugar and tobacco legs, collapsed. "With the demise of the Soviet Union, we had to change, says Antonio Ravelo Nariño, a Cuban economist. "It was like a wedding; if one person dies, you can't expect the other to go on living with the dead. We were trying to live with the dead."

The government opened the island to tourists and their dollars, but that was not enough. To control spiraling inflation, the threat of unemployment, and a grinding depression, Castro gave in to what was already happening in black markets and inside homes all over the island: he legalized the possession of dollars. He also allowed small private enterprises to flourish under tight regulations and permitted foreigners to invest in mixed ventures. "If we hadn't been allowed to fend for ourselves, put up our businesses, things would have exploded," Alejandro, the hot dog vendor by the payphone explains as he polishes the shiny aluminum countertop.

If Cubans had to scramble for hard currency to survive, so did the government. When tourist dollars were not enough to pay expenses, the government looked for ways to cash in on the remittances that relatives abroad sent to Cubans on the island. The answer came in the form of government-owned dollar stores. These quickly appeared on every corner, selling everything from Italian biscotti to television sets. The majority of Cubans, however, still lived on pesos, and with an average wage of 240 pesos, about 12 dollars in 2001 (9 dollars in 2004), families shared what they had to squeeze by on the basics. But for anything more, Cubans everywhere went and go into the streets to make up the difference between their peso salary and the dollar reality. "This is the land of magical realism," Fernando explains on the way to showing me the room he has for rent. "Incredible things happen every day so that people can go on. People invent."

Inventing a living is how engineers like Fernando end up on a Havana sidewalk convincing a tourist to follow him home. His is the story they all tell: his peso salary in a management position with a state-owned company was never enough, and since the legalization of dollars in 1993, he has been earning his dollars any way he can—selling instant photographs that he takes of couples in restaurants, renting pirated videos, and sometimes renting a room in the home he shares with his sister. Inventing.

He has no license for renting rooms, but like many other Cubans, Fernando has mastered the tightrope walk between punishable illegalities and everyday infringements that most officials ignore. Renting videos was not one of the categories of self-employment that the government legalized, but from the second floor in one of Havana's old mansions with soaring twenty-foot ceilings, peeling paint, and faulty plumbing, Fernando makes his own rules. One tape goes for twenty-five cents, a bargain next to the official government rate—five dollars a membership and one dollar per tape. What is really priceless is the selection: while state-owned video rentals limit the movies available to those that have been officially sanctioned, Fernando's solid wood china cabinet offers a range of new releases that rivals Blockbuster's shelves: *Terminator*; *Crouching Tiger, Hidden Dragon*; and three hundred others. Cubans, he explains, as he flips from channel to channel through a pirated satellite hookup, prefer action and violence. He stops at the Playboy Channel. "I don't record this stuff. A government official might look the other way if his kids are watching rented movies, but if they start watching pornography, then he might want to find out where it is coming from," he says, shrugging off the question about what would happen if he were caught. "When ordinary things become crimes, then you make an ordinary man a criminal," he says. The television set flickers. *Urban Legends*, a popular series, comes on. He starts recording.

Not all private businesses on the island are outside the law. In 2001, there were 150,000 legal, licensed businesses in Cuba, ranging from shoe shiners and plumbers to small restaurants and private homes that rent rooms to tourists. A few chosen occupations—initially 110, and later 157

A loaf of bread rests on the seat of a broken motorcycle, Havana, 2004.
Photo by Mimi Chakarova

—opened up for private enterprise in fits and starts. The number varies according to governmental whim, and in 2004, new meetings were underway to determine if the number would change. "The government tries to limit this sector as much as possible," says Roberto Orro, a Cuban economist living in Puerto Rico. "It had to accept it because there was no other option, but it was certainly against its will. There are people who are not politically faithful to the government, and now those people have the possibility of obtaining a certain economic independence."

Paladares, for example, the tiny restaurants named after a canteen in a Brazilian soap opera, were ordered shut in February 1994, with Castro accusing the owners of the still tax-free establishments of illicit enrichment. The need to create employment and jump-start the economy forced the restaurants open again weeks later, and the *paladares* were finally legalized on June 8, 1995, in Resolution 4/95, according to professor Joseph L. Scarpaci at Virgina Polytechnic Institute and State University. The informal restaurants operate under tight rules and close inspections by several government agencies that have the right—if not the manpower—to check everything from hygiene to tax compliance. These regulations squeeze many legal businesses underground. Once they disappear from government lists, the businesses that give street life in Cuba its flair—1950s taxi cabs and food vendors—flourish without taxes or regulations, making enough money to pay the occasional fines and still make a comfortable living.

Meanwhile, legal *paladares* can only serve food bought at government-owned dollar stores at retail prices. The rules say receipts must be kept handy for frequent monthly inspections that can come any time between 5:00 a.m. and 10:00 p.m. The establishments are forbidden from having live entertainment and must stay away from main streets and popular tourist hubs. But it is difficult to know to what extent these rules are respected since even legal businesses seem to follow some of the rules while ignoring others.

Take Fernando's favorite *paladar* in Santa Fe, forty minutes west of Vedado, past the upscale oceanside neighborhood of Miramar and far from where most tourists stray. We get to the seating area in the backyard by walking under the front hedge, along the house, and through the patio where dozens of caged parakeets hang amid ferns. When we emerge from the ferns, we run into the restaurant owner, who stands elbow deep in blood, dissecting fresh chicken. She prefers not to give her name.

"Our advertisement are our clients," she says, explaining why no visible sign hangs out front. Her sister, who is squatting on the floor inspecting buckets of chicken parts, is more direct: "Unnoticed, we do much better than by calling attention to ourselves." A quick glance around shows why the two sisters want to keep their secret: the first rule for *paladares*, no more than twelve customers at a time, is disregarded. This place has twelve tables. A restaurant this busy also needs many employees, which according to rules, should all be family members. Are they? "Well," says the owner, laughing with her knife in hand. "It is as if we were all a big family. Everyone puts this address in their identity booklets, so that when inspectors come . . . you know."

I wonder if all that chicken was bought from a government dollar store, as mandated by the law. These are fresh, not frozen, and in residential areas like this, a quick stroll is long enough to spot chickens scratching in the backyard, or to catch the unmistakable whiff of a homegrown pig.

A few feet away from the owner, on white plastic tables facing the ocean, the guests enjoy fried chicken and the breeze for just a handful of dollars. Far from tourist-heavy Havana, this place caters to Cubans who have thrived in the changing economy. The prices are lower than down-town—$2.50 for rice, beans, fried bananas, and fried chicken—but still in dollars. The owners have also done well, and the temptation to do even better is hard to resist.

To attract business to state-owned restaurants, the government does not allow *paladares* to serve seafood, although some of course do. With the ocean a few feet away, and family members working as fishermen, the two sisters are proud to point out that this is one rule they respect. "There are those who take the risk, but we try to stay safe," the owner says. "So many of them have been shut down, but we are still here."

As with Fernando's video business, the secret of surviving is in know-ing which rules to respect and in having a friendly relationship with your inspectors. Watching the sisters, Fernando tells me about a friend who rents rooms without a license and pays his neighborhood inspector fifty dollars a month to get away with it. "One month, he didn't have enough. He told the inspector, and immediately the man started naming the in-fractions he was committing: renting a room, serving food to foreigners without the proper sanitary precautions. . . . My friend ran out and bor-rowed the money really quick."

At an open-air market by El Malecón, Havana's main seaside walk, William, a sculptor, echoes these concerns. As he talks, he whittles ebony into the slender figures of Cuban *guajiros*, peasants, and naked *mulatas* (mulattas) he sells to tourists. "They didn't tell you to close down, but when they saw people were getting ahead in life, they started to force you to close: taxes went up all the time, until you were barely making a living, and the inspectors came at any time of the day to see if all the people working have licenses." William and his brothers make a handsome living, finishing the month with more than one hundred dollars each in a country where the average wage is a fraction of that. However, like other Cubans who first experimented with profit a few years ago, he found taxes and regulations to be an unpleasant yoke. In 1992, when he and his brothers first started selling the sculptures they made as a hobby, they paid noth-ing to the state, since what they did was illegal. In 1993, selling arts and crafts became legalized—and soon the tax hikes began, from 2 dollars a month in 1993 to 159 a month, plus a daily fee of 3 dollars for using the market. The monthly tax is fixed, independent of earnings, and another year-end tax is based on revenue.

Vegetable Market, Camagüey, 2001. *Photo by Mimi Chakarova*

Other businesses also pay taxes unheard of a few years ago: to rent a room to tourists in Vedado, the home owner pays a monthly tax of 250 dollars per room; to run a private cab that charges in dollars, the taxi driver pays 225 dollars every month. "Nowhere do people pay taxes like this," William says, shaking his head in frustration. It is hard to tell whether William is really overtaxed, or just unfamiliar with the way capitalist countries work. But even if the legal businesses pay over half their income in taxes, Cuba's budding entrepreneurs are still making a killing relative to others on the island. William's complaints about taxes have a familiar ring: he sounds like small business owners everywhere. He just doesn't know it.

"There is no small business culture in Cuba," says Mayra Espina, a sociologist with a prominent research center in Havana, the Centro de Investigaciones Psicólogicas y Sociológicas (Center for Psychological and Sociological Research). "They don't know how it works in other countries, and they feel they are being strangled by taxes and rules. When small businesses sprang up in Cuba illegally, they had profit margins of 500 percent. With 200 percent gains, they think they are suffering. This doesn't mean the government isn't tightening the screws, but of course they also have to contribute to the state, and follow rules like everyone else."

In spite of their ingenuity and flexible understanding of regulations, Cuba's entrepreneurs are "a sector on the defensive," says Gillian Gunn Clissold, a professor at Georgetown University. "The Cuban government has become much more fierce about self-employment. It definitely is tightening restrictions and imposing new ones." Santa Fe alone had twenty-two *paladares* in the mid 1990s, when self-employment had just been authorized, and Cuban families began to dream in dollars. By 2001, there were only two, and since then, the government has stopped issuing any more licenses for room rentals or *paladares*. This neighborhood is no exception.

"Self-employment was never fully accepted by the government," says Espina. "They saw it as a necessary evil, and the tension continues. When self-employment goes up, there is always a reaction: taxes go up, inspections are more rigorous, permits are no longer issued." Legal businesses may be closing, as government officials say—but they might be simply slipping off the official rolls, out of the government's grasp, and into the island's booming underground economy. There, no one pays taxes, and the only rule is to stay in business. Flourishing illegal enterprise helps Havana feel far from depressed. "There are a lot of people doing this illegally," says Eugenio Espinosa Martínez, an economist who teaches at the University of Havana. "No one knows how many, but you see them all over town."

In fact, any conversation with a restaurant owner or a stroll down old Havana's cobblestone streets will show that even Cuba's legal businesses exist on both sides of the law. Just about any curbside stall offers examples of the ingenuity that allows Cubans to survive. Instead of buying all his wood from government supply stores, William, the sculptor, whittles some of his figurines from the banisters and roof beams taken from old Havana's crumbling mansions. The taxi driver who takes a tourist home at night is likely to ask him or her to agree on a price beforehand, to avoid turning on the meter: "You pay less to me, I make a little extra money." Gisela, who rents rooms in her home, doesn't declare all the rooms she has for rent.

Joaquina, a sociology professor at the University of Havana who also rents rooms to make ends meet, explains, "This isn't the black market;

there is nothing hidden. It is the market. Period." She started hosting foreigners during the Special Period, "right around the time when even toilet paper was scarce. I decided we'd had enough." Her husband, Bienvenido, a sailor, returned home from his trips with food and clothing that
the family sold to neighbors. Paying under the table with black market
money, they moved their four-person family to a five-bedroom apartment
with two bathrooms. More sailing brought more goods for sale, and they
bought beds. Soon they had a profitable bed-and-breakfast that caters to
the visiting professors and scholars Joaquina meets through the university.

In 1997, as soon as it was possible, she legalized her business and now
pays the necessary taxes. Her business is perfectly legal, but talking over
breakfast, she explains the web of small illegalities and daily infractions
that she and others participate in. Take the bread, she says, pointing to one
of the tasteless, crumbling rolls Cubans buy at a subsidized price. "The
bakery workers stretch the government-rationed flour and oil, making
bread that weighs just a little less than it should," she says. "At the end of
the day, they make extra loaves, which they sell for a profit to people like
me." While she talks, the doorbell rings. The neighborhood pharmacist
is delivering her daughter's migraine medicine. Home delivery in Cuba?
"This medicine only comes once in a while," she explains. "He knows we
need it, and that we can pay in dollars, so he got the prescription from
a doctor he knows. When the medicine comes in, he brings it over. That
way we don't have to check at the pharmacy every week, and he makes a
little extra."

Joaquina and Bienvenido established their bed-and-breakfast and live
on the winning side of the dollar divide. They can afford home delivery,
weekends on the beach with the family, and occasional dinners in one of
Havana's *paladares*, where they drink their beers next to tourists. Like
small business owners everywhere, they needed capital to start up. In a
country where credit or loans are nonexistent, and salaries never see the
end of the month, raising money is one of the most significant barriers to
establishing even a small business.

However, the dollars sent by Cubans living in Miami, Spain, or Costa
Rica could change that. Already the more than 700 million dollars in
yearly remittances supply would-be capitalists like Fernando, who rents
videos without authorization, with seed money. He relied on money sent
by his mother and brother who live in Miami to buy the VCRs he needed

Western Union,
Havana, 2001.
*Photo by Mimi
Chakarova*

to set up his video rental business. Whether the money helped start a business or put food on the table, remittances have become a lifeline for the economy of the country and for the families receiving them. When the government legalized remittances in dollars in 1993, the country breathed a collective sigh of relief. The Cuban government used the tourist dollars and whatever it could capture of the remittances to buy basics such as oil abroad, and to keep the bare essentials of its social system in place: subsidies on basic food items, and Cuba's renowned public health and education system.

"The net balance of these measures was positive for the government," says Orro, the Cuban economist living in Puerto Rico. "They managed to preserve the regime, and people felt relieved." Adds Fernando, "During the Special Period, we went through a phase called option zero, meaning zero gas. Horses and mules were used even in cities." Even today, bicycles and bicycle taxis are common means of transportation. Cubans came close to starvation, Joaquina says. She remembers an epidemic of scurvy in Havana, when fresh fruit could not reach the city because government truckers had no money for gasoline. The advent of the dollar changed all that. But even while the American currency brought some prosperity to Cuba, dollars also brought inequality.

Salaries in state-owned companies, which employ the vast majority of Cubans, are still low, but in 2001, teachers, police officers, lawyers, doctors, and nurses received a raise. Some workers get dollar bonuses that go from five dollars to twenty dollars as incentives to keep their poorly paid state jobs, and to take the edge off their frustration. Others, like Joaquina, get a monthly supply of essential items only available in dollar stores, such as soap, deodorant, and toothpaste. However, the gap between the life these professionals lead on peso salaries and the lives of friends who can get about a hundred dollars a month in legally allowed remittances—an amount that varies depending on changes in U.S. and Cuban laws—is too deep to be affected by a few more pesos or a month's supply of shampoo. Large income gaps exist between neighbors and family members, and the relationship between work and wage is distorted by the effortless affluence brought to some families by the dollars from abroad. "This is the negative side of remittances," says Gunn Clissold, the Georgetown University professor. "In Cuba, you can live very well doing absolutely nothing if you are lucky enough to have relatives abroad. And you can work your butt off, you can be the most industrious, hard-working, entrepreneurial person on the island, but if you don't have access to dollars, your children are probably running out of food at the end of the month. It has encouraged a mentality that reward is not related to work."

The division between those with dollars and those without widens as Cubans who get money from abroad put it to work, setting up their own businesses and generating even more dollars. "This money betters the quality of life of those who receive it, but they create a difference among neighbors that did not exist before," says Marta, who rents rooms in her apartment and also receives money from her son in Miami. A picture of him posing beside his car sits on the living room coffee table. It faces away from the enormous home entertainment system that takes up a corner of the room. "A simple salary in pesos does not allow people to live with these same comforts," she says. "But I see it as a necessary evil."

Not everyone likes Cuba's new source of income or the dollar economy. Those who had bet on staying close to the party and moving up the ladder, accessing scarce privileges along the way, feel cheated. They watch as the relatives of emigrants, who used to be at best ideologically suspicious, become the new, moneyed elite. "Many saw this as a betrayal," says Fernando. "They saw their possibilities diminishing along with their salary. They wanted to be recognized for their dedication to the common project, and many really wanted an egalitarian society." The shift away from old Marxist rhetoric has been difficult, Joaquina explains. The ones who learn fast take advantage of the new system. The ones who don't, sink. "We have to educate people all over again, to teach them to live in a capitalist world, even if we are in a socialist country," she says. "Before, after ten, fifteen years working in the university, you got a car. You had the right to a car. Now, no one gives you anything, though some are still waiting."

It is dollars that count, but behind every hotel counter, every state taxi, and every dollar store is a government employee paid in pesos. The greenbacks go to the government; the employees also give a portion of their tips back to the government and then share the rest. This also holds true for Cubans who work for foreign companies doing business in Cuba. And there are an increasing number. "The Cuban workforce is excellent," says Demarco Epifanio, the head of Brazil's Cuban subsidiary of the oil company Petrobras. "But there are no links between Petrobras and the Cuban employee; we contract them through the state. If I need someone, I call Cuba Petroleum. I pay them, for example, two thousand dollars a month for an accountant. They pay the accountant maybe some four hundred pesos." The government pockets the difference. The same is true in all foreign enterprises. Employees only keep their dollar tips.

But to make sure it gathers even those modest sums and remittances, the government has established *tiendas de recaudación de divisas*, literally, stores for the recapture of hard currency. That's where Cubans must go for just about anything they need. The prices are high: three hundred dollars for a thirteen-inch television or thirty dollars for a tabletop fan. The inflated prices at dollar stores effectively act as a hidden tax on the dollars Cubans earn in remittances. Any attempt to tax this income would simply drive them underground, so government stores absorb the dollars instead. "These dollar stores?" asks Ravelo, a Cuban economist. "They're there

A Cuban tries his luck at the small business of selling goldfish,
Havana, 2001. *Photo by Mimi Chakarova*

for those who get remittances. The government gathers up these dollars,
and with them buys what it needs."

Of course, there are Cubans who do not have dollars. For their convenience, the government has posted CADECAS—*casas de cambio* or exchange booths—all over the island. There, tourists can sell their dollars,
but when Cubans try to buy these dollars with pesos, what they get
are Cuba's version of Monopoly money—*pesos convertibles*, convertible
pesos, or *chavitos*, as they are known. On the island, they are worth the
same as dollars and can be spent at any government dollar store. Leave
the island, however, and the game's over; *chavitos* have no value.

Chavitos are an unusual economic tool, and one of the more curious
aspects of Castro's efforts to reap dollars for its own uses. With these
convertible pesos in circulation, "the government does not have to sell
dollars," says Espina. "They buy dollars, which they can use, and they
sell *chavitos*, which people can still use as if they were dollars." *Chavitos*
came about when the government felt the need to reward state workers
with some access to the dollar stores, but did not want to let go of the dol-

lars it had. "Different sectors started emitting vouchers that were worth so many dollars," explains Espinosa. "Soon, there were so many vouchers in circulation that no one knew which ones were valid."

It's hard for the economy to function effectively with three different currencies in circulation, and economists agree that this measure must be limited to the period of economic recovery. How long that will take, however, is anyone's guess. There are positive signs. The economy grew modestly at an average rate of 3.18 percent a year from 1994 to 2004, according to economists in both the United States and Cuba. "We need to learn to compete within the harsh reality of a capitalist world, even as a socialist country," says Silvia Domenech, a professor of economy at the Escuela Superior del PCC, the Cuban Communist Party's school of higher education.

At the end of 2004, Castro attempted to take dollars out of the economy by making Cubans convert their dollars into chavitos and trade in the convertible pesos. But, other than giving the government an automatic—and considerable—10 percent commission on the exchange, dollars still fueled the economy and remained in circulation. Since 1993, Cuba's economy has stabilized, but in 2004, inflation showed signs of increasing, and the Cuban peso hovered at around twenty-six pesos to a dollar, compared to twenty to a dollar in 2001. The island still needs hard currency, and Castro needs more than just a stable economy. "Cuba is preparing itself aggressively for the day the American embargo falls," says Epifanio. "If it ended today, they'd be in trouble because the United States would take over with people and capital. They are trying to develop their own infrastructure so they'll be able to stand on their own."

While the island braces itself for whatever may come—real economic independence or market-driven globalization—Cuban citizens are doing the same. Fernando dreams of getting an American MBA and writes asking about the entrance exams and university applications. In Castro's Cuba, he is reading Adam Smith and John M. Keynes, soaking up his lessons in capitalism straight from the source—and inventing himself a future, wherever that may be.

The Old Cuban Cadre

Four Women Survive Manzanillo

◡ ALICIA ROCA

It's six o'clock. Rosa fumbles with the light switch; roosters crow some-where in the darkness. She pulls a chair by its back and climbs on it. She jiggles the lightbulb: a little to the left, then to the right. At last, it hums, flickers, and emits a dim orange glow.

"Hay que inventar." You have to invent, she says with a slight smile when I visit her in March 2001. It is a phrase often used in Manzanillo, a parched, sweltering city of about 100,000 in Cuba's poorest province, Granma. "No es fácil." It's not easy. Rosa explains that since the col-lapse of the Soviet Union, everything is in short supply, particularly light-bulbs. Those available cost four dollars, one-third the average Cuban's monthly salary. For Rosa, a seventy-eight-year-old widow who does not receive money from Miami relatives, lightbulbs are a luxury. So are toilet paper (for which she substitutes newspaper), toothpaste, deodorant, and shampoo.

The first thing Rosa does every morning is clean. She wraps a damp cotton rag around a wooden stick and drags it across the concrete floor. Her back is hunched, causing her spine to protrude. Her thin arms sweep slowly back and forth. "I can't live in a dirty house. My husband always wanted a clean house."

But chores were not always a priority. In 1956, Manzanillo was alive with revolution. Late that year the *Granma*, a boat carrying Fidel Castro and eighty-two men from Mexico, landed sixty miles from Manzanillo. Waiting for them was Celia Sánchez, the daughter of a provincial doctor and the woman who organized the underground network. Based in Man-zanillo, it would support Castro and his sympathizers for the next two years. For months, Sánchez moved from house to house, depending on the residents in Manzanillo to evade Fulgencio Batista's men. In exchange

Celia Sánchez, archive
photo from the 1960s.
*From the private
collection of Lydia
Chávez*

for the promise of a better future, the locals fed, housed, and shielded her
from government inquiries. With their support, Sánchez funneled guns,
supplies, soldiers, nurses, and even reporters such as Herbert Matthews of
the *New York Times* to rebels in the nearby sierras. Rosa remembers when
Sánchez stayed in a house across the street from her. And she remembers
the other women who became models for the modern Cuban woman.

Haydée Santamaría and Melba Hernández were nurses in the attack
on the Moncada barracks in nearby Santiago. The Mariana Grajales, an
all-woman platoon, fought alongside men. Violeta Casel was the first
female announcer on Radio Rebelde. Some women, including Lidia Doce
and Clodomira Acosta, *manzanilleras* and mountain messengers, became
martyrs after being tortured to death by Batista's men. The Giralt sisters, members of the underground, were gunned down at their apartment.
Countless others, now forgotten, exploited stereotypes of women as naive
and incompetent as they worked as gunrunners or smuggled subversive
pamphlets beneath their skirts.

Manzanillo was their base, and if peasants here suffered most during Batista's reign, they gained most in the early years of the revolution. The province was renamed for the *Granma* that landed in 1956. A hospital that bears Celia Sánchez's name went up, schools opened, and doctors arrived, yet now, more than four decades later, the revolution and its gains seem like ancient history. *Manzanilleras* are at the bottom of Cuba's reemerging dollar-based social strata. Gone are the fervent guerilla warriors; in their place stand everyday women with everyday struggles. Like making a lightbulb come to life.

After Rosa cleans, she starts breakfast. The process takes an hour although she is only making coffee and toasting bread. She drips liquid fuel into a spoon. Her hand shakes. She tips the fluid into a small bowl. She turns the iron burner on and places the bowl beneath it. She lights a match. Nothing.

"Le echan mucha agua al combustible." The fuel is too watered down. She smiles and tries again. It takes her fifteen minutes. The smell of gas is thick, making it difficult to breathe in the cramped kitchen, but Rosa won't open a window. She's afraid. A year ago a young boy broke in and stole Rosa's towels and iron. "They weren't even towels. They were more like rags."

She still doesn't have any towels, and her only iron must be heated over an open flame. Nevertheless, she irons her clothes every morning. "My mother always told me a woman has to look her best." Since the burglary, Rosa stays locked indoors. She always isolated herself, neighbors say, but now she only leaves to buy food and see doctors.

When she was young, life was different. This is Rosa's litany: people had morals then. Today, the young don't want to work. They look for easy ways to make money. They are sexually promiscuous. They are struggling because they do not try to better their lives. Before the revolution, poverty and illiteracy were rampant in the countryside. Over half the population could not read. Today there are options, Rosa says. Education is available to everyone. How far they go with school depends on how hard they are willing to work.

Rosa lugs water in pails from metal barrels so she can bathe. The task is difficult for a woman who suffers from arthritis and cataracts and weighs eighty pounds. As she flips the bathroom light switch, cockroaches scatter. They are the size of small rodents, with wings.

The milk arrives and Rosa is happy. She loves milk. She would drink it three times a day if she could. Every month, Rosa and other Cubans are entitled to one pound of salt, four cans of fish, five pounds of rice, six pounds of sugar, ten ounces of beans, a few ounces of cooking oil, one pound of coffee, and ten eggs. All this food can be purchased for about four pesos, or twenty cents. The elderly, pregnant women, and children under the age of seven also receive two liters of milk a month. But complications arise. Sometimes not all items are available, and people tend to run out of food toward the end of the month. Additional food must be bought at higher prices, so the poor, like Rosa, stretch their rations by having one meal a day instead of three.

After bathing, Rosa finishes the coffee. She dips a teaspoon into a jar filled with sugar and swarming with ants. She pours the milk through a strainer and splits the curd between her dog and cat. The dog takes the cat's share. The cat meows and scratches Rosa's leg. Rosa mixes the milk, coffee and sugar with a small metal spoon. "A morning without coffee is like a dark, dark night," she says.

There is a knock at the door. She cocks her head. "Voy." I'm on my way, Rosa yells. She hooks a chain on the door, opens it a crack and peers out with one eye. In a sliver of light, a boy, about five years old, holds a golden peso in his hand. He reaches into the darkness and lays the coin in her palm. "Who are these for?" asks Rosa. "For my mom." "How many does she want?" "Two," he says. Rosa takes a clay bowl from her cabinet, drops the coin in it, and removes change. She slides a tattered brown box across the table, pulls its lid off, and lifts out two cigarettes. She gives the boy the cigarettes, the change, and shuts the door.

All Cubans born before 1959 get three boxes of black tobacco, one box of blond tobacco, and four Cuban cigars a month for six pesos. Like Rosa, many sell their tobacco to buy other goods. Rosa puts the money bowl on the cabinet shelf and dribbles oil into a pan without a handle. She rotates the pan with pliers. She places her breakfast, a white roll, in the pan and browns it. She opens the cabinet and cradles a beige, intricately crocheted tablecloth. When her husband was alive, Rosa spent much of her time crocheting. Although she had a college education, he forbade her to work or leave the house without him. They never had children. Prior to marrying him and prior to the revolution, Rosa worked as a tutor for wealthy children.

Rosa unfolds the tablecloth, shakes it, and drapes it over the kitchen table. "I'm poor. I don't have much, but everything I have is yours." When

Three generations of women on the streets of Old Havana, 2004.
Photo by Mimi Chakarova

her husband, Juan, was alive, life was better. She never wanted for anything. She calls those the happy days and divides her life into two periods—when Juan was alive and now. Juan died in 1991, the same year the Soviet Union collapsed. Relatives try to persuade Rosa to move to Havana or Santiago where conditions are better, but she won't. She won't even visit. There are too many memories in her house.

As she sets out to buy milk, Rosa stands before the bedroom mirror and brushes back strands of hair with her fingers. Missing clumps reveal pink skin several shades lighter than her caramel complexion. Rosa wraps a scarf around her head to hide it. She flicks the window locks, jams a chair up against the back door, and locks the front door. "Quédate aquí. Cuida la casa." Stay here and guard the house. Sandito, the dog, barks and wags his tail. She slams the door shut and greets a neighbor. "How are you?" he asks. "En la luchita." In the little struggle, she says with a smile.

As Rosa wakes, Felicia arrives at school. Her class does not start until seven o'clock, but the bus comes at 5:30 a.m. It is too far to walk and the horse-drawn carriages, the primary mode of transportation in Manzanillo, are not out that early. Sometimes Jorge, Felicia's husband, takes her to school on the back of his bicycle, but Felicia prefers he stay home and attend to her son, José. Children stop receiving milk at seven and José is nearly eight. It is a struggle to find breakfast for him. Yesterday all he had was a piece of bread with cooking oil on it. "But there are people in worse situations. Most of the kids in my class come to school on an empty stomach. How can they think with an empty stomach?" asks Felicia. A few days ago Felicia gave one of her students a peso for a haircut. "Some of these parents just don't care."

Felicia lives near the ocean in a neighborhood called El Malecón. Her school is in the hills, in one of Manzanillo's poorest barrios. Felicia waits in the teacher's lounge for school to begin. She is a secondary-school English teacher. Secondary school includes seventh through ninth grade. Schooling through ninth grade is mandatory. After that, children with the best grades go to the pre-university level, where there are general and scientific schools. Others go to schools for military, art, or the trades. Masters and doctorates are available by invitation only. Few of Felicia's students will go on to the pre-university level.

At 7:00 a.m., students file into the classroom. The other teacher is absent, so Felicia has eighty students instead of forty. She turns on a small color television. It is time for tele-class, a new one-hour live broadcast from Havana. The government developed it five months ago in response to the teacher shortage. The same tele-class is shown to seventh, eighth, and ninth graders.

The rowdy children settle down when the television teacher begins speaking. He greets them. His name flashes on the screen. For the next hour, he speaks in English. He asks the children to repeat after him, to respond in English, to copy sentences. But they don't understand any of it and talk among themselves instead. Felicia paces the aisle shushing the children, warning them to listen. Several students walk in late. Since all the seats are taken, they sit on the floor or stand. Some cannot see the television. "I didn't know you lived so far from school," Felicia says to one latecomer.

A bell rings signaling the end of class. The children jump out of their chairs. They had no chance to ask questions, nor did Felicia have a chance to teach. Prior to tele-classes, Felicia wrote lesson plans, led discussions, and assigned homework. Now she maintains order. Some suggest taping tele-classes in order to enable teachers to pause them for questions, but there are not enough videotapes.

At 8:00 a.m., Felicia walks to the teacher's lounge and waits. She only teaches one class today, but stays in case she is needed. She is paid three hundred pesos a month, roughly fifteen dollars ($11.53 in 2004). At noon she strolls around the corner to buy a snack. She stops at a small concrete house with children in front. One little girl has a Barbie doll. The others chase after her. "Déjame ver la muñeca." Let me see the doll, says a thin, curly-haired girl in a red T-shirt.

A sign on the door lists today's specials: Pru, a root drink, Fritura, a fried corn patty, and pizza. Felicia settles on the pizza and a sugary pink drink similar to Kool-Aid. The pizza costs two pesos. It is a small, thick bread with tomato sauce and crumbled cheese. In three bites it is gone. Most people go home for lunch, but Felicia lives too far away. "Six years without lunch. I am so hungry," she says.

It will be another six hours before Felicia eats dinner. Her breakfast of coffee did not stop the hunger pangs, nor did the tiny pizza. But she would rather she go hungry than her son or husband. She often goes without to provide for them. One time she went a year and half without shoes. Today, she nearly forgets it is her thirty-third birthday. "I'm celebrating by cooking and cleaning," she says when she remembers.

Eight years before Felicia's birth, women revolutionaries founded the Federation of Cuban Women (Federación de Mujeres Cubanas, or FMC). The goal was to eradicate machismo and create a more equal society. They fought for eighteen weeks of paid maternity leave, free contraception, prenatal care, abortions, and a national day-care system for working mothers. But equality is still a distant goal. Women, especially *manzanilleras*, bear a disproportionate burden. Felicia prefers not to discuss politics. "My politics are my son and my husband, my family." While her father is not in her life, Felicia has a close bond with her mother.

It is time for an assembly. The teachers in the lounge trudge to the school yard. A doctor stands at a podium, yelling because there is no microphone. She is hard to hear, and the children talk among themselves. It is nearly one hundred degrees and there is not a breeze. The sun is merciless.

"Escuchen. Es importante." Listen, it is important, says the doctor. The doctor alerts the children to the dangers of viral meningitis. She describes the appearance of the mosquito that carries it, as well as symptoms. Fumigations are occurring across the countryside, she tells the children. Only a few people have as yet contracted the illness, but it has not been seen in Cuba for decades, and health officials fear an epidemic. They suspect a mosquito carried it across the Atlantic on a cargo ship from Africa. "Can we count on your help?" "Yes," the children shout back.

Felicia leads the children upstairs, then returns to the teachers' lounge. She makes small talk to pass the time. She opens a worn, brown book and points at a map of the United States. She smiles. "Where is Michigan?" She has a friend in Michigan. It would be nice to visit, she says. At 5:00 p.m., Felicia heads home. It is a fifteen-minute walk downhill to the horse-and-carriage stop. She hails the first one. "Hay lugar, cochero?" Any room, she asks. But all are full. Another fifteen minutes pass. At last, one with room. The *cochero* (driver) stops and Felicia climbs on.

"This is a Cuban taxi," she says with a smile. She points at a passing horse and carriage. "Would you believe me if I told you that man was once the best history teacher in Manzanillo? He quit and now makes more money as a *cochero*." Has Felicia ever contemplated quitting her job? Perhaps for a more lucrative one in the tourist sector? "No, I love my kids," she says. "I'm a teacher."

Her best friend Angel works at a tourist resort nearly three hundred miles away in Cienfuegos. He has friends from abroad who visit and leave generous tips when they check out. When Angel visits, he will hide a five- or ten-dollar bill somewhere in her house. Sometimes she will find one in a pair of pants or under a dish. It is her only access to dollars. "He knows I won't accept it if he hands it to me. We're all struggling, and he can't afford charity anymore than I can. But by the time I find it, he's already gone."

After a twenty-minute ride, Felicia pays the *cochero* one peso and begins the long walk home. When she arrives, Kevin, the dog, is whimpering. He is tied up and hungry. If she were to untie him, he would run outside and be stolen. She puts leftover rice and beans in a tin plate. Kevin wags his tail and devours the food.

Felicia's mother and José are waiting too. José's elated face is smeared with dirt. She hugs him and tells him to clean up. She prepares a bucket of water and finds a bar of soap. While José washes in the backyard, she carries a bucket of water to the outhouse and pours it into the toilet to flush it.

She changes into shorts and a tank top and walks to the kitchen. She points to the kitchen ceiling. There are several lose bricks. "Watch out.

They could part your skull." The kitchen is filled with chicken wire, bags of concrete, and scraps of wood. Jorge is planning to fix the house. They bought it for a good price because there are holes in the walls and ceiling. Mother, father, and child share a small room with a bed, a crib, and an armoire. José sleeps in the crib. They cannot afford a bed for him. Even if they could, there would be no room for one. Felicia is proud they have a home of their own. "We own this, we don't rent," she says.

Felicia's first marriage was to Salo, a man she met in college. They were happy for a while, but after José was born, he began to change. She says he became distant and withdrawn. He dropped out of school. Then he disappeared, only to resurface in jail. He had built a raft and attempted to reach the Dominican Republic. Instead, he had washed up on Cuba's southern shore. He spent four years in jail for attempting to leave.

"He asked, 'If even a dove, an animal, migrates in search of better conditions, shouldn't we humans?'" After that she divorced him. She was hurt that he had not discussed his decision with her. She was even more hurt that he would abandon their son. It was then that she began dating Jorge, a childhood sweetheart. "If it weren't for him, José and I would have starved during the Special Period," says Felicia, referring to the early 1990s when food was even scarcer.

It was Jorge who rode his bike up into the mountains in search of firewood when there was no combustible liquid to light the burners. It was Jorge who found *plátano* (banana) trees when there was no food. "You ate whatever you could because you never knew when you'd have your next meal."

Felicia makes dinner. She pours rice onto a piece of cloth. She sits at the table to clean the rice. She lifts the tablecloth to reveal a table made of wood scraps. Rusted nails jut from it. "Jorge made it." She continues picking out bugs, rocks, dirt, and discolored grains of rice. It takes fifteen minutes before she pours the rice into a bowl, lugs water in from out back, and washes the grains. Next, she cleans the beans and lights the burners.

José runs clutching a piece of pink paper. He prances around the kitchen, waving it in the air. "Look what I found today, Mami. Colored paper!"

Ana starts work at 7:00 a.m. Her job is a forty-minute walk from her home. Her boyfriend usually takes her on the back of his bicycle, but not this morning.

Today reminded her of the days when she prepared breakfast for the two older children, sent them to school, and then went to work with her youngest child in her arms. That was thirty years ago, when her husband left her for another woman. She was twenty-four then, and raised her children without any assistance. Single mothers are more common nowadays. Between 1973 and 1988, 39 percent of all Cuban children were born to single mothers, by 1989, the number had increased to 61 percent. "No era fácil." It wasn't easy. But we survived.

For the past three decades, Ana has been a cook at the Círculo Infantil, a government-run day-care center. The program provides low-cost day care for working mothers at twenty to seventy pesos a month, depending on the parent's salary and the number of children in the family. Initially, the program was free, but it became too expensive for the government. The children are between six months and six years old. They begin arriving at 6:00 a.m. and have to be picked up by 7:00 p.m. Ana is responsible for preparing their morning snack and lunch. At 9:00 a.m., children have milk or orange juice, if available. Today the children had a yogurt drink and bread. Ana would like to retire, but she needs the money. In Cuba, women can retire at fifty-five, men at sixty.

Ana and another cook are in the kitchen. It is a small room without windows. No one else is allowed in because years ago someone put crushed glass in the children's food. "Te imaginas?" Can you imagine, asks Ana. Outside, the children are divided into groups. All the workers are women. Each one has a group of ten to fifteen children. They sing songs and play with the children. One woman, about Ana's age, is in charge of the three-year-olds. She sings a song about rabbits. A boy cries as his father leaves. Two others fight over a red flower. A little girl pulls a little boy by the ear and he screams. There are not enough chairs to accommodate latecomers. "I'm so tired," says the teacher. She holds up laminated pictures glued on popsicle sticks. "What's this?" she asks. "A lion," says the crying boy. "Yes, a lion. And where does the lion live?" she asks. "In the zoo."

Across the yard, six-year-old boys sit at tables, drawing on scraps of notebook paper. A pencil breaks and the caretaker sharpens it with a knife. As the boys draw, the girls play at life-size stations made of cardboard. There is a factory, a kitchen, a beauty salon, a hospital, and cars. A group of girls plays in the kitchen. One cooks while the others sit at a table. The cook serves equal portions to each girl. "Eat all your food. It's rice, beans, and chicken," she says.

A boy passes time on the railroad tracks of Surgidero de Batabanó, 2004.
Photo by Mimi Chakarova

When Ana gets home at 3:00 p.m. she makes dinner immediately so she can have the evening to herself. Her boyfriend comes home at four. Tonight Ana is visiting a friend, Oda. Oda moved to Havana six months ago. This is her first time back. Oda is homesick and unhappy about the move. She wants to return to Manzanillo because her family is here. In Havana she is isolated, depressed, and losing weight. A robust *manzanillera* is considered beautiful. When her friends call her *flaca* or thin, it is not a compliment. They say it with concern. They pinch the pink spandex of her dress to show how loosely it fits her. "Tienes que comer, Oda." You have to eat, says her worried sister. Ana carries a *batido de trigo*, a wheat smoothie, to Oda.

Although Oda loves her husband, she is considering leaving him to come back. Like many women in Manzanillo, she sees her immediate family as her priority. She feels uprooted in Havana, though conditions are better. "Have faith in God. It will pass," says Ana. She is a devout Baptist, as is Oda. "Ponte de rodilla y ruégale al Señor." Get on your knees and beg the Lord for strength. "It isn't easy," replies Oda.

Oda's sister, Flora, needs advice too. For the twenty years of their marriage, Flora has tolerated her husband's affairs. When he was recently arrested, Flora went to visit him. Another woman was there. "Bótalo ya." Dump him, advises Ana. "There's a point where you have to say 'no more' and love yourself more than you love him. You can't live like this."

Ana knows about cheating men. She complains that Cuban men are *mujeriegos*, womanizers. "They don't want to stay with one woman," she complains. After Ana's husband left her, she met another man. She fell in love, and they were together for several years. "But he was too good looking." Women chased after him. "The women here, they don't care if a man is with someone." So Ana left him. He is a tall, handsome man with a black mustache. Even now, when they meet on the street, she can hardly resist his charms. "He wants to be with me, but who can be with a man like that?"

After that relationship Ana met another man. She was with him for eight years, but he followed another woman to Havana. Later he returned, ill and disheveled. Ana nursed him to health. "I guess I was better," Ana smiles. They have been together five years since then. He lives with Ana. "But it's my house. I own it." Ana's eyes sparkle. The pride in her voice rivals the tone with which she speaks of her children. "It's not much, but it's mine."

As Ana arrives home, her daughter Belén is cleaning. She wets a gray rag and wipes it across the counter. It is 9:00 p.m., and she just walked in the door. She too had a long day. She leaves for work at 7:00 a.m., and it is a forty-five minute walk, but she likes the time alone. "Give me hot chocolate now," demands her nine-year-old brother. She ignores him and pulls a strand of black hair behind her ear. She swats away flies with her hands. Her cheeks are flushed. "Nowww," he whines. She rolls her eyes, sighs, and lifts the milk off the cupboard shelf. They have to drink it as quickly as possible; they don't have a refrigerator.

When her mother is not home, Belén is the matriarch. As if on cue, the five-year-old twins run in. They are clad in underwear. Their petite facial features are perfectly chiseled, as if from marble. Their wavy black hair is in disarray. One twin is screeching, the other laughing. "Nina me jalo el pelo." Nina pulled my hair, says one, eyes wide with astonishment. The other continues laughing and runs out the back door.

In the living room, Belén's *abuelo*, her grandfather, and his trio make music. Two of the men are middle aged. They arrive immediately after work every day and stay for hours. Belén's seventy-year-old *abuelo* is the oldest and most experienced musician. He founded the trio half a century ago. Belén grew up with the sounds of his guitar, as did her mother.

The three men fill the house with traditional Cuban love songs, boleros. They sing of loves lost, unparalleled devotion, and beautiful women. "O mi amor, por siempre tú." O my love, for always it will be you, her grandfather croons. "Are you hungry?" Belén yells. With one hand on her hip, she wipes the sweat from her forehead. He stops singing. "Of course I'm hungry. When's dinner going to be ready?" he asks. There is irritation in his voice.

Belén prepares the rice. Melodies rise in the background. "They say it's women's work," she whispers. Belén's ex-husband, Luis, had the same idea. She thought he was romantic at first. He seemed protective, not controlling. She drew other conclusions when she found he was cheating. "Tenía otra mujer." He had another woman, says Belén. Belén and Luis only knew each other for a month before they were married. She was flattered that a man ten years older was interested in her; especially a good-looking man. It was a way to get out of the house and start a life. But the marriage only lasted nine months. Why did they marry so quickly? "Because he wanted to," she says. She doesn't want to discuss him anymore.

Divorce is common. Many Cubanas have been married multiple times. Couples can divorce easily if their marriage "loses meaning" or if a spouse is "abandoned" for six months. In addition, boys as young as sixteen and girls as young as fourteen can legally marry. By 1987, more than one-third of marriages and divorces occurred among adolescents. In 1992, a majority of married couples were under thirty. Such marriages lasted on average less than two years.

Belén's ex-husband still pursues her. He loiters outside her work. He offers to walk her home. He brings her gifts. She tells him, "I don't want anything to do with you." Just a few months have passed since their divorce, and she is eager to wed again. "Do you want to see my wedding album? The gown is beautiful." She is looking for a boyfriend, but prospects are slim. There are none at school. She yearns to be a mother and wishes she had children. She smiles at the thought. She would have some already if her ex-husband were not sterile.

Her gaze shifts. A cat jumps over the fence. It is emaciated and severely burned. Most of its black fur is missing, and its pink skin is covered with pus, open wounds and blisters. "It was caught stealing." The cat went into a house through an open window or door looking for food. Someone then threw hot water or oil on it. "It was probably a piece of meat or fish."

Nowadays, Belén works at Manzanillo's only medical school, where she is a waitress at the dormitory cafeteria. There are many *extranjeros*, foreigners, but tips are rare. For the past three years, Belén has also been a student at a trade school for restaurant and hotel workers. She has learned basic English and service skills; she has learned how to set a table and how to take an order. When she was fourteen, Belén had the opportunity to go to pre-university. Her grades were high, and teachers encouraged her to pursue college. The pre-universities are located far away in the mountains, and students spend half the day studying and half the day working in fields to develop respect for the land and laborers. After several months at school, Belén returned because she was homesick. Others say she missed a boyfriend. That was when she chose to attend the trade school. "Me gusta." I like it, she says.

Where will she be in ten years? She laughs. "I don't know. I haven't thought much about the future." She would like to work in a place with more tourists, but that is competitive. And the idea of leaving home for Havana scares her. She looks down and separates the discolored grains of rice. "I'm not going anywhere," she says.

Research assistance by Nichole Griswold

Trinidad

Life on the Margins

~ **JULIAN FOLEY** ~

Dany is a *jinetero*, a hustler.

Slouching against the white, wrought-iron fence of the Plaza Mayor, he watches weary, sunburned tourists wander in and out of a simple church the Spaniards left behind centuries ago. A policeman on the corner watches too, stoic and motionless. Behind him, a fierce orange sun slips into the horizon. When its glow fades, he disappears, out of sight. On cue, Dany is in action. He calls out to a young couple: "Hi, how are you," first in English, then in Italian. A "bonjour" finally turns their heads.

He's on them quick, flashing a sweet, jaunty smile as he makes his pitch in fluid French. He is Afrocubano, tall and dark, handsome even beneath the dingy T-shirt and faded red shorts he spends his days in. The silver rings that weigh on his long fingers flash brightly against his smooth skin. His confidence is contagious. "I can get you anything you need," he tells the couple: private lodging for two in a real Cuban home, just twenty dollars a night; a succulent home-cooked lobster served with fried bananas and fresh green tomatoes for five dollars; a guided horseback ride into the nearby Escambray mountains to visit the magnificent El Cubano waterfall and swim in its pools. He absentmindedly snaps his right hand as he talks, adding urgency to his offer. But the two have their response ready: They already have everything they need, thanks. He lets them go. Undeterred, he returns to the fence and gets ready to try again.

Dany is one of Cuba's new entrepreneurs, and this is the new Cuba. If the people of the city of Trinidad have something to sell, he will make sure the foreigners buy it. In return, he gets a cut off the top. And everything is for sale in this pristine colonial city on the island's underbelly. From the slew of government-controlled resorts, hotels, restaurants, and shops—even bars and clubs—to the counterfeit cigars sold from dark corners, a two-tiered, postrevolutionary economy has developed to divest tourists of their money.

There is no shortage of pocketbooks. Each day, sleek tour buses wobble over the cobblestone streets in the town's old center to dump their loads: Europeans, Canadians, even Americans—package tourists shipped in from the beachfront resorts on the white-sand Península de Ancón just twelve kilometers away. Over the past fifteen years, tourism in Cuba has grown from a trickle of Soviets and native vacationers to a nearly 2-billion-dollar industry, thanks to a careful opening to foreign investment. Most of the money, desperately needed hard currency to pay the island's external debt, goes straight to the government. But ordinary Cubans have found ways—legal or otherwise—to keep some of it for themselves. "Every country has a national sport," explains Dany, whose name, along with others in this piece, has been changed to protect his identity. He grins unabashedly. "Cuba's is looking for dollars."

Just on the outskirts of town a luxury tourist bus from Havana rolls into an empty lot. Eager Trinidadians are already there, pressing their faces to the metal gate that keeps them out. They know the schedules by heart.

Disoriented and groggy, I step off the bus just as the din erupts. A taxi driver grabs a couple's bags and hoists them on board without waiting to be asked. *Jineteros* and home owners wave makeshift white business cards and call out prices as the foreigners disembark, fighting to lead us to private rooms. "Ten dollars. It's my house. Very comfortable," one tells me, shoving his card in my face even after I have brushed him off. Three others follow me, two on bicycle, one on foot, up the gentle hill into town in a contest of endurance until, finally, two give up and I reluctantly give in to the third. The bus stop is just the beginning. The protocapitalist cacophony here never quiets.

In the center of town, skirting the landscaped squares and magnificent colonial mansions that tourists come here to see, open markets line the narrow, labyrinthine streets. Vendors wait behind tables laden with crafts—painted gourds, handmade maracas, and polished wood statues of drummers and dancers—for spendthrift visitors to wander through. Beautiful handmade linens hang one after another along the curving sidewalks, filling an entire alley with billowing sheets of white. "Good prices," a woman assures someone who stops to look. "Fifteen dollars," she says, to get the bargaining started. "And I'll give you a necklace for free." Just around the corner by the tall, brilliant blue wooden doors of the Galería de Arte, an old man, white sideburns peeking out beneath a dilapidated straw cowboy hat, sells photo ops with his donkey for fifty cents. Selling on the street has been legal since 1993, but with the new freedom of self-employment came hefty government license fees and taxes that divert most of these vendors' profits to government coffers. Vendors pay for the right to sell, regardless of how much is sold. Unless they have another source of income, one bad season can wreck them. So an illicit tourist sector has developed alongside the legal one, and the *jineteros* are its tour guides. "What's worse?" asks Dany's friend Manuel, who sells counterfeit cigars. "Selling cigars on the street, or robbing and begging? They call us bad names, like pimp, but we are just trying to make a living."

And a living, the people here will admit only from the privacy of their dining rooms, is something that the socialist system, even one bolstered with tourism revenues, can no longer provide. Basic goods that Cubans covet, like toilet paper or meat, are simply unavailable most of the time in the tiny storefronts that accept the Cuban peso. Instead, they must be purchased from the special stores that sell such luxuries for dollars only. A government salary that may have proven plenty to live on in the 1980s was, in 2001, worth about twelve dollars and, by 2004, about nine dollars. That buys about five bottles of vegetable oil in a country where everything from chicken to bananas is fried. "If everyone had pesos," says Dany "if I spent pesos, if you changed money to pesos, it would be fine. The problem is that everything requires dollars."

He, for one, would like to return to the days before the Special Period—the years of economic austerity that began when the Soviet Bloc's collapse left the heavily subsidized Cuban economy in freefall. "Una maravilla," a marvel, is how he remembers it. He kisses his hand and blows it to the wind. But then, he was only twelve when it started. And though it is easy to understand why he blames dollarization for his poverty, it is clearly a symptom of Cuba's dysfunctional economy more than a cause.

Dany, like most in his field, prefers to work at night, when the darkness provides cover from anyone who might be watching: police wandering around their quadrants, looking for troublemakers, or the Committee for the Defense of the Revolution (CDR) representatives—neighborhood groups that do everything from local crime watch to organizing around health campaigns and reporting on antigovernment activity. He knows where they are and is careful to avoid them, even though some people say that neither the police nor the CDRs are as watchful as they used to be.

The cobblestone streets of Trinidad, 2001. *Photo by Mimi Chakarova*

Hungry tourists looking for a good meal make for his easiest prey at this hour. Tonight he positions himself at the bottom of the *escalera*, the wide stone staircase next to the church that unfolds onto the sloping town below. A dominoes game in the street has attracted a small crowd. Lively salsa lures foreigners up the steps to an outdoor bar; further up is a mediocre state-run restaurant. Both sell in dollars only, and it is rare to see a Cuban there who isn't serving or performing. So Dany doesn't mind stealing their business. And he knows he offers a superior product.

With a sharp eye, he spots an Italian couple he found dinner for the night before and sidles up beside them. "You want to eat?" he asks in an animated whisper, slipping his arm around the man's shoulders. They remember him and pause to hear him out, laughing to each other at his persistence. His irresistible grin and impressive high-school Italian wins them over again. "Come on," he says, motioning, and they follow him obediently, trustingly, as he steers them toward the dark streets behind the plaza. He stays a pace ahead of them to avoid suspicion, and his eyes never stop moving.

"There is a lot of fear here," he tells me. And some say racism, too, despite the official denial. Manuel thinks that he and Dany get questioned by police more often than white *jineteros* because of their dark skin. But Dany disagrees. "We just stand out more when we are walking with the tourists," he says. "White Cubans blend better." White Cubans also have an indisputable advantage in the formal tourism sector. International companies catering to European elites often prefer white faces in service positions, according to Alejandro de la Fuente, an associate professor of history at the University of Pittsburgh. And these are the jobs that are more likely to earn dollar tips.

Dany glances over his shoulder one last time before he leads the Italians into the living room of a private home. Two women watching television don't even look up as the three pass through into the tiny, badly lit dining room of this unlicensed, illicit *paladar*. Dining rooms like this are hidden all around the tourist part of town, behind colonial Cuba's trademark mélange of pink, blue, or green wooden doors. Some *paladares* are legal, but the license is prohibitively expensive for Cubans who only have enough room in their tiny houses to seat eight to ten guests. Dany's services, a mere dollar or two per guest compared with up to five hundred dollars per month for a license, are cheap. So most who serve food to tourists do it quietly and keep it small enough that the neighborhood watch is willing to let it go.

Dany stays only a moment to see his charges seated at one of two rickety tables, mismatched plates, silverware, and scratched glasses laid out on a plastic tablecloth. "They want lobster," he whispers to the woman of the house. "I told them five dollars." He'll get his cut later. Within seconds, Dany is back out on the street, looking greedily for his next catch.

Dany's other big moneymakers are the *casas particulares*, the private homes in which Cubans rent out rooms to budget-conscious tourists, or to those who want a more "authentic" experience. Renting rooms was legalized in 1997, and most who do it are licensed, but proprietors who do not have the time or nerve to go out into the street to find their own customers still have to pay Dany two dollars per night for every guest he delivers. This, on top of the 150 dollars per month per rental room for the license and the yearly income tax they pay the state, means scarce profit. Many people secretly rent out additional rooms or offer their guests home-cooked breakfasts just to make it worth their while. The government justifies the fees by the heavy housing subsidies every Cuban receives, but it is also a way to keep a tight hold on entrepreneurial activity that the state still considers contrary to Cuba's socialist ideology.

The town is teeming with *jineteros* tonight, jockeying for untapped tourists. David, tired and grungy-looking beneath his five o'clock shadow, is trying to pull in anyone Dany hasn't gotten. In another life, he would be a scientist. He studied geophysics for three years before the Special Period began in 1990 and he had to give it up to work. At thirty-one in 2001, he doubts he'll go back to school, but he hasn't stopped reading and studying on his own. He has plenty of ideas, like almost everyone here, about what the dollar economy means for Cuba's future.

"The government knows that Cubans are inventive and that they will find a way to survive, but shhh," says David, leaning across the table in a dingy *paladar*, whispering. The official penalty for selling anything without a license, be it a taxi ride or a steak dinner (*paladares* are prohibited from selling both beef and lobster) is 1,500 pesos, or about 58 dollars in 2004. And Cuba has its own three-strikes law—on the third fine, it's off to prison. But David thinks that a little extra moneymaking has been tolerated here as a safety valve for discontent as long as it's kept quiet, a theory echoed by many analysts of Cuba's parsimonious capitalism.

Tolerance, though, is at least somewhat tied to economics. Through most of the nineties, government tourism revenues were on a double-digit growth path, the island was flooded with foreign visitors, and a little diverted business to the likes of David and Dany seemed relatively harmless. But in the post–September 11 slowdown, revenues actually declined, to 1.8 billion dollars in 2001 from 1.9 billion in 2000. That prompted a crackdown on extragovernmental business activities seen as competition to the five government-owned companies that have a formal monopoly on tourism services. And even though the industry appeared to be making a full recovery in 2004, a high-profile purge of top executives for poor management in 2003 suggests the government may no longer be quite so willing to share.

On this night, however, there are still plenty of tourists to go around, even with the peak October-through-April season coming to an end. Dany has made three sales already. In addition to the Italians he took to dinner, he dropped off a pair of Americans at the most expensive *paladar* in town and found rooms for them too. All in all, a pretty good evening.

A hard day's work means a night of play. Dany lopes up the hill behind the church toward home to change out of his dirty sneakers and sweaty clothes, leaving the rest of the underground tourism economy in full swing behind him. He passes a man in a doorway offering "real Cohibas, just like Fidel smoked" to every passerby. "My mother works in the factory," he whispers to the unwitting tourists. More likely, the guidebooks will warn you, they are fakes, rolled from the tobacco sweepings that ended up on the factory floor. Dany, however, insists *he* can get the real ones, but says he only offers them to tourists he has befriended.

He arrives on his sagging doorstep and squeezes through the chicken-wire gate in no time. High up on a dusty road where the cobblestones have faded into dirt, this tiny house his father built long before the revolution is too far from the Plaza Mayor to be part of the government restoration plan. The whole town is a UNESCO World Heritage Site, but although a percentage of tourism earnings goes toward maintaining its genuine Cuban character, most is reserved for the parts tourists actually see. So Dany is financing his own restoration project. His weedy side yard has already given way to a bare gray cement skeleton that will one day be a new house for him and his father. His mother isn't around anymore. She was only twenty-three when he was born and wasn't ready to settle down with his sixty-two-year-old father, so she lives in Cienfuegos, about an hour from here by bus, and has a new family.

From outside the door, Dany can hear the Soviet-made radio crackling from the dining room, where in a dark, cluttered corner his father sits with his eyes closed, rocking slowly in his timeworn chair. The bedroom father and son share is the only other room, save a small entryway and a crude kitchen. A pot of thin bean-and-squash soup is already heated up. "He is a good son," says Dany's father, getting up from his chair. At eighty-four in 2001, he is still fit beneath his brown skin, wrinkled from a lifetime of cutting sugarcane. His smile is bigger than Dany's as he lifts his eyes toward the ceiling, as if to thank God for his good fortune.

Dany sits down at an old wooden table covered with dirty white canvas. His brother, who might have helped the family, is in prison for "evading work." Dany could go to jail too if he gets caught doing what he does, but he won't get cited for being idle. He is still considered a student while he waits to be admitted to the nearby National System for the Formation of Tourism Professionals (FORMATUR) school. Even though he has been making a decent living in the past year, the forty or fifty dollars a month he makes on the street are not enough to buy the cement he needs to complete the house. For that, he will have to go to work in the formal, government-controlled, tourism industry of high-class restaurants and luxury hotels—these days the most lucrative job a Cuban can hold.

Dany pulls his dog-eared Union of Young Communists (UJC) card from his wallet and holds it up to the light. "It means I am an exemplary youth," he says, smiling. And, he believes, it is his ticket to a real job in tourism. "I'd like to be a tour guide," he says, "because I love learning languages." That and traveling the country, meeting people from around the world, staying in nice hotels, eating good food, and most important, earning dollar tips.

The school Dany has his future riding on is one of nearly two dozen FORMATUR schools in the country that train Cubans of all ages and backgrounds—from highly educated professionals changing jobs to recent high-school graduates—to serve food, make drinks, sweep floors, and greet guests. The training is mandatory for job placement even in the lowest tier of the tourism industry. The school also prepares the select few who prove their worth for management positions in one of the independently operating tourism companies that fall under the government's tourism ministry. The really lucky ones go from FORMATUR to one of the Spanish or Canadian companies that have joint ventures or management contracts in hotels around the island.

Getting into the school is no small feat. Applicants need a college degree, recommendations from local CDR representatives, teachers, and employers, and all of the things typically associated with university admissions. They will also have to pass tests on politics, economics, geography, and history, and will be screened and intensively interviewed by a psychologist. "This is a very selective process," says José Irarragorría León, the secretary general of Trinidad's six-hundred-student FORMATUR school, gesturing at the piles of papers on his disheveled desk. And given the high demand, it has to be. Irarragorría has no doubts about applicants' incentives: "What would you rather do, be in the hot sun picking fruit, or would you rather work in tourism?" he asks, not bothering to mention the dollars, tourism's real draw, as he lights a filterless cigarette in his cramped and stale office. But he denies allegations that only the most committed communists are offered the opportunity to choose.

"We try to find the best students. If a person comes straight from jail, would you want them to manage your new hotel?" he says defensively.

But picking good students, or even good citizens, is not the government's only concern. If it were too easy to work in tourism, everyone might do it, draining other sectors like agriculture and education, where salaries are paid in pesos. In the early nineties, when Cuba's drive for tourist development began in earnest, surprising numbers of highly educated people left their jobs in education and engineering to clean toilets, sweep floors, or serve beer in the new tourist resorts in Varadero and Jibacoa. If a maid earns an extra thirty dollars in tips in a month, she has tripled her government salary. And it isn't just the cash. Some employees get other perks too, like *jabas*, the monthly baskets of food and personal items only available in dollar stores—good cuts of meat, shampoo, lotion. There is ample opportunity for cheating as well. A bottle of rum only costs three dollars at the market, and a *mojito*—the lime, rum, and mint drink that is Cuba's trademark—sells for two dollars at any bar. An enterprising bartender, Dany and others suggested, could easily bring his own bottle to work and pocket the money from the drinks he makes with it.

Dany and his colleagues also maintain that given the high demand for tourism jobs, the people who run *la bolsa*, the lottery system by which FORMATUR graduates are selected for job interviews, can be bribed. "Give them fifteen dollars," he says, "and they'll pull your name." He will get to test this theory after he graduates—if he dares. "Sure tourism brings in a lot of money for the state," says David, who is surprisingly candid in his criticism. "But it also brings money to those who can get it, and that breeds corruption."

But if tourism money is creating new temptations for people in privileged positions, it is also reinforcing the loyalties of the people who have access to the good life it brings. "Everything is perfect in Cuba," says Eduardo Ruiz, who says he earns an extra thirty or so dollars in tips each month driving tourists to the beach and back in a bright yellow, egg-shaped taxi. "When you want a house, they give you a house. No one sleeps on the street here," he says. But what he doesn't say is that he, or even Trinidad, is not an average sample of Cuban life. In other parts of the country where there is no, or very little, tourism, opportunities to earn extra dollars simply don't exist. And in places less concerned with attracting visitors, government repression tends to be more open.

Even David, who lives in a tiny, bare, cement-floored apartment, knows life in Cuba isn't so clear cut. He and his wife pay ten dollars a month to live apart from his extended family. Scraping enough money together for rent is not easy. "Es una imagen," he says of the Cuban ideal. A facade, a mirage. He still takes pride in the benefits socialism has brought to Cuba—good, free education and health care the most obvious among them—but he is not blind to the contradictions the dollar economy has created.

On the street that runs behind the *escalera*, a barefoot young mother, stooping with the weight of a wide-eyed baby that clutches her side, spends her afternoons asking tourists for money to buy formula. All over town, parents and teachers are worried about their children, who have already figured out that tourists are walking candy dispensers. And then there is María, a hunched old woman with no front teeth who walks around most days begging tourists for dollars and neighbors for used cooking grease. "There are many people who just sit around and beg tourists," says Aragón, the white-haired elderly man who rents his donkey for photos. "I myself don't believe in begging, but if a tourist wants to give me something, that's different." But then, he is fortunate enough to have a donkey at his disposal.

María isn't so lucky. She doesn't have a donkey to photograph, an extra room in her house to rent out, or an old American car to offer tourists illicit rides in. "I have always been poor," she says, scurrying off nervously, as if that were explanation enough. The government does hand out a monthly ration card for staples like beans and fluffy white bread at heavily discounted prices, but it only buys the most minimum of diets. People like María, without access to an extra income, cannot afford to pay full price to supplement it. "Before the Special Period, you could eat perfectly well, just with pesos," says David. "You could buy clothes too. But now, prices keep going up and up." He blames the dollar economy for that.

But for people like Eduardo who have dollars, the good life is not an illusion. The division between the dollar-rich and the dollar-poor is visible on any street. Bright white Adidas sneakers stand out against worn-out loafers. Well-off kids in their drab yellow school uniforms crowd into dollar markets in the tourist part of town to buy sodas and little packages of cookies or candies. Flashy watches and gold chains are conspicuous next to naked wrists and callused hands.

Seventeen-year-old Chuchy is the essence of the new consumer. She has had her heart set on a career in tourism for years. Never mind the bored look on her tanned, round face as she serves customers at the state-run Restaurante Villa Real just off the plaza, writing orders on scraps of paper, or her hand, and setting down drinks under the direction of a senior server. She gives away her real motives even as she professes her love for service: her wild, frizzy blond hair is pulled back to show off aquamarine and gold plate earrings that match one of several rings adorning her childish hands. A gold-colored watch, its shine already fading, tells her when it is time to go home. These are things that in Cuba only dollars can buy, and she, like Dany, knows that a job in tourism is the fastest way to get them.

Chuchy is in her last year at a secondary school that feeds directly to the FORMATUR, where she can study for one, two, or three years, depending on how high up she wants to go. To work in one of the peso cafeterias near the Parque Céspedes, she needs only a few months of training, but to work with foreign tourists, she will need language proficiency. In the meantime, she earns enough tips doing her internship at Villa Real to keep herself well dressed. Her husband already works as a waiter, and his mother works in a gift shop at the Costasur Hotel on the peninsula. From the outside, the house they all share looks like any other on the dusty block. But inside, it is a veritable temple to all the things that tourism money buys: a Panasonic 5-CD changer, a new television, and a VCR. The family even has a car in the cinder-block garage behind the house. Their stereo was priced at 450 dollars in the dollar store. That is twice as much as it will cost Dany to put a roof on his new house.

In this egalitarian society, the disparity between people like David and María, on the one hand, and Chuchy's family, on the other, has not gone unnoticed. Even the Communist Party leaders here readily admit that dollar tips are creating inequalities and upsetting the wage structure. But discouraging tipping, as they did in the early 1990s, was ineffective, and asking workers to hand over their earnings for redistribution proved unrealistic. Boris Turiño, the frumpy but charismatic secretary-general of the Communist Party at the new Brisas Trinidad del Mar hotel (there are party representatives in every hotel in Cuba) has begun to think that tips are a good thing. "If I ask a waiter, did you get a tip, and he says no, I know that he did not give good service," Turiño says. And since Cuba's state tourism companies compete against each other for revenues, good service feeds the bottom line.

So instead of fighting the realities of the tourism industry, the government began boosting other sectors in 1999, including a 30-percent increase in public health and education salaries and productivity bonuses distributed as magnetically striped cards that can be used in dollar stores. In some industries, like fishing, where the incentives for cheating are high, salaries are paid partially in dollars. "In the Special Period, when there was no money, and when the economy was down, that's when there was a move of professionals trying to get into tourism," says Turiño. But as tourism grows—and despite the industry's recent troubles, it is expected to eventually—it will continue to pull doctors and scientist into its ranks and erode incentives for young people to get educated in higher, but lower-paying, pursuits.

Dany, for one, isn't interested in years of schooling for a job that won't put meat on his table. The beans-and-rice dinner he ate tonight, for what seems like the millionth time in a row, has left its usual hole in his stomach. If he wants the real goods, he knows he has to go for hard currency—dollars.

When he steps out the door, hollering good night to his father over the still babbling radio, Dany is a changed man. His pressed, sky blue collared shirt is open just enough to show off the flat, round silver pendant, his initials scripted across it, that hangs on a modest silver chain against his hairless chest. Crisp khaki shorts have replaced his dirty red ones, and as he strides out into the street, his new Adidas reflect the moonlight. All, he explains, are gifts from tourists.

"I never buy my own clothes," he brags, shaking the too-big "titanium" watch that hangs loosely from his dark wrist. The only clothes he could afford anyway are the ones in the peso stores, most of them donations from Spanish or even American church and humanitarian groups. "Nobody likes the stuff the state sells. Everybody prefers *el shoping*," he says, referring to the dollar stores. What he doesn't get free from tourists, he buys on the black market. That's where he got the watch and the four silver rings that clutter his hands. The cologne he wears, though, must have come from Trinidad, since the same scent permeates every street corner and stoop where young Cuban men gather.

Heading toward the plaza, Dany thinks back to the Italians and their dinner and wonders aloud if they will be going to the Casa de la Música tonight, one of five state-run clubs tucked into the neighborhoods around the plaza. If he finds them, they might pay his one-dollar entrance fee.

Or maybe the French guys he talked politics with the evening before will. Anyone, really, as long as he doesn't have to pay out of his own pocket. "Last night I had seventy pesos," he explains. "Three dollars, more or less. I could have gotten into the Casa de la Música, but I couldn't have bought anything to drink. With pesos, we can't even go out in our own country."

The nightlife here isn't really intended for the Cubans anyway. Dany can hear the music spill out of the open courtyards all around town, filling the still warm, moist Caribbean air with a riot of Afrocuban beats and the cheerful rhythms of *son*, Cuba's folk music. The medley is the same every night. Songs from the Buena Vista Social Club are played again and again, in club after club, to make sure the tourists get the Cuba they expect. Even local music is a state enterprise, packaged and sold for dollars.

Some clubs are worse than others. Dany almost never goes to Las Ruinas de Segarte, just around the corner from the Casa de la Música. There, twenty-year-old Daniel, dressed in African-print pants and a baggy green shirt, his Chicago Bulls hat left behind on a corner table, begins the night's show by raising his powerful, pitch-perfect voice over a pulsing drum beat. He has been singing since he was seven, when his father and uncles began teaching him the music and languages of Santería, the Afrocuban religion that was one of the few tolerated by the revolution. He plays everything—the timbales, the guiro, the claves.

At Las Ruinas, Daniel accompanies himself with a huge, handmade beaded gourd that showers pellets of sound into the microphone. A thicket of wires connect a beat-up amplifier to an old tape player that records performances, night after night, onto tapes sold later for a little extra profit. Three men seated behind the timbales join in with a deep, insistent rhythm that propels a motley group of costumed dancers, who act out the work of the slaves that toiled in the sugar plantations here until they were freed in 1886. From their midst, a handsome woman in purple silk emerges, straight-backed and haughty. Waving a hand broom impatiently, face impassive, she shoves a straw hat toward a German man sitting in the front row. He has seen this before and reluctantly pulls his wallet out again. She moves on.

"It is all for the saints," Daniel says after the show. But it is clearly for the tourists' money too. At the end of the night, when everyone else has gone home, the dancers and the players divvy up the tips, dollar by blessed dollar. Each of the players and dancers in Daniel's group also earns a

Waiting for tourists,
Havana, 2001.
*Photo by Mimi
Chakarova*

small government salary. As for everything else here, there is a set process for becoming a musician and performing for the tourists—schools, tests, provincial auditions—that controls who plays what and where.

Dany's friend Manuel is one of the luckier musicians. His band has built up an international reputation, so for him playing music means travel opportunities that most Cubans will never have. Half of his group is currently in Mexico performing, and although he was not allowed to go this time, he expects to go next month. He will even get to keep some of the profits they make. All it takes, Manuel claims, is an invitation from abroad. While he waits, he sells cigars on the street. It is easy to see from his Rolex watch and brand-name clothes that he's good at that too.

In the end it is me that gets Dany into the Casa de la Música, an old red brick courtyard with arched passageways and a lit-up stage on the back of the *escalera*. A stern policeman is standing near the door when we arrive, his conservative green uniform almost comical next to the skimpy spandex dresses the Cuban women wear. He is probably just doing his rounds, but Dany won't take the chance of walking in with his new friend. Cubans accompanying tourists are automatically suspect, and he doesn't feel like being hassled. So instead, barely hiding his embarrassment, he takes my dollar outside and walks in ahead of me, looking around for his friends and an empty table. He spots Manuel, already talking to some foreign young women. The Italian couple is here too. Dany slaps the man five, puts his arm around him, and before long, the man hands him four dollars for a bottle of Havana Club Silver Dry rum. That's three dollars less than the Italians would have been charged. Passed around the table with a can of Coke, the bottle lasts as long as the music does.

Dany and his friends are not the only locals at the club. It is one of the few places in town that has dancing, and that is what the Cubans come for. The courtyard is full of sexy young men and women dressed for flirting. When the salsa rhythms start, the dance floor fills up with bodies moving fluidly together, swinging in time to the rattling maracas and singing guitars. The irresistible motion and insistent invitations soon lure the tourists up from their seats. They are conspicuous in their clumsy steps and the sporty shorts and sneakers they spent the hot day in.

The end of the night, when the band reels in the wires and the stage clears, is when the real fun begins. The pumping bass of Cuban rap comes blaring through the loudspeaker, and suddenly everyone is up, stomping and thumping and rapping along. There are mostly young people left, and even the visitors know what to do. This is what Dany has been waiting for. This is Cuban time.

Later, walking home, Dany passes a group of young Cuban women, tube tops hugging as tightly as their spandex skirts, with an entourage of tall, pale-skinned foreigners. "One, two, three," he counts out loud, taunting. "Four, five. Five girls for four guys?" he asks. "Two for one. I guess that is the Cuban way." There is a fine line here between a good time with a Cuban "girl" and outright prostitution. Dany wouldn't think of pimping women ("straight to prison," he explains), but there is nothing to stop women from accepting a few drinks, maybe a new dress, from a tourist, and going home with him for a few more dollars. I overheard a couple of men complain, though, that like everything else here, the women aren't as cheap as they were a few years ago.

Tourism has been called the locomotive of Cuba's economy. Its dollar revenues surpassed those of sugar for the first time in 1996, and, if the industry continues at its pre-2000 growth rate, it will remain the primary source of hard currency to service the country's 12 billion dollar debt. But if the Dominican Republic and Cancún are any indication of what is to come, this economic model has a price: local populations become inputs for, not participants in, a foreign-owned industry; local economies are shut out by the all-inclusive Caribbean resorts that send profits out of the country; and once-distinctive coastlines become generic beaches, where the only thing native is the help.

Despite the Cuban government's effort to control the industry's impact through strict regulations on ownership and hiring, tourism and the dollar economy it has spawned are already redefining Cuba's priorities. People who once gave the proverbial middle finger to their powerful northern neighbor are increasingly dependent on its currency. Highly educated engineers, doctors, and teachers—the products of Cuba's fabled education system—are giving up their careers to drive taxis and scrub hotel bathrooms. The tenet of income equality that underpins socialism itself is being allowed to disintegrate in the name of economic growth.

Everything Cuban, especially here in Trinidad, is up for sale: music, art, even women. Everything except the land. And like in any export-based economy, the good stuff is appropriated for the foreigners. But those same dollars that are driving women to prostitution and the elderly to begging are saving ordinary Cubans from reliance on a government that can no longer feed them. Dany is angry that he needs dollars, and yet desperate to get more. It disgusts him to see the women he went to school with cozy up to tourists, but even he relies on a tourist to buy him a drink or pay his way into a club.

Dany doesn't ask for much: a house big enough for him and his father to live in comfortably; a bus ticket to Havana to visit his sister, so he doesn't have to hitchhike for an entire day to get there. But for these things, he has to have dollars. "I want to live in Cuba forever," Dany says passionately, tapping his hand to his heart the way people do here when they talk about their country. "But *with* money." He fingers the pendant at his neck and wrinkles his dark forehead as he looks out over the Plaza Mayor. On nights when he is sad, he comes here to watch the stars, taking over one of the benches that during the day belong to the tourists. From here, he can listen as the music dies down and the bars slowly empty out, as the hushed voices of couples dissolve into the darkness, as the footsteps of the foreigners fade away. At last, when the quiet settles in, the town belongs to him again. And from where he sits, it is easy to understand why he wants to stay. "With enough money," he says, "Cuba is everything."

Research assistance by Pedro Mosqueda

PART TWO ~ *Breathing*

Hip Hop Pushes the Limits

It is a late Friday afternoon in Havana, and an old man in a worn-out tuxedo opens the doors under the flickering green and red neon of Cabaret Las Vegas. A poster on the wall, its corners curling, advertises the usual cabaret fare: live salsa, banana daiquiris, and beautiful women. But the people standing outside with me are not tourists looking for an exotic thrill. They are mostly young, mostly black, and dressed in the latest FUBU and Tommy Hilfiger styles. And despite the one-dollar cover charge—steep for most Cubans—the line to get in is long.

Once inside, I see two young Afrocubans on a small stage in the back. One is tall and languid, the other is shorter and in constant motion. They wear baggy jeans, oversized shirts, and sprinkle their songs with "c'mon now" and "awww' ight." But while it's clear they admire American hip hop style, Yosmel Sarrias and Maigel Entenza Jaramillo rap about a distinctly Cuban reality, and offer some commentary on U.S. life as well: "It's time to break the silence / This isn't what they teach in school / In search of the American Dream / Latinos suffer in the hands of others."

"This music is not for dancing. It's for listening," a young man wearing a Chicago Bulls jersey tells me. He waves his hand high in the air. "And for Cubans, believe me, it takes a lot to keep us from dancing." Entenza crisscrosses his arms as he moves across the stage, and the crowd follows him, word for word. Sarrias stands toward the back of the stage, delivering a steady flow of verse. The audience is enrapt. Anónimo Consejo—Anonymous Advice—is one of Cuba's top rap groups, waiting for the next big break: a record contract and a living wage to do what they love.

The key to that big break—producer Pablo Herrera—is in the DJ's booth, looking down at the two rappers. "What you're seeing is Cuba's underground. I'm talking about the empowerment of youth as a battle spear for a more conscious society," he says to me in English so flawless that he's sure he lived another life in Brooklyn. And he looks it—from the braids in his hair to the New York attitude. Herrera and a fellow representative of Asociación de los Hermanos Saiz, the cultural arm of Young Communist Union, put on the weekly hip hop show. With more than 250 rap groups in Havana alone, he chooses each Friday night's lineup carefully. "I can't work with everybody, I'm not a machine," Herrera says with a shrug. "I mostly go with what I like."

But even with Herrera's approval, the world for young rappers here is full of contradictions. They believe in Cuba, but they're not ideologues—they just want to make music from their own reality. Anónimo Consejo's lyrics are edgy, but getting too edgy could end their careers. Each day is a political and social balancing act.

Cuba's fascination with hip hop is more than just a passing teenage fad. The Cuban government now sees rap music—long considered the music of American imperialism—as a road map to the hearts and minds of the young generation. Far more likely than their elders to complain about Castro, young Cubans are the question mark of the island's political future. And in recent years, more and more have started voicing their discontent by rhyming—on buses, street corners, anywhere a crowd might gather to listen.

Young Cubans have long consumed American pop culture like junkies, waiting to watch the next smuggled hit from MTV or VH-1. For young Afrocubans in particular, the popular music of black America is replacing salsa as their music of choice—especially hip hop. With its hard-driving beats and street-smart message, rap often depicts a powerful and distinctive black identity. In Cuba, where Castro's government promotes the idea of a color-blind society, this idea has revolutionary potential.

But a full-scale hip hop rebellion has not happened yet. So far, only one Cuban rap group has made it big—Orishas. That group was also a Pablo Herrera creation, back in the early 1990s. Then they called themselves Amenaza, or Threat, and Herrera says they were the first rappers to explore racial identity and challenge Castro's ideal of a colorless society. Tempted by an enticing record deal with a European label, the group traveled to Paris to perform in 1998—and stayed.

Sarrias and Entenza look at Orishas with both awe and disappointment. Once abroad, the group made hits, but they did so by adding Cuba's beloved salsa and rumba beats to their music. As their singles climbed the foreign charts, Cuban rappers back home criticized them for selling out to commercial pressures to evoke Cuban nostalgia. "Salsa makes it easier

Entenza on stage,
Havana, 2001.
*Photo by Mimi
Chakarova*

for older people to accept rap music. But it's not what Cuban youth are really listening to," Sarrias says. He and Entenza want Anónimo Consejo to succeed by sticking to rap and not jumping onto the salsa fusion bandwagon.

The Orishas success story reveals the contradictions inherent in marketing the music of youthful dissent. On the one hand, many Cuban rappers claim to eschew the materialist nature of mainstream American rap music, but at the same time, foreign record producers often seduce them with stories of big contracts and lavish lifestyles abroad. Kali Akuno, a Berkeley-based organizer for the Malcolm X Grassroots Movement who leads trips to Cuba, says the temptation to stray from revolutionary ideals is strong. "There is the danger of people on [the foreign] side of the Cuban rap scene serving more as exploiters. When people come to Cuba to make records with rappers there, they want to sell a product. But where is the money going? That's a major concern."

All of these pressures bear down on a passion that began as a hobby. When they met in 1993, Entenza, then thirteen, and Sarrias, seventeen, were just kids looking for fun on an island so depressed that scores of their compatriots were building rafts out of everything from Styrofoam to old tubes to take their chance at sea. Entenza and Sarrias watched them from their homes in Cojímar, once a sleepy fishing village near Havana. By the time they were adults, the government had built dozens of Soviet-style high-rise apartment buildings there.

For relief from the dog days of 1993, the two young men and their friends hung out at Alamar, a sprawling housing complex nearby. The kids entertained themselves in a big, empty pool, improvising, break-dancing, and listening hard to the American music coming from antennas they rigged on their rooftops to catch Miami radio stations. They heard songs like this one: " 'Cause I'm black and I'm proud / I'm ready and hyped plus I'm amped / Most of my heroes don't appear on no stamps," rhymed Public Enemy in "Fight the Power." Sarrias was hooked. "Their songs spoke to me in a new way. There was nothing in Cuba that sounded like it."

Or talked about issues that Afrocubans had only begun to face. Cubans have been taught to ignore race, and the revolution tried to blur color lines by opening all professions, universities, and government offices to Afrocubans. Officially, race all but disappeared as a part of national discourse. But increasingly, race has become an issue in Cuba. If Afrocubans benefited most from the revolution, they have also suffered the most during its crisis. Every Cuban needs dollars to survive, and the bulk of the easy money coming in remittances goes to white Cubans because it was their relatives who left early on. Darker Cubans also face discrimination getting the island's best jobs in the tourism industry. Skin color—despite the revolution's best intentions—has once again become the marker of a class divide. Many Afrocubans say this happens because Cuban society is inherently racist, while hotel owners are likely to say that European tourists—the mainstay of the Cuban tourism industry—feel more comfortable with white faces. The truth is probably somewhere in between.

Cubans of all shades are quick to deny the existence of racism on the island. They point to the many interracial couples walking the streets as proof that prerevolutionary hang-ups about skin color have all but vanished. But many will admit to a more subtle social prejudice that takes the form of police harassment and racial profiling. "Cuban racial categories are much more fluid than in the United States," says Nadine Fernández, an anthropologist at Florida International University. "It's a question of facial features, hair texture, and skin tone that decides what category you belong to, and it depends who you talk to. Police harassment and discrimination are everyday experiences for many black Cubans, but a vocabulary of black oppression doesn't exist here."

That is changing. As more international academic research develops around race on the island, more Cubans have made contacts within the African American intellectual community and have begun to share their ideas. For years, Castro positioned racism as a problem outside of the country. But a growing number of Afrocubans wonder if that was not just a way of displacing the racial question at home.

Kali Akuno has been involved with the hip hop scene in Cuba since the mid-1990s. He first went to the island for the second annual Cuban rap festival, where he participated in roundtable discussions with Cuban artists and other African American artists and scholars. "The government response initially was not enthusiastic. There was this sense that both hip hop and rock music were coming from a gringo imperialist perspective," Akuno says. "Hip hop was very racialized there, as it was here. The government's attitude was 'we don't want this music to divide Cubans.'"

Sarrias and Entenza grew up in a neighborhood with few white Cubans. They live in substandard housing, with constant police presence. Like disaffected youth everywhere, they looked for role models that gave them a sense of pride. In school, when Sarrias tried to talk about his African ancestry, teachers called him unpatriotic for thinking of himself as something other than Cuban. He turned to his mother to find out more about his African roots, and before long, her stories became his lyrics: "In my poor bed / I read my history / Memories of Titans / Africans kicking out the Spanish."

She also taught him about Santería, Cuba's African-derived religion that has outlasted any political regime. "In school, they taught him about slavery, but they didn't go into depth," his mother says, standing in the dirt yard in front of their small, clapboard house. Lines of laundry hang to dry in the hot sun. A single mother, she washes her neighbor's clothes in exchange for a few extra pesos each month. Sarrias weaves her lessons throughout songs like this one: "If you don't know your history / You

Entenza and his mom embrace in his room covered with posters of basketball players and hip hop artists, Havana, 2004. *Photo by Mimi Chakarova*

won't know who you are / There's a fortune under your dark skin / The power is yours."

He sought other teachers as well. He and Entenza often stop by the house of Nehanda Abiodun, an African American woman who calls herself a political exile and was a member of the Black Liberation Army. There the two young men receive informal sessions about black history, poetry, and world politics. The messages in their music, says Abiodun, come naturally. "They were born in a revolutionary process where they were encouraged to ask questions and challenge the status quo," she says. It also comes from their daily lives: "Their parents, their experiences on the street growing up, what's going on in the world."

If expatriates like Abiodun serve as historical guides, African American hip hop artists give them their beat. "It was amazing to hear rappers from another country worried about the same issues I was," Sarrias says. Alternative rap artists like Common (Sense) and Mos Def have been traveling to Cuba since 1998 as part of the Black August Collective, a group of

African American activists and musicians dedicated to promoting hip hop culture globally.

Even while unsure about the movement, the Cuban government welcomed American rappers because of their support for the revolution, says Vera Abiodun, codirector of the Brooklyn branch of the Malcolm X Grassroots Movement, and part of the collective. Cuban youth responded to the rhythm, but also to the visitors' obvious pride in being black. "We didn't know how huge this would become in the beginning," she says.

Just as black Americans did in the 1960s, Afrocubans in the 1990s began to embrace their African heritage. "Every time that the police harass me, I don't feel like being here anymore," Sarrias says. "When that happens, the first place I think about is here," he touches an African amulet hanging around his neck and refers to the power he associates with his ancestry, compared to the belittlement he can feel from others because of his color. "When I feel African, I don't feel black." And for many young Afrocubans, rap music, not the syrupy lyrics of salsa, validates the ancestry they have been taught to overlook.

Sarrias and Entenza admire heroes of Cuban revolutionary history like José Martí and Che Guevara. But they also look up to Malcolm X, Mumia Abu-Jamal, Nelson Mandela, and other black icons. They and thousands of other young Cubans heard Abu-Jamal's son speak at an anti-imperialist rally two years ago. And when the young rappers talk about meeting American hip hop artists, their faces beam.

Their musical style reflects the love. Like that of their favorite American groups, N.W.A., Method Man, and the Roots, Anónimo Consejo combines politically charged lyrics, most written by Sarrias, with Entenza's playful vocal delivery. Because of limited technology on the island, their sound sounds more "old school" than the slickly engineered music produced by American rappers like P. Diddy and Jay-Z. Perhaps because of this lack of pretension, Cuban hip hop has become the darling of the American underground rap scene. Socially conscious rappers and cultural exchange groups have come to the island in search of what many consider the pure essence of hip hop. Even when they do not understand Spanish, visitors to the island come away with a positive impression of *el rap cubano*.

Eli Jacobs-Fantauzzi is just one of a growing number of hip hop pilgrims who go to Cuba in search of the true underground. It is the more progressive element in hip hop culture that focuses on social justice and racial equality in its music. Since 1995, when rap musicians decided to hold a hip hop festival each August, more and more American and European hip hop devotees have shown up in Cuba—often with recording equipment and CDs in hand. The word in the close-knit underground community is that Cuba is where it's happening. "It's been a dream of mine to go to Cuba for a long time," says Jacobs-Fantauzzi. His eyes light up as he watches the video footage he shot of the sixth annual hip hop festival in Havana. He bounces his head up and down to the beat and sings along with Magia, the female MC of Obsesión, one on the long roster of Cuban rap groups to perform alongside some of the best-known hip hop artists of the U.S. underground scene. "My first impression of hip hop in Cuba is just that it's raw, like these people do it for the love of it," he says, hitting his fist in his palm for emphasis. "Right now I feel like hip hop out here in the States is really diluted and people like it for other reasons: money, girls, cars, whatever it is. But out there, they do it for a love of the music, 'cause they're not really getting much from it. They're not getting the Bentleys or the big diamonds—that's not going to happen in Cuba."

Even in poverty, the frequent foreign visitors and word-of-mouth popularity give Anónimo Consejo a certain cachet in Cojímar. "What bug crawled out of your hair and ran around all night?" A middle-aged woman yells at Entenza as he walks by her front porch, his long Afro gently bobbing in the wind. "People around here think we're a little crazy," he grins. "But they love us anyway."

But you cannot live on love alone. That's where Pablo Herrera comes in. A former Havana University professor who taught English and hip hop culture, Herrera is both a devotee of African American culture and passionate about Cuba. He has also emerged as Cuban rap's main spokesperson internationally and at home. In a country where the government controls just about everything, rap proves no exception. In the early 1990s, police regularly shut down hip hop shows and labeled rap as imperialist music. But Herrera and other hip hop disciples waged a publicity campaign to revamp rap's troublemaker image. Writers like Ariel Fernández published numerous articles on rap in state-run newspapers and cultural journals, while Herrera helped organize committees on its relevance for the revolution. Herrera reminded the old guard that the younger Cubans needed a voice and that rap music was their chosen form of expression. "The purpose of hip hop is serving the country, not being an antagonistic tool," he says. "The idea is to improve what is already in place."

His efforts were rewarded—in 1998 Abel Prieto, the minister of culture, officially declared rap "an authentic expression of *cubanidad*" and began nominally funding the annual rap festival. Even Fidel Castro himself rapped along with the group Doble Filo at the national baseball championship three years ago. With Castro's blessing, Prieto recently funneled about 32,000 dollars worth of audio equipment to rappers through the Young Communist Union's cultural arm.

Although officially accepted, rap is still in its infancy. Herrera is the producer with the most equipment to make Cuban rap groups sound professional. Herrera works out of his sun-filled studio with a turntable, a mixer, a drum machine, a sampler, and cartons of classic Cuban LPs. It's a simple setup, but by Cuban standards, it's a soundman's paradise. "Since most music here is not really produced electronically, there's not many people who can do this," he says.

Now that the Orishas remake of Compay Segundo's famous tune "Chanchan" can be heard all over Havana, rap music is more popular than ever in Cuba. Herrera hopes Anónimo Consejo can achieve the same stardom—without defecting from *la patria*, the homeland. In a shirt with the words "God is a DJ," Herrera shuffles through a stack of CDs and smokes a cigarette while Sarrias and Entenza sit on his couch, intently studying every page of an old *Vibe* magazine. "Yo, check this out." Herrera finds what he's looking for. "En la revolución, cada quien hace su parte." In the revolution, everyone must do his part. Castro's unmistakable voice loops back and repeats the phrase again and again over a hard-driving beat. Herrera nods to Sarrias, who takes his cue: "The solution is not leaving / New days will be here soon / We deserve and want to always go forward / Solving problems is important work."

Herrera may not be the only rap promoter on the island, but rappers say he is the one best connected to the government. As a key member of the Hermanos Saiz, Herrera has rare access to music clubs like the Las Vegas. Any rapper who hopes to be seen at a decent venue must first get the association's approval, and that can only happen if their music is seen to serve the revolution. But having equipment does not necessarily mean an artist becomes a government puppet. According to Nina Menéndez, a San Fransisco–based music promoter, breaking into commercial distribution depends on personal connections within the industry more than towing the party's line. "Many people whose politics seem outside of official discourse have no problems getting access and even receive a state salary," she says.

In the Cuban hip hop world, there is a strong tradition of alternative distribution methods—mainly smuggling records on and off the island. The Cuban music industry has been slow to catch on to hip hop, especially because most Cubans—and foreigners—prefer more traditional music. Resources are limited for most rappers, particularly for those who are young and still unknown. But Menéndez feels this will change naturally as Cuba's hip hop scene grows. "Hip hop is emerging as a new genre of Cuban music, but it is still in the development stage," she says.

Herrera's mission is to help speed that process along. He is the unofficial ambassador of Cuban hip hop for the flood of foreign reporters, musicians, and record producers coming to the island in search of the next big Cuban musical export. He discovered Anónimo Consejo in the mid-1990s at the first rap festival. "I work with them because their music is really authentic," Herrera says. "I like their flow, but what is really striking is what they say . . . so mind-boggling."

Up to a point. Cuban rap—and Anónimo Consejo is no exception here—pushes the envelope, but not so far as to offend the government. The duo has become a favorite at state-sponsored shows, warning young Cubans against the temptations of American-style capitalism. In the song "Appearances Are Deceiving," they rap, "Don't crush me / I'm staying here / Don't push me / Let me live / I would give anything for my Cuba / I'm happy here." Their nationalist pride recently helped them land a contract with a state-run promotion company. All that means, however, is that their travel expenses are covered when they tour the island and that they receive a modest paycheck, usually around 350 pesos each ($13.50 in 2004), after each major show. That money does not go far in an economy increasingly dependent on U.S. dollars. And it is getting harder to convince their parents that a rap career is worthwhile.

Entenza quietly slips out of the recording session at Herrera's studio, not to return all afternoon. Later he says that he was upset and needed to cool off after an argument he had had with his mother that morning. "She says that I'm a grown man now, and she's tired of supporting me. She thinks that I should get a real job," he says, twisting the end of a braid between his fingers and looking at the ground. "She doesn't understand that this is what I want to do—this is my job." In the mid-1990s, both

Entenza and Sarrias decided to forego Cuba's legendary free university education and to devote themselves to making music. They both still live at home with their mothers, depending on the state's meager ration cards to eat. Herrera is trying to help them pay the bills. "They are already the top group in the country," he says. "They deserve a very good record deal, and they deserve to be working at a studio every day making their music." But when their session is over, they still need to borrow a dollar to catch a bus back home.

Just as young Afrocuban males complain about being stopped for criminal activity, young Afrocuban women are quick to point out the injustices in their own lives. Job opportunities and salaries have plummeted since Soviets pulled out, and women more often than men are responsible for holding households together financially in *la lucha*, the daily struggle for survival. The only sector of the economy that is booming is tourism, and most of those highly coveted jobs go to lighter-skinned women. In the hotel industry, *buena presencia*—good appearance—is a job requirement often equated with whiteness. The one area of tourism wide open to women of a darker tone is Cuba's thriving sex industry. Though officially frowned on by the government, prostitution is widespread on the island, where in almost every restaurant older tourists can be seen dining with beautiful young women of color.

The island has long appealed to American and European men looking for a good time. Visions of the sensual *mulata* are a prime marketing tool for Cuban tourism—the government even invited *Playboy* magazine to run a feature on the "girls of Cuba" in exchange for free publicity for the island's tourist facilities. Nadine Fernández, an anthropologist at Florida International University, says the *jinetera* has become a racialized category. "The allure for foreigners is the exotic *mulata* image. Even women who are socially white in other contexts alter their appearance to be *mulata*, trying to look more mixed by curling their hair or being very tan, because that is what sells."

Anónimo Consejo is one of many rap acts to criticize Cuban women for coveting material goods enough to sell their bodies to buy them. "Men here have a hard time dating our own women because we can't afford to buy them the things tourists can," said Entenza, with a roll of his eyes. "That's not right. Our songs try to remind girls what's really important in life."

For Pablo Herrera, there's only one formula for success, in Cuba or any-where. "Write great lyrics, have dignity, and be hard working," he says. But it takes more. In late 2001 Cabaret Las Vegas closed its Friday hip hop show to make room for a more traditional salsa crowd. "That's the way it goes in Cuba," Entenza says, bitterness in his voice. "With salsa comes the money." Later El Atelier opened for a weekly night of hip hop and remained open in 2004.

But the first and last refuge of Cuban rap has been the complex in Ala-mar. Located on the eastern side of Havana, on the other side of a long tunnel, Alamar was once billed as a shining example of communal living. In the 1970s, the giant housing complex was Fidel Castro's pet building project. More than thirty years later, rows of crumbling white buildings look out over the sea, far from most jobs and services. Few white faces lean from the rows of windows, watching the action below. It is here, in a giant empty pool, where Cuban rap began and continues. Every Fri-day night, Havana's aspiring and already established rap groups pace the pool's concrete steps and strain to be heard over a lone speaker in a cor-ner. For only five pesos, hip hop fans can make the long trek out here to hear what they won't hear on the radio: the music of their generation.

Anónimo Consejo has to pay the entrance fee like everyone else and mill with the crowd. Entenza sips from a small bottle of rum and greets his friends with high fives, while Sarrias cuddles with his girlfriend off to the side of the pool. This is their territory—everyone knows them, and no one cares much if they have a record deal. Here, they are already famous. When it comes time to perform, the sound system fades, and in the middle of one song the CD skips, leaving the duo with no background music. Sar-rias glares angrily into the hard light coming from the DJ's booth. They start again, but their energy is low. Next, a group of five young rappers come out grabbing their crotches and doing a poor imitation of the Ameri-can gangsta poses they've seen on TV. Entenza cheers them on, but Sarrias sulks on the sidelines. "I'm tired of this place. There are always prob-lems," he mutters.

Despite their lyrics about staying put in Cuba, they want more. "We are waiting around for an angel to come from abroad who recognizes our talent and is willing to invest a lot of attention and money in our project," Entenza says. But celestial intervention moves slowly. In 2001, Anónimo Consejo appeared on a U.S.-produced compilation called *Cuban Hip Hop All Stars* (Papaya Records), and they were featured in recent issues of

Source and *Vibe* magazines. They received the chance to travel around the United States, performing in various alternative hip hop shows, and in December 2003, they went to Venezuela to perform. But so far, none of that has translated into a deal or dollars.

"Sometimes I think we're supposed to live on hope alone," Entenza says back at his mother's house where his bedroom is plastered with magazine photos of NBA basketball stars and his favorite rap musicians. Then he hikes up his baggy pants and goes outside to wait for a crowded bus to Herrera's studio. A couple of British record producers were supposed to swing by to hear Anónimo Consejo lay down some beats. You never know, he says as he climbs aboard, this time it could be their big break.

Research assistance by Eve Lotter

Authors Who Knew or Know the Limits

~ EZEQUIEL MINAYA

In March 2003, seventy-five so-called dissidents, some of them independent jour-
nalists and librarians, were arrested and sentenced to up to twenty-seven years in
prison. Included in this sweep were Raúl Rivero Castañeda, who is profiled in this
piece, and Héctor Palacios Ruiz, who ran an independent library with his wife and
helped with the Varela Project, which has gathered more than 30,000 signatures to
request a referendum on basic rights. At the end of 2004, Rivero was released.

I missed him again, this time by only ten minutes. For about four days, I
have been combing Havana for Pedro Juan Gutiérrez—poet, novelist, and
journalist. I want to talk to him about his writing, Cuban writers after the
revolution, and censorship. But above all else, I want to hear his thoughts
on exiled poet Heberto Padilla.

I have stopped by underground libraries, the apartments of independent journalists, and even the crowded hangouts lining El Malecón that
Gutiérrez wrote about in his latest novel, *Dirty Havana Trilogy*. All I've
got to show for it is a messenger bag full of illegal dissident writing, a
dozen new titles from the many Havana bookstores, and more offers of
sex than I can afford.

Depending on who you ask, *Trilogy*—an international hit—may or may
not be banned in Cuba. Government officials have told me that it is not
widely read in Cuba because it is not a good book. It is typical of the
Cuban writing so popular overseas, one writers' union official told me. It
has a dash of anti-Castro—though Gutiérrez never directly names him—
and a lot of sex, the official complained. But not just sex, he continued.
"Hot *Cuban* sex," he said in a mocking tone.

People on the fringes of the state—reporters transmitting pieces critical
of the government to the United States via the Internet, librarians operating out of apartments without state sanction, writers estranged from
government-run art institutions—have told me that some works are just
not read in Cuba. "Censorship, that's your word," one nervous writer said

to me; "all I'm saying," he continued, "is that *some things are just not read in Cuba*." "Stop asking these questions," another writer advised, "you are going to get yourself or me in trouble."

"Yes, Pedro Juan is in town," I had been told several times. "Yes, he was here but a day ago," a renegade librarian said. At an independent library in Miramar: "Oh, you missed him by a couple of hours." At the independent library Dulce María, just blocks from the official writers' and artists' union, UNEAC, the caretakers—the married couple Héctor Palacios Ruiz and Gisela Delgado Sablón—say that I was off the trail by just ten minutes. "If you see Pedro Juan again, tell him I just want a little of his time," I plead. The three of us are sitting in a small back room in the couple's shabby apartment. The room is the extent of Dulce María, and, they say, a peaceful place to live when books aren't being tossed into the streets by soldiers.

Palacios Ruiz, in his loud, booming voice says that Pedro Juan knows I am looking for him. "He was considering it," says Palacios Ruiz, who has been in and out of jail because of his own writing and Dulce María. He promises to put in a good word. And as long as we are talking about favors, he says, could I do him one? Could I, he asks, carry his latest collection of essays—which include a letter he had written his wife during his latest stint in jail—to the United States. I say yes, but "please make sure that Gutiérrez gets my message," I add. "Sure," he says, "but you make sure you don't get caught with these"—he waves the thick sheaf of papers. "Do you think Gutiérrez will want to talk about Heberto Padilla?" I ask as I prepare to leave. "I don't know," Palacios Ruiz responds. What's left to say?

Plenty. How is the once international symbol of Cuban censorship remembered by notable Cuban writers living on the island today? What does Padilla's fall from grace and subsequent exile mean to Cuban writers? Could it happen again? How has Cuba changed?

On September 25, 2000, Heberto Padilla, a visiting writer and professor at Auburn University in Alabama, failed to show up for class. His students went in search of their professor and discovered him in his apartment —dead of natural causes. Padilla, sixty-eight, had suffered from heart problems. He had recently split from his wife, the writer Belkis Cuzá Malé, who was living in New Jersey at the time. Students barely knew the Cuban writer. But at the time of his death, Padilla was considered by

Havana, 2004. *Photo by Mimi Chakarova*

many writers still on the island to be one of Cuba's greatest living poets. In the next week, I'm going to visit some of them.

Back in Havana, Raúl Rivero Castañeda—a poet, journalist, and friend of Padilla's—remembered the news of Padilla's death zipping by on television so quickly that it took him a few minutes to fully understand. Rivero tried to imagine what the last years of Padilla's life had been like. Did Padilla—whose vocation as a poet immersed him in Spanish—ever grow accustomed to hearing so much English? How had Padilla handled the winters? Did he ever miss Cuba? Rivero had not forgotten Padilla. No Cuban writer could. But Padilla is remembered not only for his contributions to poetry. His story is that chapter in the Cuban Revolution that signaled the end of the honeymoon between Castro and his writers: *el caso Padilla.*

In 1968, Padilla—already a respected poet and journalist—entered the annual literary contest of the National Union of Writers and Artists (UNEAC). His entry, a collection entitled *Fuera del juego* (*Out of the Game*), offered a scathing critique of the government's iron grip on intellectual life. It had only been seven years since Castro's remarks at a conference of intellectuals. Having recently declared the Cuban Revolution a socialist one, Castro wanted intellectuals to do their part for the cause. He instructed: "What are the rights of writers and artists, be they revolutionaries or not? Within the revolution all; against the revolution nothing." That same year UNEAC was formed in imitation of the Union of Soviet Writers.

Padilla chafed under the restrictions. In *Out of the Game*, he wrote:

> The poet! Kick him out!
> He has no business here.
> He doesn't play the game.
> He never gets excited
> Or speaks out clearly.
> He never even sees the miracles.

An international and independent panel of judges awarded Padilla the nation's highest poetry prize, the Julián del Casal award, for the collection. The writers' union, however, declared Padilla's poetry "ideologically outside the principles of the Cuban Revolution."

No action was taken against Padilla until three years later, in 1971. Padilla was reading from his work at the writers' union when authorities arrested the poet. Among the tight-knit community of writers, the subsequent weeks of his absence produced the inescapable question of the season in Havana, "Where is Padilla?" He reappeared a month later and addressed many of the same people he stood before when he was detained. This time, however, he read a scathing indictment of himself and many other literary notables and friends. He condemned, among others, his wife. His public confession complete, he disappeared again. But this time, in full view. Though released from custody, Padilla would not be published for nearly a decade. He was also forbidden to leave Cuba. Friends and family avoided the thirty-nine-year-old writer, and he and Cuzá Malé lived an internal exile.

Word of *el caso Padilla* spread around the world. Soon notable leftist intellectuals began to retract their support for the revolution. A petition requesting the release of Padilla was circulated and signed by many. The diminished prestige of one man was becoming a costly loss of face for a country that, surrounded by real and imagined enemies, could not afford to lose friends. Finally, Castro decided that it was time to let Padilla go.

Cuzá Malé, who now lives in Texas, told me that Castro came to their house personally and said to Padilla, "You can go. Come back when you are ready." Padilla, then forty-eight years old, never saw Cuba again.

Antón Arrufat: *El Rehabilitado*

Central Havana is far removed from the tranquility of El Vedado, home of several state ministries, and the grandeur of Old Havana. This section of the city feels like a tough New York City neighborhood, with a similar insularity, a sense that residents are caught, like satellites, by the pull of the place. This is where Antón Arrufat, a national award-winning writer, has lived for much of his life, on the top floor of a two-story house. Like many other buildings in this part of town, it is a crumbling beauty.

Four men—ranging in age from their mid-twenties to late thirties—are hanging out on the stoop of Arrufat's house. Walking near them, I can smell booze even though it's 10:00 a.m. They are arguing over the compensation for a favor. One of the younger guys—a squat, barrel-chested man—insists, in slow, drawn-out words, that the agreed price was a half bottle of rum. One of the older men, skinny and jumpy, his voice rising, disagrees. He distinctly remembers hearing a full bottle and "mira, no vengas con mierda, coño."

I ask them if this is the home of Antón Arrufat. For a moment, they eye me, as if they don't understand the question. One of them responds, "Yeah, of course he lives here, everybody knows that." They look me over and can tell I'm not Cuban. One of them decides to help the foreigner out. "You know—what are you, Dominican? You know, *dominicano*, that Arrufat won a national award, don't you?" "Yeah, yeah," another one chimes in, "he also has a new book out, a book of essays." "*Coño*, I've got to get it," he adds.

At the appointed time, Arrufat walks out onto his wrought-iron balcony and casually waves me upstairs. I'm surprised by the lavishness of his apartment. The big rooms and high ceilings seem like they belong in New York's Dakota, not in one of Havana's poorest neighborhoods. "This neighborhood is very promiscuous, very crowded, very crime-ridden," he says, adding that fame protects him. No one messes with "the writer." And, he's clearly one. The walls are lined with bookshelves filled with every imaginable title. Throughout the tidy, quiet apartment hang and

Antón Arrufat next to his books, Havana, 2004. *Photo by Mimi Chakarova*

stand several paintings and sculptures. A small dog scampers between rooms, apparently pleased to be hosting company. Arrufat, a tall, solidly built man with broad shoulders and a soft middle, is quieter. His hair, caught up in a short ponytail, is gray, and he is wearing a plain white T-shirt and shorts. In his sixties, he wears thick eyeglasses that barely soften an intense gaze.

Besides the national literature prize, he also won the 2000 Alejo Carpentier prize for best novel with *La noche del aguafiestas* (*Night of the Spoilsports*). I was introduced to Arrufat a day earlier at the writers' union. "Here is a true genius," the man said. At the moment, Arrufat is Cuba's most celebrated writer. But it wasn't always so.

In 1968, the same year Padilla won the poetry award, Arrufat took top honors in the drama category for his play *Siete contra Tebas* (*Seven against Thebes*). The play, critical of the Marxist-Leninist regime, tripped censor alarms. The writers' union condemned Arrufat's work as containing "conflictive points in a political context that were not taken into account when the winners were selected." The play has never been staged in Cuba. And so, much as Padilla, Arrufat was imprisoned in silence. But he stayed, refusing to budge from the section of Havana he has called home since 1959, when he returned to Cuba at the age of twenty-four. "When the revolution triumphed, I was living in the United States. I was living in New York," he says. But once Castro rode into Havana, Arrufat returned home to a Cuba brimming with possibility. "It was a moment of great energy, of great happiness, of great vitality. It was like breaking everything that had existed before—just destroying it. We didn't know if with good intentions or bad, if what should have been done had actually been done or not, but that didn't matter then, what mattered was the enthusiasm of the moment, the magnitude of the time."

He became part of a group of writers known as the Generation of '50 that included Pablo Armando Fernández, César López, Manuel Díaz Martínez, Fayad Jamis, Heberto Padilla, and on and on and on. "It had the feel of a family," he says. The group established its own identity by sweeping away the old literary regime. "We belonged to a less transcendental generation," he says. "We used colloquial language, conversational language. We used the language that was around us. Metaphor was eliminated." In illustrating the difference between the writers of the fifties and the older writers, Arrufat quotes—nearly sings, really—a poem about fireflies by José Lezama Lima. He takes a poet's pleasure in every word, but "he never says the word *firefly*," Arrufat says. "I would have just said *firefly*."

T. S. Eliot, William Carlos Williams, Denise Levertov, and the Beat poets all influenced Arrufat's generation. "We tried to write a poetry whose musicality was destroyed by the poet. When a real musical verse came to mind, we busted it up, fragmented it, we made it rougher, more arid, less musical, less melodic." The writers soon, however, turned their critical eye to what was happening to the miracle that had brought them home. The revolution had begun to change, repressing homosexuals—many of whom were writers and artists—excluding the religious, and demanding complete adherence to the party line. Within the revolution all, the saying went, against the revolution nothing.

One writer, Ambrosio Fornet, called the late 1960s and early 1970s the "gray period," but Arrufat says now, "It was absolutely black." It lasted about six or seven years, Arrufat says, and during that time the government wanted writers to copy rigid Soviet realism and produce proletarian morality tales. They were also pushed to write children's literature, to impart to the youth the virtues of the revolution. But it was also an attempt, in part, Arrufat tells me, to steer writers away from controversial topics.

But it failed, Arrufat says, with him, with Padilla, and with a few others. They challenged the miracle and paid the price. "I was largely excluded for fourteen years," Arrufat says. Forbidden to publish, Arrufat shelved books in a library. But, the author says, he was going to stay in Cuba. Padilla, he remembers, was struggling with the idea of leaving. "He chose to leave," Arrufat says, without rancor of Padilla's departure. "I don't criticize him for it. I think it's fine. I chose to stay." "His life was made a little impossible, all those things that are done so a person will go overseas, things that would make people who were accusing him appear to be right. So it was 'look, he was an enemy, look how he ends up leaving.' "

Arrufat stayed and, over time, became "rehabilitated." Arrufat attributes the recovery to the natural development of the nascent revolution. "Things just went about changing." In part, he says, the government reconsidered its campaign against writers because it looked bad. "It became a serious problem for the revolution." Many of Cuba's friends, Arrufat says, "were displeased." With his reputation salvaged, Arrufat and others, including Fernández, López, and Lezama, were published again, but rarely overseas. Writers who wanted to do so had to submit their manuscripts for review, and the government further discouraged it by restricting writers' abilities to accept dollars.

But publishing in Cuba changed dramatically with the fall of the Soviet bloc. In economic crisis, the state slashed—along with everything else—publishing budgets. The number of titles dropped by two-thirds over a five-year period. Only 2,500 to 3,000 copies of any new edition were printed. Many writers wanted out. In a move as dramatic as the legalization of the dollar in 1993, writers were permitted direct publishing contracts overseas. It is a move that many credit with staving off a mass exodus. Arrufat is at the forefront of a wave of Cuban writers who now publish internationally, once considered a crime. Grijalbo-Mondadori, a Spanish publisher, released Arrufat's *Antología personal* (*Personal Anthology*) and also plans to offer *La noche del aguafiestas*. Even Abel Prieto, Cuba's minister of culture, publishes outside Cuba.

Though Arrufat makes it clear that he has not lived outside Cuba since

1959, he travels often. He has spent up to three months visiting Spain and Mexico and five months visiting family in Saint Paul, Minnesota. I ask him if his life is what Padilla could have had had he stayed. "I think so," Arrufat says. "I think so." But freedom has its limits. I ask Arrufat about President Castro's comments during the annual Cuban book fair. Castro told visitors that there were no prohibited books in Cuba. Arrufat gives me a long, steely gaze. "Well, here, I don't think there are prohibited books." He stops for a moment. "There are books that don't enter. There are books that don't enter. That don't enter." He repeats the phrase softly, letting it trail off. "Well, that's enough," he says suddenly. The interview is over.

My search for Pedro Juan has hit rock bottom. I've just paid over twenty dollars to two *jineteros* (hustlers) who say they can find anybody in Havana. "Yeah sure, we know the writer Pedro Juan." I met them at a jazz club. We can show you the real Havana, they say with inviting smiles.

Pedro is the good-looking one of the two. He is tall and an unbroken shade of dark brown. He has a shaved head and big, sparkling eyes. Manny is the brooder. He is heavyset and wears a baseball cap low. As we walk toward El Malecón, Manny asks, "Do you like girls? How about some real Cuban rum? How about some Coke?"

A block away from the sea, two police officers stop us. The muscular men wear neat brown uniforms, shirts tucked in, tight over their broad shoulders and big arms. They address Pedro and Manny with disdainful formality; come here comrades, IDs comrades, stand still, comrades. They ignore me and pull Pedro and Manny several feet away. I'm told to wait. I can't hear what he is saying, but Manny is explaining the hell out of himself. He is waving his hands with an urgent look on his face. Every once in a while, after one of the officers asks a question, Manny just vigorously shakes his head; no, no, no.

The officers approach me. "Sir, do you know who you are hanging out with?" one of them asks. My friends, I say and smile. That man, he points to Manny, has been in jail for robbing tourists like you. "No me diga," I say. Don't tell me.

"Now, Sir," he continues, "have these men sold you any tobacco or rum?" Though he is out to stop a black-market transaction, I think to myself, he has stumbled across something better: an American with a satchel full of dissident ramblings. "Don't get caught with these," I can hear Palacios Ruiz say. At worst, I would be arrested, questioned, and deported. But Palacios Ruiz said he would catch hell again if anyone found his writing in the hands of an American journalist. "No, Sir, no rum, no cigars," I say. "Can we check your bag, Sir?" "Of course," I say. I do my best imitation of a bumbling foreigner. "Oh, I dropped my notebook, it's a little dark on this side of the sidewalk. Oh, there goes all my change. Well, I guess you can't really see inside the bag. Let's. . . . What do you say we cross the street to get under those streetlamps." "No, no, Sir, it's fine," the officer says. "Have a good night." Thank God Havana police don't carry flashlights, I think to myself. My heart is racing. How does Héctor live with this fear?

Raúl Rivero Castañeda: *Inxile*

Neatly arranged on a small glass coffee table in the Central Havana home of Raúl Rivero Castañeda—an award-winning poet and internationally acclaimed journalist—are small, framed photographs in various sizes. They form a triangle, the tip of which is a picture of a young girl. The second tier is two photos of teenagers. In all, there are about ten frames. Blanca Reyes, Raúl's wife, points to each picture and says a name and then whether the person lives in Cuba or Miami. "He's gone," she says about her son. "She's gone," she says of her husband's daughter from an earlier marriage. There is no emotion in her voice. Two years later, in March 2003, Rivero is arrested, and by April he is sentenced to twenty years in prison.

But that night in 2001, Rivero is still free and he's running late. He is, no doubt, working on a story, his wife says. I sit in one of three rocking chairs in the small living room. There are a few photographs on the walls—portraits of young people bearing a resemblance to either Rivero or his wife. There is a small television, the small coffee table, a larger, round wooden table against the wall, and the rocking chairs. The floor is tiled in dingy linoleum.

We are joined by the silent and slightly hunched mother of Rivero. She slowly shuffles to a rocking chair and sits down. Reyes takes from me a small duffel bag filled with medicine, vitamins, video cassettes of children's television programming, and a digital video camera. Their friends in Miami sent the care package. We strike up a conversation. We talk about the movie *Before Night Falls*, based on the life of exiled Cuban writer Reinaldo Arenas. Reyes, who knew the writer, remembers Arenas as a rude, blunt, moody character who said whatever was on his mind, no matter the consequences. She says the actor who played the lead caused a buzz in Central Havana when he moved into Arenas's former home. She hears the actor is up for an Oscar. She recalls an editorial in the few, slim pages of the official newspaper, *Granma*, saying that it would be a victory of politics and not art if he won the award. Later that month, he loses.

The light from the open balcony begins to dim. Over the next round of strong, syrupy coffee, the talk shifts to politics. Rivero's mother gets up, slowly shakes her head, and shuffles out of the room. Reyes cannot contain a small chuckle, nodding her head in the direction of her mother-in-law.

Rivero finally comes home. He is of average height and stocky. He enters the living room, sees me, smiles, and walks forward, hand extended. The three flights up have left the heavyset smoker out of breath and speaking in short, clipped bursts. He has one more thing to do before his day is done, he says. It has something to do with his journalist network. "I'm sorry," he says, "it can't be helped." In moments, I'm standing in the hallway, the door closed behind me. The meeting is rescheduled.

A couple of days later, Rivero keeps the appointment. He is relaxed, but his face is still a light shade of red. He sweeps his thinning blond hair with his hand often. He is casually dressed, with the top buttons on his striped shirt open. He is wearing shorts and slippers. He chain-smokes throughout the conversation, whittling to the butt one Marlboro after another. We sit in rocking chairs, facing the balcony and its view of Central Havana's rooftops. "The same thing that is happening with the Cuban family," he says pointing toward the photos around him, "is happening with the literary Cuban family—there is division."

"On one side of the divide are writers that work with the government and collect all the perks: travel, book parties, conferences," he says. "Many of them were once sanctioned," he says, during the gray period, but have returned to good graces with a vengeance. "Pablo Armando Fernández was sanctioned for about ten years because of the Padilla case, Antón Arrufat, César López, all those people had problems. But they have returned and are now in absolute harmony with the government." It was once that way for Rivero. "I, once upon at time, also made that pact. I moved in that world, when I supported the government." That was before he crossed over to the other side of the divide.

Rivero was one of the first generation to get a degree in journalism from the University of Havana after the triumph of the revolution. He eventually became a senior correspondent for the state news agency. He was also successful with his art. In 1969, the writers' union gave him an award for his poem "Papel de hombre" (A man's role), and in 1972 he won the Julián del Casal award for the book *Poesía sobre la tierra* (*Poetry on Earth*). He also served as the right-hand man of the first president of the writers' union, Nicolás Guillén.

But in 1989, Rivero, like Padilla before him, grew disenchanted. He quit his position at the writers' union. And in 1991, he completely broke with the government when he joined nine other writers in composing an open letter to Castro, asking for greater freedom of expression and the release of prisoners of conscience. "When we signed the letter, there were ten of us. [Members of the group] began to leave immediately. People were attacked. María [one of the signers] went to jail for two years. Reasons were found to arrest them. I wasn't a member of any political party, so I was left here. But we got harassing phone calls. People saying they were going to kill us in our sleep." Rivero says that, as happened with Padilla, friends and family stopped visiting.

"We spent many years in a very bad situation. I'm telling you, we sold everything we had, everything, clothing, everything, because we had nothing. I couldn't publish." Rivero says that crowds of his neighbors would gather beneath his balcony, yelling threats at "the family of traitors." He says the yelling has stopped, but his home still gets searched by police from time to time, and his phone is tapped. "On television they have a program called *Roundtable*. They have said on that show that 'Raúl Rivero is a reactionary counterrevolutionary who receives money from the U.S. Interests Section.'" In 2000, President Castro referred to Rivero as a drunk. Rivero, who admits to having had a drinking problem, has been sober for years.

Of the ten signers of the open letter, Rivero is one of the few left in Cuba. In 2004, he is still in prison. But that night in 2001, he was indignant when I asked why he decided to stay. "Why should I leave? This is my country."

Rivero is an independent journalist and professional *inxile*, a name

Raúl Rivero Castañeda, an independent journalist who was arrested in March 2003 and sentenced to twenty years in prison. Family photograph, published with permission of Ricardo Trotti of the Inter-American Press Association.

he coined in 2000 in a *Miami Herald* article. *Inxiles* are, Rivero wrote, writers who still live in Cuba but openly oppose or at least criticize the government and as a result are kept from publishing and often face harassment. Arrufat was an *inxile*, he says, as were Lezama and Fernández. "But the first *inxile* was Padilla," Rivero claims. "Heberto was left completely alone; all of us younger writers completely distanced ourselves from him. After having much of the same things happen to me, I understand more than ever [Padilla's suffering]."

"You can't call people because you don't know if they are scared to meet with you." He gives the example of a friend—who Rivero asks not be named—who still moves in official circles. If anyone was to find out that they still spoke, he says, his friend would be at risk of losing his job and status in the community. So, if they were ever to run into each other in public, his friend would probably ignore Rivero. The latter wouldn't blame him. "He's not a bad person. He just lives in Cuba," he says with a smile.

Rivero is openly harassed, but other writers, he says, are kept in line by more subtle means—a change from the open repression of the gray years. "Don't forget that here the state is the only employer, the one owner of everything. [The government] used to insist that [writers] show publicly their loyalty to the country. Now, if not that, at least try not to write in opposition, keep quiet, in a very discrete way." If a writer steps out of line, Rivero says, his or her requests to travel are suddenly denied and invitations to conferences and events stop coming. And in the case of continued and open defiance, Rivero says, these people lose their jobs and are left to the ravages of poverty.

In 1994, in the midst of his own precarious financial situation, Rivero was contacted by an exiled Cuban journalist living in Spain, who commissioned two columns. That was when, Raúl says, the idea for an independent news service began to form. A Miami contact gathered the financing for a Web site and Cubapress was born. "We try to have people from all over the country. It's hard, because it's hard to get people in the remote provinces, and it's hard to train others. At the moment, we have sixteen reporters." Reporters dictate their work over the phone or smuggle it overseas over black-market Internet lines. Wages are around twenty-five dollars a month, which in Cuba, Rivero says, is enough money to survive. In 1997, the French foundation Reporters sans Frontières (Reporters without Borders) honored Rivero and Cubapress with its annual award. He was unable to attend the award ceremony, he says, because of fears he would not be allowed back into Cuba.

He now knows how Padilla felt, Rivero says. And he is happy he was able to tell him before Padilla's death. Before Padilla died, Rivero was on the phone with an editor in Miami. After they were done talking business, the editor said that she had somebody there who wanted to say hello. "It was Heberto," Rivero says. "And I told Heberto, 'You must have suffered a lot because it's exactly how much we are suffering now,' but it must have been a lot worse for him, because he didn't have some one like Heberto Padilla, in exile, to talk to him." He pauses and buries his chin in his hand.

Rivero talks a bit more. But soon the seemingly boundless energy Rivero had at the beginning of the interview wanes. He lends me the only copy of his latest poetry collection, published in Spain. Outside, while waiting for a taxi, I open Rivero's book and begin to read at random. I stop at the poem "National Pride": "None of our officials are rich / None have estates, factories, or companies / None have accounts in Swiss banks / Nor do they want them." I can't help but be surprised.

Alberto Guerra: *El Muerto*

Even by the lofty standards set by street after street of haunted, crumbling mansions in El Vedado, UNEAC, the writers' union on the corner of 17 and H, is impressive. It is a peach-colored, two-storied mansion with marble columns, ringed by the thin bars of a black iron fence. Just off to the side of the front entrance and down a small stone path, artists sit in the Hurón Azul Café, enjoying the rays of the midafternoon sun, quietly talking at small tables. The porch is also peopled with groups talking in undulating volume about painting, film, writing, art. There are young people who could pass for New York bohos, and older conversationalists who have a more rigid informality to them, as if they were on a corporate picnic. This is the place that the world comes to when it wants its fix of Cuban culture. Want a trio of folk musicians plucking out revolutionary arrangements? An Afrocuban poet? A Cuban sculpture? This is where you go.

Alberto Guerra, one of the young stars of Cuban writing, prefers to stay away. He stays at home, in the far-flung Havana neighborhood of Playa, seated in front of his computer, chasing his dream, his foremost ambition, of being a great writer.

In 1976, Castro decreed that basic cultural centers were to be built in each of Cuba's two hundred municipalities. These centers were a museum, a cultural hall, a movie theater, an art gallery, a bookstore, and a library. It was in those cultural centers, especially the library, that Guerra, and many of the young writers of his generation, first discovered literature and their own talent. It was there that during the international furor over Padilla, he says, he studied, gaining a solid intellectual foundation. But now, all Guerra wants to do is write. He quit his job at UNEAC and has withdrawn his membership in the Communist Party. "I try to stay as distant as I can so I can *write*. That's to say I don't engage in a social life. Because the more of a social life, the less intellectual intensity. So I stay here. Here in my neighborhood, in Reparto Flores, in my house, writing," he says.

Guerra is in his forties, but can pass, with ease, for someone ten years younger. He lives in a modest one-bedroom house with his wife, who also defies her age, and their teenage daughter. Guerra, black, with a shaved head, is proud of his heritage. One of the few adornments on his wall is a portrait of one of his ancestors, Tiburcio Naranjo, one of the first Afro-cuban officers in the Cuban military.

Guerra is very pleased that I have come to speak to him. I read one of his stories in the UNEAC literary magazine and saw in it a quality that I had not seen in any of the other pieces in the union's literary offers. The story, "El muerto" ("The Dead Man") is a muscular, taut story that only uses commas, no periods, and tells the tale of a young Cuban who assumes the identity of tourist. "I wanted to take a look at the situation in Cuba of the presence of tourists. But I decided to look at it through the eyes of an average Cuban."

The story opens with the first-person narrator in a hotel bathroom stall, counting *fulas*, street slang for dollars: "Seated on the can, my man, with the door nice and shut, I count the money and I can't believe it, my lord, I say to myself, I count it again, slowly, with my pants at my ankles, as if I was wrapped up in the business of taking a dump, so the employees and the curious suspect nothing, nine hundred bucks is not a dream, I say to myself, real, constant, I count them again." The narrator then decides to wear his new identity out on the town, carrying himself with the mixture of stupidity and arrogance, according to the story, typical of tourists. "Soy un yuma," I am a *yuma*, the narrator says to convince himself that he is passing in his guise, *yuma* being slang for a tourist from either the United States or Europe. As a tourist, the unnamed narrator sees Havana open up to him. Women throw themselves at him, drawn to him by his money. Bartenders, who would otherwise not look twice at him, busy themselves, almost exclusively, to his comfort. Hotels that do not permit Cubans to enter, open up to him and his money.

In a sense, contemporary Cuban literature has come full circle with Guerra's short story. In 1950, Nicolás Guillén wrote an essay entitled "Josephine Baker in Cuba." The piece opens with a scene in which a hand-wringing clerk of the national hotel turns the singer away because of her dark skin. El Nacional was off limits to black people and all other Cubans who could not afford its exorbitant prices. Guillén writes that the hotel might as well have been a part of another country, dropped into the middle of Cuba. It was not for Cubans.

Today, with the legalization of the dollar and the country's increased dependency on tourism, the government does not allow Cubans to step into hotels and other tourist areas, unless they work there. Not only black people but all Cubans are subjected to apartheid-like laws. This is the environment that Guerra wants to capture. The Havana overrun by young girls from the countryside who come to work the streets. It matters little that some of these women are college educated because their jobs, if they have any, will only pay a fraction of what it costs to survive. It's a Havana where socialist ideals vanish as the need for dollars becomes the ruling principle. The narrator of "El muerto" ends up gorging himself on all the food and drink he can buy. Then, in a vivid scene, he throws it all up. "I'm happy when my work connects with someone," Guerra tells me.

His wife is giving him the cold shoulder today. She is upset that he has quit his job at the writers' union. But Guerra saw his position there as little more than a distraction. He has to write. A black man has to prove himself twice to measure up to standards in Cuba, he says. Nobody, certainly not anyone in the union, is going to give him what he wants, a place in the Cuban canon. He's going to have to take it. And he's made progress. In 1992, he won a major writing award. And he also accompanied Miguel Barnet on a reading tour of Germany. Barnet, head of the culture ministry's Fundación de Fernando Ortiz and a major writer of an older generation, thrilled Guerra when he mentioned that many years earlier he had gone on the same tour with famed Mexican writer Juan Rulfo. "That's the first time I ever felt like a writer," Guerra says with a smile.

Guerra's generation is called the "the newest of the new." But even though his generation is celebrated as the next big thing, there are already, he says, a group of younger writers preparing to charge up the literary hill. "We have yet to fully arrive and already we're being challenged," he laughs. We smoke cigarettes and talk writing for hours. But he doesn't seem to want to talk about Padilla. Finally, he relents. Of course, he says, he's heard about Heberto Padilla. Who hasn't? "Sure, it can happen again," he says. He seems reluctant to pursue the topic. "Look," he finally says, "I just hope it doesn't happen to me."

I have pretty much given up on finding Pedro Juan, but I decide to stop by Dulce María one last time to see if my luck changes. Palacios Ruiz is happy to see me. After coffee and cigarettes I ask if he has had a chance to speak to Pedro Juan about seeing me. Yes, he says, he was able to meet with Pedro Juan one last time before he went back home to another province. "I'm sorry," Palacios Ruiz says, "he did not want to talk to you. He doesn't want any trouble."

Dancers Who Stretch the Limits

~ ANA CAMPOY

The lights are dim and the red velvet curtain is up. Hundreds of expectant eyes stare at the bare stage. They know he's coming—they read his name on the program—but a split second later, Rolando Sarabia still takes them by surprise. Before the first chord, he flies onto the stage like a disc soaring through the air. One, two, three, four. Is he ever coming down?

He does, but only long enough for the audience to catch its breath. Then Sarabia takes flight again, blurring the air as he spins and lands perfectly balanced. Unlike him, the audience, a rowdy crowd of university students, bureaucrats, blue-collar workers, grandparents, and school children, is in motion. They hoot, cheer, and whistle as if Sarabia had just hit a home run. But the delicate shoal of white tutus that suddenly flutters on stage reminds them that they are at Havana's Gran Teatro and not at a baseball game. The corps de ballet is perfect—not a wing out of place—and it is clear that Sarabia, while exceptional, is not an exception.

If such flawless dancing is expected in London or New York, where the upper class, dressed in suits and gowns, waits until the end of a piece to clap politely, it is a staggering feat in a small country where the masses, not the elite, are the aficionados. Among them sits their idol, Alicia Alonso. Nearly blind but completely in control of the company that she has dominated for longer than Fidel Castro has ruled the island, she oversees her life's work from the central balcony. Alicia, who like Fidel is known to everyone by her first name, created her own revolution. In less than thirty years she erected a dance establishment from the ground up, indoctrinated Cubans in her art, and produced dancers sought after by the best companies in the world. But will it survive Alicia? "Ballet in Cuba will surely continue," Ismael Albelo Oti, ballet expert and official of the Ministry of Culture, told me. "How, is what nobody knows."

The story of Cuban ballet begins with three children who loved to dance, Alicia Martínez and Alberto and Fernando Alonso. Fortunately for them, they belonged to a privileged class that appreciated good ballet and brought the biggest stars of the day to Cuba. But when the Great Depression hit their island, the wealthy could no longer afford to import their entertainment, so they created a moneymaking scheme, a ballet school at a mansion in Vedado, a well-to-do neighborhood in Havana. As its manager served Laura Rainieri de Alonso, an art-loving, progressive pianist from an aristocratic family who ignored the rules of machismo and sent her two boys, Fernando and Alberto, to train. But the majority of students at the Escuela Pro Arte Musical were girls, among them Alicia. She was Cinderella-charmed—slipping into her first pointe slippers at the age of ten because her feet were the only ones in the school to fit into them. But she also pushed herself hard. She danced the main roles with Alberto and fell in love with Fernando.

Like any talented dancers from a small country, the three young Cubans soon outgrew the local scene. So Alberto left for Monaco; and Fernando and the fifteen-year-old Alicia eloped to New York. There, they practiced ballet during the day and kept house in a Spanish Harlem tenement at night. A baby, Laurita, soon joined their household. But child rearing did not keep Alicia away from barres, the slender wooden poles dancers use to practice. Sometimes she paid fifty cents to take a class in a West Side church with Enrico Zanfretta, a master of the Italian school of ballet. When she could afford it, she paid a dollar to take class with Alexandra Fedorova, a veteran of the recently disbanded Ballets Russes directed by Serge Diaghilev. After losing out to opera for the later part of the nineteenth century, the Russian impresario had put ballet back on the main stage in the early 1900s with avant-garde productions to music by Stravinsky, costumes by Picasso, and choreography by Nijinski. But with Diaghilev's death in 1929, his company collapsed and its dancers made do in New York and elsewhere. "At that time there existed no big ballet companies that maintained a repertoire and shows for even part of the year," Alicia writes in her book *Diálogos con la danza* (*Dialogues with Dance*).

Only Broadway offered steady work. Its chorus lines were the sole option for starting dancers like Jerome Robbins, Nora Kaye, and Alicia. She danced in the Fritz Loewe musical *Great Lady* and Ethel Merman's *Stars in Your Eyes*, but the bright lights and lavish productions failed to match her dreams. The American Ballet Caravan came closer. Run by Lincoln Kirstein, it was one of the first efforts to create an institution of American ballet. Though short-lived, it was filled with talent, including William

Dollar, Lew Christensen, and Alicia. When it fell apart, Lucia Chase, a dancer and millionaire, put up the money for a new company, called Ballet Theater. Its star was Alicia Markova, an English dancer known for her Giselle. Her name was really Alicia Marks, but she had added "ova" at the end to make it sound more Russian—thanks to Diaghilev, everyone who was anyone in the ballet world of the time wanted to be Russian. "She seemed to laymen to float in a mist," wrote choreographer Agnes de Mille. But one day Markova got too sick to float. None of the dancers dared step into her spotlight—except one. Twenty-two-year-old Alicia Alonso, who refused her producer's suggestion to Russianize her name, took Markova's place. After her performance, George Schaffe, a ballet paraphernalia collector, went backstage, untied Alicia's pointes from her blistered, bloody feet and kissed them. "For history," he said as he ran off with the shoes.

In a dance documentary, critic Ann Barzel explained Alicia's powers. "Alicia Alonso is a great ballet technician, but there are more things than what people think is technique: there is virtuosity and there is technique. Alicia has both." In practice, this means that Alicia could not only raise her legs higher and bend her back farther than anyone else, but she could also do it more elegantly. George Balanchine, then forty-three, made use of Alicia's abilities in his *Theme and Variations.* As with all his dancers, the choreographer pushed Alicia to bring out her best. He set a routine of steps for her, and when she did them perfectly on the first try, he created an even more complicated combination for her. The result was a "show-piece" of virtuosity, wrote Walter Terry in the *New York Herald Tribune* after its debut. "Alicia Alonso danced the principal role commendably. Its fleetness of action, the long sweepingness of its patterns were in complete harmony with this dancer's basic gifts."

By the time the Ballet Theater broke up a year later, in 1948, Alicia had danced all the important roles, and the Alonsos were ready to go home. Within months, they had started Cuba's first professional company, the Ballet Alicia Alonso. "She was the famous one," Fernando said explaining the name of the company and later of the school, Escuela Alicia Alonso. But Alicia's fame was not enough. Money was scarce and to finance her Cuban plans, Alicia returned to New York where Chase's old company had been reconstituted as the enduring American Ballet Theater. The accolades for Alicia continued. "Technically perfect, dramatically forceful and very much human," wrote the *Daily Express* in 1953.

"One of the greatest ballerinas in the world." But in Cuba, her company struggled despite modest government help. After General Fulgencio Batista overthrew the elected government in a 1952 coup, even that disappeared. The dictator insisted that the troupe earn its subsidy by becoming part of his government. The Alonsos refused. Alicia wrote a public letter to condemn Batista's "bribe" and organized a national tour to denounce it. In white tutu and full makeup, she appeared at the end of each show to promise that she would not set her pointes again on the Cuban stage until Batista left it.

But behind closed doors, the company kept dancing. At their ballet school, Fernando, Alicia, and Alberto innovated. "We took a little from the Russian school, a little from the English, some of what we had learned in the United States, and put it together," says Fernando. At the time, Russian technique had overshadowed the more traditional Italian and French schools and dominated the ballet world. Fernando took its strength, combined it with the fast footwork from the Italians, added a good dose of Caribbean sensuousness, and made it all "the Cuban school of ballet."

The shirtless Sarabia dancing at the Gran Teatro epitomizes Fernando's project. Although his toned body flows through the combination, each step is executed with clinical precision. Unlike the Russians, who emphasize arm work, or the Danish and Americans, who focus on legwork, Cubans use their whole bodies to dance. But gracefulness does not make Sarabia less macho than any Cuban out on the street. When his partner walks in, their dance becomes flirtation. It took Sarabia eight years of training to dance like that and Fernando more than twenty to develop the system to teach him how to do it, but neither could have developed in Cuba without Fidel Castro.

While the Alonsos worked in the studio, the *comandante* and his *barbudos* fought in the sierras. A few months after they marched into Havana and Batista left the Cuban stage forever, the revolution knocked on the Alonsos' door. Alicia was away and Fernando was reading a book when their daughter Laura announced the visitors. "Tell them to come up," he said. In walked Fidel Castro and one of his collaborators. Sitting at the edge of the bed, they talked with Fernando about world and local politics for hours, until Fidel said, "I came here to talk about ballet."

"I always have time to talk about ballet," Fernando recalls saying. "How much money do you need for the ballet company to start up again?" Fidel asked. "I don't know, *Comandante*, 100,000 dollars," answered Fernando. Fidel, Fernando says, gave them 200,000. "The revolution was a beautiful thing in the beginning," Fernando says. So was the future of the ballet. It had revolution pesos and a full-time star to back it up—three really, Alicia, the dancer, Fernando, the director and teacher, and Alberto, the choreographer. Rebaptized as Ballet Nacional de Cuba to match its funding, the company also showed revolutionary zeal. With the same passion that Alicia had rejected Batista, she embraced Fidel and gladly put on green fatigues to dance a work choreographed by the Soviet Azari Pliezlatzky, who also played the role of El Comandante. Shortly after the revolution, the government declared that ballet was "one of the most elevated and beautiful artistic manifestations" and that it would strive to make it available to "all social classes, preferably to workers and other popular sectors." Dancers took their new role seriously. They performed on makeshift platforms set in factories, in schools, and in countryside cane fields.

The prima ballerina even got on her knees to harvest the national product—the ballet later switched to planting coffee because cane cutting was too harsh on their bodies. But she also trained her corps relentlessly, and in 1964, when her dancers traveled to the international ballet competition in Varna, Bulgaria, the rest of the world got its first glimpse of the Cuban miracle. "Before the competition we realized there were some Cuban names, but we did not think anything of them," says Arnold Haskell, an English ballet expert who attended. "And remember that we at Varna thought we knew everything about the world of ballet and that nothing could surprise us."

The Cubans did. The technique that Fernando had developed years earlier and that the three Alonsos had perfected mesmerized. At the end of the competition, the Cubans walked away with gold medals. The Alonsos' experiment had worked, and now everyone wanted a part of it. Suddenly, says Haskell, "Everyone in the ballet world talked about Cuba." Countries from Mexico to Argentina dispatched their dancers and teachers to the island to pick up the new expression. And like the doctors and the *guerilleros* sent to the third world by Castro to represent the Cuban Revolution, the ballet sent its dancers to France, the Soviet Union, and Japan.

But not all those who left were ambassadors of the new order. In 1966, during the starkest period of homosexual persecution in Cuba, ten male dancers defected on a tour in Paris, leaving ballerinas without partners. Already the Alonsos had trouble getting little Cuban boys to pull on leotards instead of baseball jerseys, so, taking a lesson from the Soviets,

A ballerina takes a moment to rest, Havana, 2004. *Photo by Mimi Chakarova*

they started to recruit children in the countryside, offering them scholarships and molding them under an eight-year training system that included everything from history to technique. By 1968, the first generation of dancers was ready to take the stage.

One of them was Jorge Esquivel. Now a teacher at the San Francisco Ballet, a ponytailed Esquivel remembers being recruited from an orphanage in Havana. "The Cuban government gave me everything, an education, a place to stay and to eat," he says. By this time, the Alonsos' school had turned into the government's Escuela Nacional de Danza. And very much like the regime bureaucracy, it spread out until it covered every province on the island with a branch where children could learn ballet, drama, and gymnastics, as well as history, math, and literature.

To make sure *tendus* and pirouettes were identical in Havana and the rest of the island, teachers went back and forth, and still do. Once a year, the best graduating students from the elementary schools are selected and transferred to the middle school in Havana for five more years of training. "We were lucky," says Esquivel, "we had Alicia, the dancer and international figure; we had Fernando, the director and the teacher; and we had

Alberto, the choreographer; it was a triangle that helped ballet in Cuba go forward." This system created a unique style passed on from generation to generation, says Esquivel, a trait lacking from his American students' education. "They want to say they have studied with many different professors, but it is impossible to acquire a style like that," says Esquivel, "You need continuity."

Esquivel got it. After wearing out the bottoms of his slippers on the school floors for eight years, he moved straight to the Gran Teatro in 1968. He was eighteen and danced with Alicia, then forty-seven. She played Giselle, he Prince Albrecht; she Juliet, he Romeo. On stage they looked like the perfect couple, she the beautiful, supple princess and he the strong, charming prince. Despite her age, the critics loved them. A year after the partnership was formed, the Mexican newspaper *El Día* wrote of the forty-eight-year-old ballerina, "The miracle of vision dances, and when she does, we know what it is to dance and to dance perfectly. The prima ballerina of the world." And when Alicia was forty-nine and almost blind from a series of operations to correct detached retinas, the German *Leipziger Volkszeitung* wrote, "Artistic grandeur shines on her. At once spectacular and pure."

But as time went by—Esquivel was Alicia's partner for eighteen years, or until he turned thirty-six and she sixty-five—the prince got tired of the princess. Alicia, he says, ruled more like the mean stepmother than like Cinderella. Dancers who obeyed went on tours; those who balked stayed at home. But even the ballerinas who behaved found few rewards other than travel. "Alicia wanted all the good roles for herself," says Esquivel. His wife at the time, Amparo Brito, won the gold medal in Varna when she was eighteen years old, but Alicia failed to move her up to important roles until she turned forty, an age at which most dancers have retired to teaching. "We were like pawns on a chessboard with someone moving us around at their convenience," says Esquivel. "Alicia stopped being human, to mistreat people. She wouldn't pay us our money."

The Esquivels were not the only unhappy ones. Fernando divorced Alicia in 1974. "Alicia and I started to have a lot of differences, so I left to Camagüey," he says referring to an Eastern city where the ballet company struggles to survive today. When he was head of it, the Ballet de Camagüey was successful, but competition with Havana for ballets and dancers tired Fernando. At the beginning of the Special Period in 1990, he left for Mexico City to direct the Ballet Nacional there. Later he moved to the northern city of Monterrey to direct a local ballet company and later to head the dance department at a local university. Alberto, the ballet's principal choreographer, dealt with Alicia's temperament by traveling frequently, but by 1993, he, too, had had enough and left permanently. He is now in Miami, teaching at a community college and staging works to Gloria Estefan music. Esquivel did not wait that long to say good-bye to Alicia. In 1986, he left the ballet and continued dancing independently in Cuba and occasionally abroad. On a tour in Italy in 1992, the prince finally defected. "I was tired. I wanted my freedom," he says.

Esquivel's critique of Alicia can begin to sound like a Miami Cuban's rant against Fidel, but he concedes to the prima ballerina what no exile would to El Comandante: "She is a genius." Many agree. Despite limited vision, Alicia managed to dance from one end of the stage to the other, captivating audiences in Cuba and far beyond. "She moves in life. Her feet, her torso, her arms, neck, and eyes, are one continuing action, taking their dynamic from her meaning. She talks. Her heart is open. Here is the essence of a dancer. It is her core she gives us; it is our core," wrote Agnes de Mille. She choreographed Alicia in the days when she could do thirty-two *fouettes*, the ballet equivalent to a triple axel in ice-skating or a grand slam in baseball.

Alicia can now barely walk, but in Cuba her admirers remember her performances as though they were yesterday. "I never saw her make a movement without any meaning," says Miguel Cabrera, the ballet's historian. And then he relates the time when Alicia was dancing Giselle. Her dress got caught up in one of the props and ripped. Instead of looking embarrassed, Alicia took a look at it, and a great sadness overcame her. She went up to her stage mother to show her how her pretty dress had ripped. Then she continued to dance. Another time she went out on stage with her costume half open, but she managed to zip it while she danced before anyone noticed. "That's her art, she transformed a very embarrassing situation, an accident, into art," says Cabrera.

This art was made available to all Cubans. The prima ballerina performed on every stage on the island—established or improvised—at proletarian prices. Even the post–Special Period entrance cost remains low: five pesos or twenty-five cents. As a result, ballet followers more resemble a sports crowd than the aristocratic elite who first brought the dance form to Cuba. Fans yell and roar in the middle of a performance. Dancers have had to stop in the middle of their routines to bow because the applause drowns the orchestra. Bouquets are thrown left and right to the favorite dancer of the moment, and when fans disagree, they come to blows.

On the night Sarabia danced, I met one of those fans, Pedro Vidal, a thirty-nine-year-old unemployed electronics technician with a black mustache and a part in the middle of his hair. Like most ballet-goers, he was dressed casually in jeans and loafers. He told me he had not missed a ballet show since he was six and Alicia was forty-seven. Like other children who watched her on TV or in public shows at stadiums, Vidal wanted to be a dancer. But he was too fat and instead became a loyal fan. I realize how loyal at his small apartment a few blocks from the Gran Teatro. It is actually more like a hallway than a full apartment, with a bedroom just big enough to fit a bed, a small dresser, and a table with a TV and a VCR, which he carefully protects from the dust with a piece of cloth. When he removes it and puts in one of the many carefully marked tapes that fill his dresser, the windowless room decorated with posters of kittens and bikinied girls is transformed. It becomes a theatre where the ballet dances solely for Vidal: "Every time you see a performance, you learn more and grow. I can tell you that I don't know the names of all the steps, but I know when the dancers do them well."

He watches them in Havana and follows the company on tours around the island. And when the dancers are resting, he gets his ballet fix in his small apartment. "I watch these tapes all the time," he says. "This is Diana and Acteon. I must have watched this one more than seventy times, and look at my skin, I still get goose bumps." Of Alicia's Giselle, he says, "The theater almost fell with applause." But if Giselle never aged, Alicia did. In another of Vidal's tapes, Alicia is in her late sixties. A stiff figure appears on stage suspended by what must be, has to be, a very strong dancer. She is more like a sack of potatoes in a pink dress than a ballerina. She is lowered to the ground and turned to one side, then to the other, her hands clinging to the dancer's neck to avoid the floor only a few feet below. Her face carries an expression of pride. Her partner's face, however, one of pure angst. Later, Alicia's grandson, Iván, who danced with her during her last days, tells me the experience was frightening. "Standing on a stage is difficult enough, now imagine standing on it with your grandmother and, even more, struggling to not let her fall," he says. Her fan Vidal just shakes his head. "It was very embarrassing at the end," he says; "she should have retired in 1985." Instead, she danced until she was seventy-four.

Alicia was eighty-three years old in early 2004. Still, she can hardly move or see, but she has kept a strong grip over the ballet. For more than thirty years, she has been the company's director, choreographer, and *maître*, and none of these titles is held in name only. Like a girl playing Barbies, Alicia decides what everyone wears, who gets the car, who the motorcycle, who will go abroad, with whom they will dance, and, of course, what they will dance. For the most part, they dance whatever Alicia has created, a fact that has as much to do with money as her attachment to the classics. The Sociedad General de Autores y Escritores de España (General Society of Authors and Writers of Spain) registers Cuban works and pays their authors royalties any time they are performed outside the island. Since Alicia determines the repertoires, she also gets paid frequently.

But tough economic times have forced the prima donna to loosen her rein on the company. No longer do dancers who want to dance abroad have to defect. Alicia allows them to take contracts in foreign companies, but as she did fifty years ago, she requires them to send part of their earnings to fund the ballet. José Manuel Carreño dances for the American Ballet Theater under those conditions, and so does Carlos Junior Acosta at the Royal Ballet in London. Alihaydée Carreño, current first dancer and cousin of José Manuel, is about to leave for Washington, DC, on a similar contract. Lorna Feijóo, the other star dancer of the moment, just returned from Costa Rica. Feijóo goes on tour several times a year and although she, too, has to contribute to the company's coffers, she keeps some of the dollars. It shows. She wears a designer black velvet leotard. Her silver toenails sparkle on her deformed feet. After class, she slips on some cargo capris and grabs her leather purse that can only be Spanish or Italian. She walks to the door, head held high.

Other dancers' salaries do not stretch that far. They wear imitation Nikes and backpacks, or slide-in sandals like those sold in the tourist market in Havana. And in 2003, fifteen to twenty of them left, saying they had too few opportunities and too many restrictions in Cuba. The dancers want to experiment with more modern fare, and the culture ministry is well aware the ballet needs some new choreographic blood. Its officials, too, were sitting in the audience a few years ago when the Washington Ballet performed in Havana. In fact, it was through their efforts that the American company was able to visit and present modern pieces danced to jazz. "They loved it, they thought it was so neat," says Kara Skolnick, the manager of the Washington Ballet, "audiences were on their feet."

Marta, a twenty-four-year-old dancer still remembers the single male body dancing in ways she had never seen before. "His sole presence filled the stage, he was a great dancer, he had good turn and good jump, but the way he moved . . . I don't even know what you call that," she says. Like a solitary ballerina twirling in a music box, the Ballet Nacional is mostly isolated from the ballet world. As a result, it already lags several decades.

But the Ministry of Culture is investing in ballet's future, one that might be more in line with modern styles. The Escuela Nacional de Ballet, for many years at the Gran Teatro, where it competed with the company for space, has recently moved to new quarters fully equipped with remote-control air conditioning, computers, fresh paint, and redone floors. On any given day, its practice rooms are filled with aspiring ballerinas who want to be the next star and meet exacting standards to get there.

To select students for a recent parade, teachers lined them up in rows. "Take off your skirts," one of them demanded. Then the winnowing began. "The one on the left, the one next to her, you at the other end," the teachers commanded, and one by one the selected dancers sat down on the side, knowing they had lost out. A tiny ballerina burst into tears. "They do it every year," said Edilsa, one of the dancers from Mexico who paid tuition to attend the school, "they don't want the fat ones to be in the parade." Although she looks thinner than 99 percent of the fifteen-year-olds I know, she too was rejected.

This is daily life for dancers in training. Only a handful of them will go on to become the next Sleeping Beauty or Cinderella at the Gran Teatro, and preparation is an endurance test in itself: same-sex ballet classes, couple ballet classes, modern dance classes, and rehearsals. The school puts on several programs a year. They are mainly composed of classics, but this repertoire is unlikely to last. On a Saturday morning, little boys and girls in tights and tutus and tiny crowns are ready to rehearse *Almendrita*, a fairy-tale story, when a blast of Jamiroquai, with its modern mixture of soul, jazz, and disco, interrupts them. They cannot resist and follow the sound down the hallway to peek through a door. They see a young modern dancer at work. He is staging a new choreography for the older students, and the children like the crazy moves. They have seen (and done) *Almendrita* many times. This is new. And—it is allowed at the bal-

Eduardo Blanco demonstrates a step routine to his dancers,
Havana, 2004. *Photo by Mimi Chakarova*

let school where Alicia offers a master class, but is no longer in charge.
Here, dancers are exposed to the avant-garde.

Beatriz Abreu, a seventeen-year-old student who is about to graduate,
studied Maurice Béjart, a quirky and innovative French choreographer,
for her thesis. After she presented it to a panel of three judges, including Albelo, she was pleased. "He is wonderful," she says to me afterward.
"He has a modern version of *Giselle* that is incredible; the second act takes
place in a mental institution." It is not a place Alicia's Giselle would ever
find herself in, and the dancers understand this. "Every day the ballet is
loosing something. It is stagnant," says Abreu. Might this have something
to do with Alicia, I asked her. "Of course, it is because of Alicia."

Her influence is hard to shake off, as George Georges, the choreographer in the room the younger students peered into can attest. The dancer
from the Compañía Nacional de Danza, Cuba's modern dance company,
had ambitious plans for the work he is staging, but the students' torsos

are too stiff and their heads too caught up in technique. "Damned Balanchine," he says. "This is shit. You are not doing it right. Forget you are a dancer; is this the way you walk on the street?" he asks walking with his toes pointing out. "Yes," the dancers answer. "Well, that is not the way a normal person walks on the street. Close your legs, relax your back. Just walk normal. Let's try it again." He switches Jamiroquai back on.

Less than a year ago, a student from the school was staging similar works in that very classroom. He is waiting to fill the empty choreographer slot at the company. "I am the first to say that it is important to conserve the classics, but we must also do new stuff," says Eduardo Blanco, the twenty-year-old who trains daily with the ballet. What he has in mind are the contorted and asymmetrical moves from modern dance. "It is not the same thing to make a *tour jeté* and cry 'aaaaahhhhhh' in the middle of it as to do it with a little arm," he says stretching his right arm gracefully in the classical form. "That has been done a thousand times. In ballet, everything is invented already." He is trying hard to innovate. One of his creations includes a girl wearing a pointe shoe on one foot and a charac-

Dancers perform a modern piece at the Ballet Nacional de Cuba, Havana, 2001. *Photo by Mimi Chakarova*

Rehearsal of "Tiempo de danzón," Havana, 2004. *Photo by Mimi Chakarova*

ter shoe on the other, and another is about a couple with AIDS. In 2001, these works had only been staged at the ballet school, and it was hard to imagine Alicia letting him move such experiments to the Gran Teatro. But she did. And in 2004—despite the defection of five Cuban dancers in the previous year, or maybe because of it—Blanco presented one of his new works, *Danzón*, at the Gran Teatro, and the audience loved it. Blanco, the son of a dancer and a musician, says he choreographs from music, and if he is sometimes frustrated with Cuba, he has negotiated a relationship with Alicia that works for him. Yes, he wants to work abroad, but only if he can return to Cuba.

On one of the nights I attended the ballet, Sarabia stood on stage with a backdrop resembling a giant swatch of flowery fabric for one of Alicia's ballets. The dancers, attired in costumes the color and shape of cotton candy, twirled about gently. Wearing a pink coat and sash, Sarabia was almost lost in the fluff. A devoted Backstreet Boys' fan, he would probably feel more comfortable in baggy jeans and a backward cap, but he says the fairy-tale ballets have not gotten to him yet. "Right now, I am not bored, but I don't know if I can do this all my life," he says. But even if he leaves, the bench is full of well-trained dancers ready to take his place. "The problem is that for such a small island, we have a very good school of ballet, one of the best in the world," says Albelo.

And everyone knows they have Alicia to thank for it. On one night when the Gran Teatro is filled to capacity and waiting for the curtain to rise, the audience stirs. I turn in my seat to look up at the balcony. There above us is Alicia, dressed in a tunic with her head wrapped in a scarf à la Margot Fonteyn, her eyes hidden by large sunglasses. The audience rises and bursts into applause. Unable to stand, the old dancer is held up by two attendants. "Bravo, Alicia! Bravo!" a woman yells, her voice breaking. The diva nods and then sits to watch.

Research assistance by Anar Desai

Interlude

A Photo Essay

∼ **MIMI CHAKAROVA**

A man emerges from a makeshift window,
Trinidad, 2001.

Carefree children in the town square after a game of baseball, Surgidero de Batabanó, 2004. ⌒ Life for the elderly in Cuba is a daily struggle, especially for those living in small towns, like this woman, without the financial assistance from relatives abroad, Austrailia, 2004.

A young couple flirts after a wedding ceremony overlooking Paseo de Martí, Havana, 2004. ∽ Flower vendors, Havana, 2004.

A girl steps through the broken doorway of a church while the police question a man on the street, Havana, 2004. ∾ Central Havana, 2001.

Marriage ceremonies take place in beautiful, colonial buildings throughout Havana. It is common to schedule four to five in an afternoon with couples, relatives, and friends patiently waiting their turn. Havana, 2004. ∽ Public art in Central Havana, 2004.

Portrait of a young woman, Camagüey, 2001.

Since most Cubans rely on public transportation, buses are extremely crowded and involve long waits. Havana, 2004. ∾ Young couple, Havana, 2001.

Ice cream stand in Old Havana, 2004. ⌒ Flower girls, Havana, 2004.

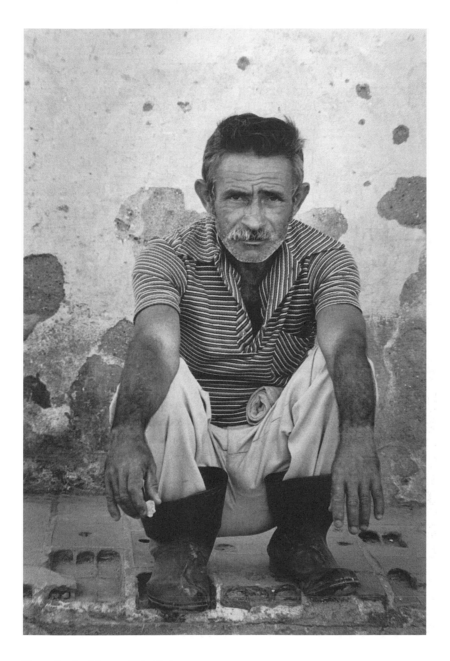

Portrait of a laborer, Trinidad, 2001.

Elderly man rests in front of his home in Old Havana, 2004. ⁓ Veterinarians in the countryside trim a horse's hair before an immunization, 2004.

Men fish and drink rum under the hot sun, Surgidero de Batabanó, 2004.
～ On the open road, Trinidad, 2001.

Housing on the outskirts of Camagüey, 2001. ∾ Illegal cockfight in a neighbor's backyard, Havana, 2004.

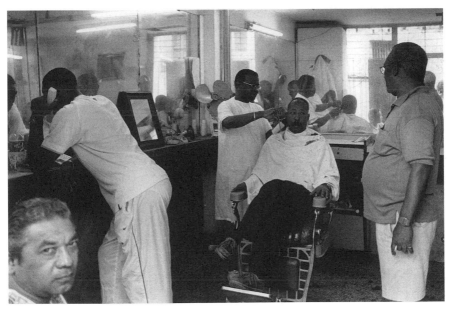

Boys play basketball on a makeshift court, Havana, 2001. ∾ Barbershop, Havana, 2004.

A group of schoolboys practice shooting at a recreational gun range, Havana, 2004. ∽ Victory billboard, Havana, 2001.

Birds fly over the Plaza de la Catedral, Old Havana, 2004. ⌒ Boy with Halloween mask, Parque Central, Havana, 2004.

Neighborhood gym, Havana, 2004. ⟳ Photographer sets up his 1920s view camera in front of the Capitolio to take pictures of tourists for one dollar each. Straight ahead is Gran Teatro, which also houses the Ballet Nacional de Cuba. Havana, 2004.

A British tourist wraps his hands around the hips of a young Afrocuban girl, Havana, 2004. ∽ Little girl attempting to help her father jump-start his car, Bejucal, 2004.

Riding lesson, Trinidad, 2001.

PART THREE ~ *Surviving*

True Believers

∼ OLGA R. RODRÍGUEZ

I knew I had arrived at my destination when I saw the hammer-and-sickle emblem outside the door. My walk there had not been through the Florence you see on postcards. Few corner stores, ice cream or flower shops operated on this side of the Arno River. I was there to meet Alessandro Leoni, a founding member of the Communist Refoundation Party, a faction of the Italian Communist Party that survived the party's breakup in 1991. Tall and slim with a bushy mustache discolored by years of smoking, Leoni opened the door to an office filled with smoke and posters of Lenin, Stalin, Che Guevara, and Antonio Gramsci. He lit cigarette after cigarette as he spoke of solidarity, equality, and the rights of the poor. For more than four hours, he talked communism, Cuba, Mexico's social problems. The smoke swirled around us.

Five years later, I remembered that episode as I walked down El Malecón in the sweltering sun of Havana. Flanked by the calm and clear Caribbean ocean and the old, deafening cars, I wondered whether foreigners who had moved to the island during the 1960s remained as supportive of the Cuban Revolution as Leoni had been when we spoke in 1996.

I first visited Rosa María Almendros, a Spanish contemporary of Leoni's who moved to Cuba after the triumph of the 1959 revolution. "It was a dream come true," Almendros says one afternoon sitting in her Havana apartment. "We knew with Castro in power it wouldn't take long before a just society would be created." Almendros and her husband at the time, Edmundo Desnoes, a Cuban journalist and author, watched the film clips of Fidel Castro, dressed in his now legendary olive green combat fatigues and his rifle tossed over his shoulder, as he marched triumphantly through the streets of Havana on January 8, 1959. Cubans filled the streets to welcome the man who promised to fulfill the dreams of José Martí, the father of Cuba's independence. More than 1,300 miles away in New York City, Almendros and her husband joined the celebration.

Already they had followed and raised funds for the Twenty-Sixth of

July Movement, Castro's rebels. It didn't take long—twelve months to be exact—before they moved to Havana. The years that followed, Almendros says, fulfilled her expectations. The *barbudos*, the young, rugged revolutionary heroes of the Cuban struggle, walked the streets of Havana and lived and worked among the Cuban people. Cubans packed the Plaza de la Revolución to listen to a young, passionate, and defiant Castro challenge the United States. Legends like Che Guevara and others were being made, and revolution was the muse of Latin American intellectuals, poets, and painters. Sympathetic foreigners watched the island transforming, and many became part of it.

"In Spain we lost a battle, but in Cuba we won the war," says Almendros, whose father fought in the Spanish Civil War against Franco. "There was a lot of hope for what Cuba could accomplish. It was a revolution based on faith." Cuba and Castro enticed foreigners, like Almendros, to leave comfortable lives and come to the island to cut cane and teach reading and writing. Some replaced doctors and university professors who left, while others worked in the new government. For their part, the young, enthusiastic idealists from the United States and all over Latin America came to experience a revolution. Hope for the future became the essence of Cuban life and their personal lives.

Forty years later, few foreigners remain. Some defend the revolution with a conviction that has lasted more than four decades. The island, they say, will remain true to its revolutionary values, even in the face of tourism and the dollarization of the economy. Others have nowhere else to go and find themselves stuck on an island frozen in time. For them, the revolution has been reduced to a memory. But not for Almendros. In her seventies now, her support for Castro's revolution remains unconditional. When I step into her apartment, she's sitting in a rocking chair two sizes too big. She is barely five feet tall, pale, and wears bright red lipstick. Her brown, shoulder-length hair, without a trace of gray, matches her long, flowing black, white, and brown tie-dye dress. "The 1960s were a time when anything was possible and when other Latin American countries were looking toward Cuba for inspiration," Almendros remembers as she peeks through a pair of glasses with the right lens cracked right through the middle. "I am happy here," she says. "I have everything I need. I don't worry about anything. I have never been materialistic."

Staying has not been easy. Some of what life was like in the early years—the isolation especially—is captured in her former husband's book, *In-*

Police officers drink juice in front of a furniture store, Havana, 2004.
Photo by Mimi Chakarova

consolable Memories. He left in 1979 and says in 2004, "I left when the Communist Party declared itself the conscience of society and took control of culture. I thought, as a writer, that I was, in literature, the conscience of society." But Almendros remained and is happy she did. Her apartment is in a decaying building with an elevator that rarely works and a set of stairs so dark you have to feel with your feet before you take a step. Inside, the walls are filled with artwork and crafts from the different countries she has visited. She has old books piled high in the corner of a terrace where she likes to eat breakfast and watch the waves of the Caribbean ocean crash against El Malecón. In bookshelves scattered around the house she keeps books about museums, painters, art history, and ones written by the Latin American authors she has met. She shares her phone line with a neighbor who has not been able to get one of her own. The artwork she collected has come in handy. "I had to sell a painting to be able to fix the leak on the roof," she says, then quickly explaining, "The government does not have the resources to take care of things like that."

Some of the paintings and books are from renowned Cuban and Latin

American artists she met during the 1960s when she worked as the director of information at Casa de las Américas, Cuba's main cultural center and publishing house. It was founded in 1959 by Haydée Santamaría, one of two women arrested with Castro during the Moncada attack, the 1953 failed attempt by Castro's rebel movement to start an armed uprising against Fulgencio Batista.

Casa de las Américas became the headquarters of leftists, intellectuals, and artists who, during the 1960s, visited the island often hoping to duplicate the Cuban Revolution in their countries. Many of them, Almendros points out, failed to accomplish what Castro achieved. But she has met them all. Roque Dalton, the Salvadorian poet, communist, and forefather of the Frente Farabundo Martí para la Liberación Nacional (Farabundo Martí National Liberation Front), or FMLN, the leftist guerilla movement, became a legend after his own comrades killed him in 1975. Víctor Jara, a Chilean poet and singer, was killed by Augusto Pinochet after the 1973 coup that ousted Salvador Allende, the socialist president. "Víctor taught me how to sign with my hands," Almendros says. "We would be in different corners of a room, and we would talk by signaling. Did you know they smashed his hand before they killed him?" she asks without expecting an answer.

Even though Almendros and her husband aided Castro's rebel movement, she did not feel worthy of the revolution. "We felt we did not deserve to come back," she says. "We had done very little to help." But when they heard rumors that Cuba was going to be invaded by the United States, she willingly left her marketing job on Fifth Avenue to defend the revolution. By the time the U.S.-backed anti-Castro Cuban exiles landed at the Bay of Pigs, Almendros and her husband were there, mobilized and ready. "We were in our posts," she says. Almendros worked for Casa de Las Américas, her husband at the Ministry of Education. "I felt I had done something to contribute," she says. More than she could in New York, where she found people caught up in "fashion trends, materialism, and shallowness."

Even now, Almendros's faith in the revolution remains, and she tells me that "this has been a profound revolution, but not a bloody or cruel one." Moreover, it changed more than her life. In El Rosario, a village in Oriente province, she witnessed a whole town go from a place where people were infested with parasites to a place that Fidel Castro would call "an example for others to follow." It was while at El Rosario that Almendros met Castro, a man she describes as "a mortal protected by the gods." "I remember seeing his jeep approach and feeling like I was going to faint," she says putting her hands on her face. "He had come to get a report about the progress in our town, and I was so nervous that I would not remember all the details. I panicked."

She had met important men before. She had eaten with Che Guevara, Salvador Allende, and countless personalities of the Latin American literary world, but meeting Castro was different. "I was shaking like a leaf," she says. "He asked about the three tractors that he had sent on such and such a date in 1970. That's when I realized that the myth about his memory was a reality." "He turned to me and said 'and you little girl?'" she laughs. "I was forty-one at the time. But I guess my height has always made me look a bit younger." Castro asked what she was doing there. "I said I was doing social work. But I said it with a Spanish accent, and he noticed. He talked with a Spanish accent also and we laughed." He left without asking any questions, but told Almendros she had done great work and should be proud of it. "I was so relieved he had not even asked any questions that I did not even think about just having met the *comandante en jefe* [commander in chief]. When he left, it was as if I had cut burnt cane all day, as if someone had just beat me up."

Almendros says the only time her faith faltered was in the 1960s when some of her homosexual friends faced persecution. "This was hard on people," she says, but prefers not to talk about specific cases. "You have to understand, the government recognized its mistake before it was too late." But the 1960s are long gone and struggling to survive has endured. The challenge now is to maintain a balance between socialism and the capitalist ventures that fund the revolutionary ideals.

So far the biggest change has been the legalization of dollars and tourism. For Almendros dollars and tourists are necessary evils. "When the government first announced they were bringing in more tourists, the first thing I thought was how this was going to rot Cuban society," she says. "It makes me remember Pancho Villa [the Mexican revolutionary] when he said, 'be afraid of the dollars and not the bullets.'" She thinks for a second, "I know Fidel will not let that happen." She pulls out her album and proudly shows me her collection of photos of the *comandante en jefe* that she keeps. These memories, she says, make her grateful for having experienced a revolution that will continue, "Even when Fidel is no longer among us."

If only that optimism translated into reality, I thought after I left Almendros. It is hard to imagine a bright future for the Cuban Revolution when you see Havana trapped in a time warp. Contradictions abound. Cubans come up to me and start a friendly conversation that ends in a business transaction of some kind; colonial buildings in decay still look royal; and the deafening Studebakers, Chevys, Fords, and Cadillacs from the 1940s and 1950s move among the modern cars. I think of Almendros's reference to Pancho Villa and wonder if he wasn't right. Dollars, not bullets, will bring change to an island struggling to hold onto a more than forty-year ideal.

For Jane McManus, an American who moved to Cuba in 1969, the island's contradictions give proof that the revolution is coming to an end. McManus, in her eighties, moved to Cuba early on. Disenchanted with the U.S. Left, she wanted to live in a socialist system. The experience, however, has been bittersweet. "When I first arrived, I worked very hard as you always do when you are enthusiastic about something," says McManus, a lanky woman with short white hair and piercing blue eyes. "But that kind of enthusiasm no longer exists. In the late 1960s, people would do anything for their government, not anymore. You can't sustain it. Revolution is a moment."

The daughter of an IBM executive, McManus grew up in an upper-middle-class household in New England. Her father voted Republican and her mother became politically active late in life when she joined a liberal organization that promoted political and social equality. "But she also kept her rich friends," McManus says. "She just did not talk about politics with them."

It was while McManus was studying at the University of California at Los Angeles that she started to become political. It was 1941, and the United States had declared war on Japan and entered World War II. She witnessed the roundups and internment of Japanese American students at UCLA. "That was my first radicalizing experience," she says. While World War II raged, she decided to go to Spain. Her father had "all these right-wing" connections that made it possible for her to enter the country. Once there, she met with people who had been victimized under Franco. After a year in Spain, McManus returned to the United States and went to work as a reporter for the *Baltimore Sun*. It was there that she experienced what she calls a "deeper radicalization" when she saw how blacks were mistreated and discriminated against. It was the mid-1940s, and segregation was stringent. "I was becoming more and more radical," she says. "I was working at the *Baltimore Sun* when the atomic bomb was dropped."

Winston Churchill's 1946 speech warning that an "iron curtain" would cut through the middle of Europe changed her life. The cold war had started and with it the persecution of left-wingers in the United States, she says. At the time McManus was covering the United Nations for the *New Republic*. But she soon ended up on a blacklist and work dried up. "I never had such a good job again," she says. From there she went to the *National Guardian*, a progressive weekly in New York City cofounded by John T. McManus, her second husband and a well-known figure in progressive politics who ran for governor of New York as the American Labor Party candidate in 1950 and 1954. The magazine was one of the few publications to openly denounce Senator Joseph McCarthy's hunt for communists.

Although McManus says she was never a member of the American Communist Party, she might as well have been. "Our telephones were tapped," she says. "We would get strange calls at night. Every time I traveled, I was always harassed when I would come back to the U.S. But I did not mind being harassed. It's part of the game." By the 1960s, McManus had become a full-fledged leftist, involved in both the Black Power and the antiwar movements. Her husband had died a few years earlier, and she was looking for a new start. When Cuba's *TriContinental* magazine offered her a job as a translator in 1969, she took it.

At the time, Castro's government was in desperate need of professionals to replace the middle class that had left for Miami. He invited university professors, doctors, psychologists, journalists, and anyone else willing to take part in the creation of the new Cuba. For McManus, the decision proved an easy one. The best years of the Left in the United States were over. "I loved Cuba already because I had been here several times," she says. "I knew people were very enthusiastic, and if anybody was going to make it, it would be Cuba."

McManus says she began to lose faith in Castro in the 1970s, and she now no longer believes in the revolution. She openly criticizes Castro's policies and describes his government as a "military dictatorship." "I was never so blindly partial," she says. "Most Americans are quite uncritical. They are a lot more starry-eyed than I am. I could easily see there was nothing being done to develop the country. As long as the paternalistic relationship continued with the socialist bloc, there was no need to produce. And now we are living the consequences of that."

A collage in a museum displays the word *Fidel* written with the blood of a youth who died for the revolution. *Photo by Mimi Chakarova*

McManus supports herself as a freelance travel writer and translator. And, like many other Cubans, her family in the United States sends dollars. But before she became disenchanted, she eagerly contributed to the revolution. She worked as a translator for *TriContinental* magazine until the late 1970s. She also became a member and eventually president of the Union of North American Residents, a group that the U.S. government described as "a propaganda apparatus of the Cuban government." When it existed, the group of about thirty American expatriates, "a hundred when there was a party," would show their support for the Cuban Revolution by marching, waving American flags in Havana parades on May 1 for International Workers' Day.

It was at one of the meetings of the "American Union," as it was known among the members, that McManus met William Lee Brent, her current husband and a former member of the Black Panther Party. In 1968, Brent shot and seriously wounded three San Francisco police officers in a robbery-related shoot-out. Then in June 1969, while free on bail, Brent hijacked a TWA airplane from Oakland bound for New York City to

Cuba, where he has been in exile ever since. He is still wanted by the United States government for robbery, the shooting of the officers, and the hijacking.

Brent spent twenty-two months in a Cuban jail suspected of being a spy. After his release, he worked on a sugarcane plantation, graduated with an arts degree from the University of Havana, taught English to high school students, and worked as a journalist at Radio Free Havana, a place where many Americans work. "The one thing we all had in common was our respect and unbridled admiration for Fidel Castro," wrote Brent in his autobiography, *Long Time Gone*, about the American Union. That respect started fading after Castro no longer liked the idea of their organization.

"Cuba began its policy of trying to reestablish diplomatic relations with other countries, so it became very inconvenient to have all these outspoken crazy exiles, who did not believe in their own governments, organized and visible," McManus says. "We became sort of troublemakers, so by the late 1970s, the Cuban government disbanded all unions." Brent, one of seventy-seven American fugitives living on the island, sits in the living room and nods in agreement as his wife speaks. He refused to share his opinions on Castro and the current situation in Cuba. In a previous interview, he had said he did not doubt Castro would turn him in if that would serve him. "Politics is politics," he said in the 1998 interview. "If the big man thinks he can get some advantage out of peddling me to the Americans, he'll do it."

Like McManus, Americans who live in Cuba are a select group of journalists, translators, teachers, artists, people who have married government officials, and those running from the American government. There are more than five hundred Americans registered with the U.S. Interest Section. But this number only represents those on the island for business purposes. How many people are there for purely ideological reasons is hard to know. "There are no more than a hundred," a U.S. diplomat claimed. "They no longer have the ideological fantasy that this is paradise." Those on the island for ideological reasons include people who ran away after they committed crimes in the United States and found a safe haven in Cuba during the 1960s and 1970s. Americans living in Cuba fall in a legal gray area since, under U.S. federal law, no American citizen is allowed to work for a foreign government. But in Cuba, anyone who works is working for the government.

Most of the Americans I encountered were unwilling to talk to me. The main reason they gave was that they wanted to maintain ties with the United States and be able to travel back and forth. Sure the government knows they are there, they said, but they felt uncomfortable drawing attention to themselves. A few of them freelance for major news networks and felt their jobs could be jeopardized. "You really put them in danger by writing about them," the diplomat agreed.

McManus was the exception. "The Cuban government does not really care what foreigners think," she says. Many Cubans share her opinions but they don't express them because "it's too close to the truth and too close to the top," she says. It almost seems as if this is the first time McManus has shared these ideas. She's anxious to talk about the lack of democracy. "You have to have a society that is run by rules and regulations," she says. "But I think there is a difference between a country that is run by law and order and a country that is run by hierarchy." She talks about Castro's inconsistencies. "He just inaugurated a statue of John Lennon," she says, incredulous. "He was the one who banned the Beatles back in the 1960s, but now they are OK."

Nonetheless, she is content to stay on the island. "I have no desire to go back," she says as she pets her long-haired dachshund. I have no house there. I have good medical care here and a very nice house." McManus lives in a quiet and airy apartment in Miramar, a tranquil and swanky residential area outside of Havana, where children play in parks and where Cubans and foreign businesspeople jog, walk their dogs, and take strolls down Quinta Avenida. Havana's Fifth Avenue, it is filled with colonial-era mansions that serve as embassies or as headquarters for major corporations doing business in Cuba.

McManus recognizes that she lives a privileged life because she has access to dollars. "If you can live better, it is easier to tolerate other things," she says. "Foreigners don't have to scramble around to find where their next meal is coming from, or stand in line eternally or go to hospitals that are filthy and don't have medicine."

It is not that foreigners have more rights than Cubans, she says. "We get to do things that Cubans do. It's just that we have more money to do them with. If there is not enough in my ration, or if I don't like an item, I can always trade it or give it away, but I can always buy things at the dollar store." Not only does McManus have access to dollars, she is also able to travel, a luxury very few Cubans enjoy. Even if they have the money, Cubans must be invited by someone abroad to get the government's approval to leave. McManus goes to the United States every year, to visit her husband's relatives in California or to see her family in New York. "This year I am going back to my grandson's wedding in Maine," she says.

If McManus is critical of Cuba now, she still remembers being a believer. "Before, it was much more egalitarian," she says. "Everyone lived comfortably without dollars. But after the Special Period, it was obvious Cuba had to open up to capitalism. Before, everything was a barter relationship, oil for sugar, troops in Angola for everything else we got from the Soviet Union." McManus says she is just saying what she and many of her Cuban friends see. "There's a lot at stake, not just personal power, but the goodies," McManus says as she opens the door to her terrace to let the warm wind in. "The people at the top live a better life."

McManus came to Cuba lured by the revolutionary dream once tangible. Her idealism is long gone, and what keeps her on the island is her husband. After all, Brent is still wanted by the United States. Since Cuba has no extradition treaty with the United States, the couple feels safe living on the island. It also helps that they live in relative comfort. I wondered if McManus would be as critical had she experienced the stifling violence and poverty of most Latin American countries. To a certain extent, McManus is like many American expatriates who go to other countries looking for a fuller, more meaningful life.

For most foreigners, life on the island is harder than it would be in their home countries, but they live a lot better than most Cubans. They have access to dollars, can travel, and many form part of the government bureaucracy. Soledad and Felipe Rodríguez, a Salvadorian couple that moved to Cuba at the start of the Special Period, are the exception. Home is a massive, 1,400-unit apartment building. Three more Soviet-style buildings just like it complete their neighborhood. The fact that you have to walk a couple of blocks to catch a taxi fails to bother them. Nor does the small apartment. Their tiny living room serves as a dining room too, and they keep a desk and bookshelves in a corner for when their daughter comes to visit from a Havana University campus outside of the city. The deep blue refrigerator has to be kept in the living room as well since the kitchen is too small. The wall is taken by huge paintings of Fidel Castro and El Che. "The small painting of Charlie Chaplin is kept because Soledad is a fan," says Felipe, referring to a painting set above a couple of old armchairs made functional after their holes were covered with duct tape.

Soledad and Felipe Rodríguez, both in their forties, have lived in the

An elementary school in Old Havana, 2004. *Photo by Mimi Chakarova*

same building since they arrived in Cuba in 1990. They have lived through the harshest of times, yet they describe Cuba as, "a paradise, a dream come true, and an example for El Salvador to follow." For them, life here could not be better.

While McManus began to tire of Cuba's revolution, in the 1970s, Soledad was working to duplicate it in El Salvador. Soledad, her guerilla name, and the name she likes to be called by, is articulate and affable. A woman with brown skin and eyes and dark, short hair, she is sharp and full of energy. She smiles as she speaks of the time when she first got involved with the FMLN, one of the leftist guerrilla groups that had a part in El Salvador's violent civil war during the late 1970s and the 1980s. She was just seventeen years old and still in high school. For Soledad, joining the guerilla movement in the 1970s was more than an ideological pursuit. The deplorable situation the country lived in and the daily sense of insecurity prompted the two of them to take action. "We wanted to change our reality," Soledad says, and then adds, laughing, "What we wanted was to build heaven on earth. We did not understand why we had to wait until after death."

During the war, countless corpses would be left on the side of the roads to teach people a lesson, Soledad says. The Salvadorian government waged a psychological war of repression. But Soledad and Felipe continued to participate in the FMLN. Their awareness and activism developed from the discussions at her church. "We never spoke about Cuba," Soledad says. "We had heard of Fidel and of El Che, but we were living our own reality. We never thought we would end up here."

"It was through our priest that we started to develop a social conscience," Felipe interrupts. Felipe "el Gato" ("the Cat") Rodríguez wears a bright red T-shirt with FMLN written in white letters, but he does not fit the profile of a guerilla fighter. He is barely five feet, two inches and fragile—he lost a kidney in the late 1980s, and the other had to be removed in 1993 as a result of not having access to health care. His skin has the yellowish tint of dialysis patients, and he has to stop every few minutes to take in air. But he is alive, and it is thanks to the Cuban Revolution. "If Cuba had not offered to help us, he probably would not be here." Soledad says.

The two came to Cuba thanks to a program to help those who have participated in social movements throughout the world. They arrived at the beginning of the Special Period and watched as some 33,000 people left Cuba in 1994 when Cuba's economic situation became intolerable. But the scarcity and the harsh times reinforced Soledad and Felipe's faith in the revolution. "Scarcity was nothing new," Soledad says. "We were used to it in El Salvador. Sure you have things there, but if people don't have money to buy them, it's as if they were not there."

During the Special Period, the Cuban economy basically found itself in freefall. Nevertheless, Felipe received the medical attention he needed during the eight months he was hospitalized after his surgery. "What would we have done in El Salvador?" Soledad asks, knowing firsthand the difference between Castro's communism and El Salvador's democracy. "We wouldn't have been able to pay for his surgery, all the medical attention he needs, and the expensive medicine." Soledad, who works as a teacher's aide, talks of how during the Special Period the unemployed were guaranteed a portion of their salary. "In El Salvador, if you lose your job, that is your problem," she says. Of course there were lots of things missing in Cuba during the Special Period, the couple knows, but in El Salvador there was always a sense of anxiety. "We had some comforts, but we also had debts," Soledad says. "There was always insecurity.

People there can't go to university. They have to work to help support their families."

The only criticism the couple has of Cuba is aimed at those who complain about the country's present situation. "They used to live in a glass ball, and they want things to be like when the Soviet Union was around," Soledad says. Cubans nowadays don't appreciate the revolutionary values of hard work and solidarity like they used to, Soledad says. And they don't appreciate its benefits. "In Cuba," Soledad likes to point out, "everyone who wants a university degree can get one." The best example is their only daughter who is on a full government scholarship, studying to become a teacher. This, too, could never have happened in El Salvador, her mother says.

Soledad and Felipe first left El Salvador in 1982, when the civil war there was in full force. Soledad's brother had been shot by paramilitaries, and one of their comrades, after being arrested and tortured, gave their names to the government. Soon after, men dressed in civilian clothes came looking for them. "I always told my mother not to open the door if those knocking were not in uniform," Soledad says. "The ones in civil clothes were the death squads," Felipe adds to make sure I understand the situation they lived in. The men knocked on their neighbor's door. The next day, Soledad and Felipe left and ended up enlisting with the Nicaraguan Sandinistas. "We had to help somehow," Soledad says. "That's when we realized our struggle was not limited to El Salvador. We were fighting an international cause."

In 1979, the Sandinistas had toppled the government of Anastasio Somoza, and by 1982 they were waging a war against the American-backed Contras. Felipe was part of the reserved battalions, and he fought on the front a few times. Soledad was part of the committees for the Sandinista defense, something like the Committee for the Defense of the Revolution in Cuba. "We wanted things to settle down so we could go back to El Salvador," Soledad says. "When we were about to return, Felipe got sick. That's when we decided to come to Cuba."

The failure of the FMLN to take power in El Salvador resulted from the divisions within the movement, Soledad says. The FMLN signed a peace agreement with the Salvadorian government in 1991 and the following year became a political party. "We didn't accomplish what we fought for," Felipe says. "There is still a lot of work that needs to be done." But it was

View of Vedado and parts of Miramar seen from the twenty-fourth floor of the Hospital Nacional Hermanos Ameirjeiras, the largest hospital in Latin America, Havana, 2004. *Photo by Mimi Chakarova*

not that the Left in El Salvador was finished, Soledad says. "Now we have to use politics and not weapons."

The two have not yet lost hope and wish to one day return and help El Salvador become more like Cuba. "Do you think this is possible?" I ask. "In the next few years, I doubt it," Soledad says while laughing. "But we hope to go back and at least help in ending government corruption." I realized that it was their idealism that kept them going. They keep in touch with Roque Dalton's widow and other Salvadorian exiles who have made Cuba their home. It is here that they can still find people who share their ideals and where they can plan how to influence change in El Salvador. Imagining a better future for El Salvador will have to do for now. They will not be going back to their native country any time soon. Doing so would mean Felipe not getting the life-sustaining medical attention he needs.

While Soledad and Felipe imagine, Almendros and McManus remember that moment when revolution was palpable. "Revolution is a moment," McManus told me. But it was that moment of revolution that gave Almendros the opportunity to see a whole village go from a place where illiteracy was as rampant as parasites to a place where children grew up to be engineers, doctors, teachers. It was also that moment that allowed McManus's husband to find a safe haven in which a prison cell was replaced by a classroom. It was that revolutionary moment that gave Felipe a second chance in life.

That was the moment that I was trying to understand and to a certain extent relive when I first went to meet Leoni back in Italy. Compared to now, it seems the 1960s were a time when idealism came more easily, a time when people cared about more than just their material well-being. It was a time when social justice and equality were thought of as possible realities and not just as the fantasies of radicals; a time when heroes were more than athletes and pop stars. But that moment is long gone. And now Cuba is a paradox of idealism and authoritarianism. Now, these foreigners are torn between the idealism of the past and the harsh reality of the present. And all we, my generation and I, have left are the heroes of an earlier generation.

Research assistance by Osvaldo Gómez

Socialism and the Cigar

~ **DANIELA MOHOR**

The warm smell of tobacco floats through the room of wooden tables piled high with tobacco leaves. Sitting at their desks like children in a classroom, more than one hundred Cuban workers hand-roll some of the world's most sought-after cigars: Montecristo, Cohiba, Romeo y Julieta. As they work soft leaves over rougher tobacco, they listen to a morning radio sitcom. "The man's face is the face of a dog," a radio actor says, but no one rolling cigars pays much attention. Instead, workers chat among themselves. While they joke, even holler across the room, their fast fingers effortlessly grasp the brown leaves and shape the cigars. Despite the daily production quota of more than 120 cigars per worker, the atmosphere seems relaxed and friendly. Most of the hand-rollers are young and have known each other since childhood.

The Juan Casanuevas factory was inaugurated in January 2000 in the small town of Pilotos, deep in the fertile land of Pinar del Río, Cuba's traditional tobacco-growing region. Named after a local hero of the 1959 revolution, the factory is the direct result of the tireless lobbying by the town's farmers. A group of tobacco growers from the Pilotos major agricultural cooperative made an uncommon move in the late 1990s: they approached Fidel Castro in person and asked him to transform the abandoned military base into a cigar factory. They had two purposes: to create new job opportunities to keep their children in town and, in their words, "to serve the revolution." Castro could hardly resist what appeared to him a potentially lucrative venture coupled with revolutionary fervor. The farmers won him over.

Pilotos's new factory is one of some sixty cigar operations playing a critical role in the country's post-Soviet economy. Desperate for hard currency in the early 1990s, the state turned to the sectors that generated the highest dollar revenue: tourism and export tobacco. While the price of raw tobacco, which is controlled by the government, is roughly ten cents per pound, a box of Cuban cigars in Spain sells for as much as five hundred

Packaging Cohibas for a government cigar shop in Old Havana, 2004.
Photo by Mimi Chakarova

dollars. The market is profitable, and Cubans know it. New brands and
new sizes of cigars at different prices have appeared in the past decade,
and every season new workers are incorporated into the industry.

There is no question that the factory's ultimate goal is profit making,
not keeping the spirit of the revolution alive in its workers. But Pilotos
is still a throwback to the old days of socialism. Unlike factories in more
urban areas of the island, workers in Pilotos are still unconditionally devoted to the socialist system. The cooperative and the factory are indeed
near perfect examples of socialist efficiency based on solidarity, moral
stimulation, and patriotism. "The country is a single entity, the factory is
a single entity, and it has a single owner: Fidel Castro," Piñaldo Franco,
the director of the Pilotos factory, said without irony. Everyone had a role
to play in the production, and all laborers were equally important, Franco
claimed.

Isolation, the cooperative's profitability, and the inheritance of rural
areas' support for the revolution have preserved Pilotos from the disillu-
sion prevailing in bigger cities. Like many of Pilotos's 5,000 residents,

Orlando Acosta, the factory's production supervisor, takes pride in the tobacco work he has done over a lifetime. He is a quiet but friendly man with a soft voice and a brown moustache. At the factory, people simply call him Rolando. "I was born under a tobacco tree," he jokes in the small storage room where raw material is handed out to the rollers. "So I know a bit about tobacco." On weekends, when he can escape family duties, Rolando goes to the *vegas*, or tobacco fields. There, he relaxes and "forgets about work."

Moving from growing tobacco at the local cooperative to managing an industrial factory was no small task. Rolando and two other cofounders had to learn everything from selecting and stemming tobacco leaves to hand-rolling cigars and quality control. For thirteen months they attended class in Havana and visited other factories in Pinar del Río, which is located three hours southwest of the island's main city. By June 1999, they were ready to open a hand-rolling school in the factory and receive the first group of workers: seventy-three people took the first class, including Rolando's wife. Since then, dozens of new recruits have been selected and trained every season, contributing to the production's steady increase from 1.4 million in 2000 to more than 2.5 million the following year.

Underlying such efficiency is the state's recent decision to create an economy based on incentives and the private accumulation of wealth—two principles of capitalism Castro spent forty years trying to reject. With the crisis, the government dug up an agricultural law from the late 1980s that permitted independent tobacco farmers to use idle cropland to grow tobacco. The state provided other incentives as well. The government still sets the price of tobacco and furnishes fertilizer and agricultural supplies, but productivity counts. The more farmers grow, the more they earn, and part of their income is in dollars. The same incentives apply to factories. Workers receive 6 percent of their wages in dollars and extra money for each cigar they make above their daily quotas. At the Pilotos factory, some workers have doubled their twenty-four-dollar monthly pay.

The incentives have worked. Between 1996 and 2000, the number of cigars exported rose from 70 million to 118 million, with the goal of exporting 200 million. In 2004, Habanos S.A., the distribution company for Cuban cigars, declined to give a number on exports, but in 2003, an official said, Cuba earned 240 million dollars from cigar exports. Most of the merchandise goes to Europe, which accounts for 72 percent of the exports. But Cuban cigars reach all markets, including consumers in American cities. Despite the embargo and strong antitobacco campaigns, an estimated 11 million cigars are smuggled into the United States every year.

When Cubans want to cut off someone's rambling speech, they say: "Don't tell me the whole history of tobacco." Indeed, the significance of tobacco in Cuba goes beyond its potential to help save the island from the dollar crisis. "Talking about tobacco is talking about the national cultural identity," said Zoe Nocedo, director of the Museum of Tobacco in downtown Havana. "It is not only a fundamental product for the economy, but a product that helped the development of the history of Cuban culture."

By the time Christopher Columbus "discovered" Cuba in 1492, the Native population had already organized many of their rituals around the tobacco tree or *cohiba*. They smoked to communicate with divinities, and they used the plant as medicine to cure skin diseases and cuts. Columbus's crew took to it easily, and it did not take long for them to send the leaf home. After unsuccessfully trying to prohibit tobacco imports in 1717, the Spanish Crown instead decided to control its cultivation and sale. With the creation of the island's first cigar factories, the tobacco industry took center stage in Cuban history. To entertain themselves, the rollers hired readers, who read news and literature from around the world—a tradition that gave the island's workers a reputation as the world's most educated. It did not take long before they started organizing and incrementally acquiring political power. They participated in all major strikes affecting the country. Later, they supported José Martí's fight for independence in the 1890s and Castro's revolution. But the workers' revolutionary fire has been extinguished by the regime they helped put into power. Nowadays, readers' fare is often limited to *Granma*, the national paper, and romance novels. Or they simply turn on the radio.

Children in maroon school uniforms play peacefully under palm trees in the main square, women with colorful umbrellas quietly walk around during the hottest hours of the day, and bare-chested men ride slow-moving horses. More than four decades after the revolution, it is hard to believe that there was ever turmoil in Pilotos. Still, some residents remember more chaotic times. Francisco Rodríguez, a gray-haired man with dark eyes known as "Pancho," was twenty-eight when Castro's revolutionary army defeated president Fulgencio Batista's troops. He still remembers the days preceding the victory. "Many people supported the revolution, and you could see the revolutionaries run in the streets to hide from Batista's National Guard," he says, standing in the quiet main square and pointing out the roads where the *clandestinos* used to hide. "The guard would arrest anyone they suspected of causing trouble or posting revolutionary signs." But the atmosphere was never too volatile. Early on, Pancho said, Pilotos residents were supportive of the revolution. "At midnight on December 31, 1959, a sergeant announced that Batista had lost," Pancho recalls. "There was no conflict. At dawn, the local National Guard had already surrendered to the new authorities."

At seventy, Pancho looks fragile but fit. A wicker hat folded on the sides protects his tanned and wrinkled face from the sun. His expression reflects a life of hard work. He has been a tobacco grower in Pilotos for decades. The cooperative, new buildings, new schools, and new medical offices are wondrous to Pancho. "Before the revolution, there was no asphalt on the streets," he says. "The town was only the main square and a few houses around. . . . The rich people were those who had a house, a field, ten farmers, and a tractor. Today the cooperative has more than the rich people used to have."

Piloteños have been smart enough to flaunt the success of their tobacco cooperative to the government. And the government has been quick to send much-needed infrastructure money their way. Since it was created in 1979, the cooperative's steady stream of revenue has led to the construction of new housing and the centralization of rural schools. It has also supported a number of initiatives in the community, such as sponsoring an institution for special education. With the construction of each new building, or the unveiling of new programs, a certain innocence has been lost. "At the beginning, the revolution gave everything for free," says Pancho. "But then it understood that it needed to exchange what it gave for people's work."

A few blocks from Pilotos's colonial square, a wooden arch indicates the entrance to the cooperative. Its name is written in colorful letters on the arcade, and right behind the structure, a blue concrete house hosts the administration's office. A hundred feet away, humble wooden shacks complete the commune where farmers and their families have settled. Behind their shacks, wide tobacco fields expand to the horizon. Each room in the office is decorated with posters honoring socialism. In the hall, a large frame with pictures of Castro visiting the cooperative hangs on the wall.

On the opposite side of the room, by the main door, a document similar to a diploma is posted. It says "National Vanguard–Socialist Emulation" and is the award given to Cuba's most productive entities.

In a sector where small farms are commonly considered more efficient than cooperatives, the Pilotos organization proves an exception. Profitable ever since it opened, it is now one of the collectives growing the largest numbers of leaves in the country with the highest yields per area. In more than two decades, its membership has grown from 52 to 364 farmers. In the early 2000s, the workers cultivated 2,000 acres of arable land.

In exchange for pooling their land, their tools, and their machinery, the state gives the workers housing and priority access to fertilizers, machines, and construction materials. They also get a minimum wage equivalent to ten dollars a month and additional money for the sale of their surplus. "Each one of us receives an advance of two hundred pesos," explained Daniel Suárez, the director of the cooperative. But if the income from the production in excess winds up being higher than anticipated, the extra money is equally distributed among farmers.

As a good *piloteña*, Zoe Valdés, the cooperative's accountant who is not related to the exiled novelist of the same name, always walks around with a colorful umbrella to protect her from the sun. In the two decades Valdés has spent working at the cooperative, she has passed through it hundreds of times. She knows the location of every field and every warehouse. On her way to the fields, she greets members, inquiring about their children, their parents' health, or just getting the town's latest gossip. The first fields across the commune are covered with a thick, white gauze that forms a sort of translucent tent and contrasts with the vibrant green of the tobacco trees underneath it. "This is the shade-grown tobacco," said Valdés, indicating the field with her umbrella. "It's for export wrapper leaves. The sun-grown tobacco is used for everything you can't see in a cigar, for the filler."

Valdés, like many in Cuba, respects tobacco planters for the dedication their profession requires. Because of the fragility of the crop, they have to visit and care for each one of the plants at least 150 times in a six-month season. The season starts in October, with the preparation of the soil. The fields are plowed while, simultaneously, the tobacco seeds are sown in the cooperative's seedbed. Twenty-five to thirty days later, the seedlings are transplanted to the field. During the first month and a half

Portrait of a man with pipe, Camagüey, 2001. *Photo by Mimi Chakarova*

following the transplanting, the farmer has to constantly irrigate, weed, and fertilize the crop. Forty days after the transplanting, harvest begins at the base of the plant and progresses over the next twenty days to its top. With a surgeon's skill, the harvester threads each leaf through the top of the center vein and ties the leaves to a pole for drying. The leaves dry in humidified barns for forty-five to sixty days. Then they are removed from the pole and placed in bulk to cure for twenty-one days. Because of its complexity, tobacco growing never adjusted to the communist vision of large state farms and government-run cooperatives. Instead, most of the traditional family-scale tobacco farms were preserved. "It would be impossible to have great extensions of land because half of the harvest would get lost," explained Nocedo.

The great care, however, does not generate great profits. The state is the only buyer, and so small farmers end up making most of their profits from other crops that they sell at farmers' markets left uncontrolled. "Tobacco is basically one more expense," says Pedro, an independent farmer near

Pilotos. But without growing tobacco, the state will not permit him to grow the vegetables that do pay well. He explains the economics. In one year, he says, he earns 500 to 600 dollars on tobacco, but his expenses leave him with profits of only 150 to 250 dollars. This is not enough to support his wife and two children, so he grows other crops and raises pigs and chickens.

The Pilotos cooperative uses the same strategy as a small farmer. Tobacco is grown on only 30 percent of the arable soil, which is divided into areas managed by small groups of farmers. The more experienced growers head the groups. The same principle applies to other crops, such as rice, beans, and soy. The farmers grow more than 1.3 million pounds of tobacco leaves, produce 40 tons of pork, and nearly 70,000 liters of milk. It is enough to meet the state quota, earn some extra income, and feed the workers. No one in Pilotos is complaining. At the corner table of the cooperative's main refectory, Valdés smokes her tenth cigarette of the day. Over a copious meal of rice, beans, and yucca she praises country life. "Farmers today have a better life than Cubans who live in Havana because they produce for their own consumption," she says. "A country house has everything you can find in Havana."

Some of Havana's houses do have more commodities than the farmers' shacks, but while most residents of the capital faced dramatic food shortages during the early 1990s, Pilotos farmers always managed to feed their families. Because of tobacco's special status in the country's economy, tobacco growers were among the few farmers who kept receiving subsidized fertilizers during the Special Period. That allowed them to maintain both their tobacco and food-crops production.

At the Pilotos factory a mile away, the Cuban flag flaps in the wind and a bust of José Martí, the island's hero of independence, welcomes the workers. Short palm trees fringe the paths curving around the different units of the plant: the stemming department, the warehouse, the packing center. The hand-rolling school is in one of the back buildings. Sitting at a table on the left side of the classroom is Marta, one of two instructors. She is a petite but voluptuous woman. Her thick black hair is pulled up in a bun and her baby blue dress elegantly marks her waist. A group of new recruits surrounds her and watches her smoothly shape a cigar. The students already know that the appropriate placement of the different kinds of leaves is critical to the quality of each cigar. Each of the leaves that Marta names has a specific function: the *capote* comes from the lowest part of the tobacco tree and is used as the inner covering of the cigar filler; the *seco* is the central leaf of the bush and helps the burning; the *volado* is a smaller leaf and enhances the flavor of the cigar, while the *ligero* comes from the highest part of the tree and gives strength to the blend. The *picadura*, finally, is the lowest grade of tobacco chopped in small pieces.

"You pick the *capote*, stretch it, and stem it," she explains while clipping the top of the leaf's midrib between her thumb and her index finger, then rolling the leaf around her fist to pull out its stem. "Set the two halves so that they overlap each other," she continues, loud enough to be heard by all her pupils. "With two leaves of *seco* make the shape of a fan, add a leaf of *volado*, half a leaf of *ligero*, and some *picadura*," she adds. "Then roll the whole in the *capote* and put it in the presser." The filler of the cigar is ready. In the tobacco industry, workers say, not one leaf is wasted.

In the factory, conservation is seen as a way to contribute to the economy and the country's prosperity. Every morning hand-rollers are given stacks of leaves of different kinds and weights. Prime material dispatchers carefully write down on a report book the amount of leaves each worker receives. The quantity of material dispatched is equivalent to a specific number of manufactured cigars. Keeping record of the prime material given out and the finished products received at the end of the day is a way to make sure no tobacco is wasted or stolen. But tobacco is not the only thing workers avoid to waste in Pilotos. Any kind of collective endeavor "to help the country," as they say, is rewarded. That includes collecting glass, paper, and cardboard. Among the multiple national recognitions it has received since its opening, the factory counts an award for its recycling effort. A few months earlier, workers had been honored for donating blood.

While the students in the hand-rolling school wait to release the filler from the presser and proceed with the wrapping, workers in a building nearby take a break. High on a wall, a sign says, "Tobacco turns thoughts into dreams." An Italian coffeemaker spurts out its first brown drops. Among the high piles of cedar boxes that cover most of the room's floor—this is the packing room—a woman pulls out three tiny cups and puts a few spoons of sugar in each of them. To be good, Cubans say, coffee must be strong and sweet. The woman's name is Mirenza, and although she does not belong to that section of the factory, she spends part of her day there. Her job is to take care of the *escaparate*, the humidified room where the cigars are stored until they are shipped to Havana. But the facility is still small, and so she has plenty of time to help her *compañeros* in other sections of the factory. "We are farmers' children, we're used to working hard and helping each other," explains Mirenza while pouring the coffee in the cups. "If we have to work extra hours to meet the production plan, we just do it."

The whole organization of work at the factory aims to foster solidarity among workers and a devotion to the nation's collective well-being. Workers are permanently stimulated. The factory, for example, keeps the wages as equal as possible. Despite a hierarchy in the ranks, supervisors do not necessarily have a higher income than hand-rollers. Their basic salary in pesos is higher, but the percentage they receive in dollars is lower. It is a way to avoid big differences in the salaries. A hand-roller who exceeds his or her quota can eventually earn more money than his or her superior. The factory uses moral incentives as well. Workers are regularly honored for the zealousness they put into their labor and their involvement in political activities. Every six months, the most outstanding worker can take his or her family for a fifteen-day vacation in a house the cooperative owns on a beach near Havana. Such policies, added to the small town's natural sense of community, shape the convivial atmosphere prevailing in the factory.

Despite the mechanical aspect of their labor, workers around Mirenza maintain their good humor. As they paste paper ribbons on the corners of the cigar boxes, stick bands on the cigars, or put them inside individual aluminum tubes, they take small sips of their coffee and chat, competing with the loud and omnipresent radio speakers. On the opposite side of the room, four men stand behind high tables lit by neon bulbs. Two of them classify the finished cigars according to their color; two others put them in the boxes. Each box must have cigars of one color only. Sorting them is a task that requires much precision, since the factory has identified as many as eight colors and sixty-five nuances. After being packed and sealed, the cigar boxes are ready to leave the factory. Twice a week, trucks come from Havana to pick up the boxes and take them to Habanos S.A. headquarters.

Despite the factory's rigorous organization and tight quality control, in the past few years, experts have said that the new cigars on the market are less flavored than older Habanos. *Cigar Aficionado* and even *Granma* have reported that international cigar merchants are worried. Cuba's eagerness to sustain its economy is hurting the fine reputation its cigars have enjoyed for decades, experts say. The efforts made to boost the production to monumental levels in the past few years have led to a significant decrease in the quality. An industry expert in Havana does not even bother to deny the difficulties. "It's hard to maintain export quality in the current situation of the country," says Beatriz Garrido, a specialist in marketing at Habanos S.A. "We made a big effort to incorporate a lot of new workers but had little time to train them."

The government, however, has become more conscious of the degree to which tarnishing the reputation of Cuban cigars could injure the country's economy. The state has tightened its Soviet-like control so that imperfections can be identified at any stage of the manufacturing and sent back to the workers. And in 2000, Habanos S.A. started a joint venture with Altadis, the distribution company of its main Spanish and French clients. The deal meant new financing, but it also opened the way to a new policy centered on quality rather than quantity, officials say. Cigar smokers are waiting to taste the results.

Most of the day, the entrance of the Partagás factory in Havana is frenzied. Located behind the Capitol, in the heart of the city, Partagás has nothing in common with the Pilotos factory except that it manufactures export cigars. With 750 workers, Partagás produces its own brand and hosts Cuba's most visited cigar store. Built in 1845, it is also one of the island's oldest factories and one of Havana's main tourist attractions. Every forty minutes in the internal patio of the Spanish-style stone building, the factory's guides call out tours in English and French. Groups of about ten people follow them into the fresh storage room and take the narrow stairs leading to the second floor where the cigar manufacturing takes place. Every room of the factory is crowded and hectic. In the long and tight gallery where the tobacco is stemmed, the visitors have to stay in line to navigate through the two rows of workers. Next door, hundreds of laborers roll cigars in a wide and bright room. The workers, mostly women, call out to tourists while they cross the room. They ask for candies, gum, pens. "Come sit near me and have a picture taken," says one of them. "Just do it, go ahead," holler her friends. Photography inside the factory is not allowed but for a larger tip, the guide will look the other way.

Workers here rarely mention socialism and are more interested in how much money they can make than in the craft of rolling cigars. "I like the job because you make more money than in other sectors," says a woman who has worked in the factory for twelve years. Others in the room agree, but say that it is still not enough to live. "Like everybody, we have to work it out some other way," says one of the workers.

Since the crisis of the early 1990s, most Cubans engage in other work besides their official job to make ends meet. Often, that means working illegally, driving tourists for dollars, being their guide for the day, or selling cigars on the black market. On the block around the factory, men constantly approach tourists offering any brand of premium cigars for a cheap price. To convince them of the quality, the men say they have gotten the cigars from a relative who works in the factory. That does not necessarily mean they are the best. Many times, the cigars circulating in the black market are either those rejected by the factory's department of quality control, those given to the workers as a daily quota, or those manufactured in illegal factories. But no matter how variable the quality of contraband cigars, many tourists still choose to buy them. The price is compelling. A box of Montecristo Number 4, for instance, costs $72.50 in the state stores, but only $20–25 on the street.

The black market is active outside Havana too. Around Pilotos, some independent tobacco growers break the law and sell part of their crops to individuals. A young man from the area said he bought tobacco from a farmer near Pilotos at fifteen cents per pound and sold it to illegal hand-rollers in Havana for one dollar a pound. He stopped out of fear that he would be caught and be subjected to a jail sentence of fifteen years. But the visibility of cigar smugglers in the cities seems to indicate a certain leniency in the enforcement of the laws. Even those whose business is harmed by the black market appear to be understanding. "Contraband is a problem that has to do with the situation of the country more than with tobacco," said Juan Moya, who works for a company in charge of the distribution of Cuba's export products. "The black market is a way for Cubans to make money."

Few resist the temptation. When asked if some Partagás cigars are sold in the streets, one of the guides of the Havana factory lowers his voice and says: "It happens, as everywhere, but people working here don't do it because they could lose their job." After a pause he asks softly: "Do you want cigars?"

It's a question that no one ever asks in Pilotos. But here, too, the administrators control their workers. At the end of a hot and humid day, the factory's loudspeakers resound with each hand-roller's daily performance. "Worker number eleven: 130 cigars, 126 good, 4 deformed, 96.9 percent of quality," says a man's voice. "Worker number fifteen: 144 cigars, 5 with twisted top, 96.5 percent of quality." After workers have heard their quality results, they leave the buildings in small groups, chatting and teasing each other. "How many cigars did you roll today?" one young man asks another. "Just thirty," the other replies, joking. At the exit door, a security guard makes sure they have not stolen any cigars. But no one takes the control very seriously. "Should I take my pants off too?" jokes one, while another grotesquely twirls around pulling his T-shirt up and showing the flat pockets of his shorts. Little upsets their good humor. They grab their bikes, pass the fence, wave at each other, and head home. Behind them, dust clouds the road.

Cubans Log On

behind Castro's Back

~ JOHN COTÉ

The rooftop apartment in Central Havana has black iron bars on the front window and door. Jagger, a German shepherd, growls and charges the doorway, his lean head pressed against the iron as he snaps at the visitors. Antonio Cuesta, a gangly twenty-six-year-old Cuban with a crew cut, takes Jagger by the collar and chains him to a yellow hallway door grooved with claw marks. "Guard dog," he says and flashes a smile. "When my mom's here alone, he won't let anyone in."

Not quite comfortably out of Jagger's reach in the front room sits Cuesta's passion: a patchwork computer, the parts borrowed from friends or bought on Cuba's black market. Before he sits down, Cuesta, who has already asked that we not use his real name, looks at his visitors. "If I get caught telling you this, it's thirty years," he says. "They'll send me to a place no one would ever want to go." With a few mouse clicks he brings up a list of pirated codes to access the Internet. He selects one, and the modem dials. It doesn't work. The code's legitimate owner might be logged on, or maybe the system is experiencing a glitch. "Sometimes different phone lines in different areas go down," says Cuesta. He shrugs and clicks another icon. "So I have eleven accounts."

Hackers must be resourceful to survive in a communist world, where fraying infrastructure, snarled bureaucracy, and draconian security services are the norm. But cyber-criminals like Cuesta are not simply survivors; they're an indication that Fidel Castro may be able to limit access to the Internet but that he is unable to fully control its inherently democratic world. Ever since the government embraced *la revolución digital*, the digital revolution, to make state-run companies more competitive, it has tried to control popular access. For the most part it has proven successful. Black-market Internet accounts like Cuesta's are rare simply because most Cubans don't have phones and can't afford a computer. That's a predicament true in much of Latin America. In 2001, for example, there were twenty personal computers for every 1,000 Cubans, according to the World Bank. That compared to twenty-two per 1,000 in El Salvador, ten per 1,000 in Nicaragua, or sixty-nine per 1,000 in Mexico.

The government controls the island's Internet provider that goes through two gateways. Home Internet accounts are restricted to foreigners, company executives, and state officials. Access codes are required to log on to the country's 3,600 legal Internet accounts that suffice for a population of 11 million. In addition, about 40,000 academics and government workers had legal e-mail accounts, half of them with access outside of Cuba, said Luis Fernández, a government spokesman. But in January 2004, the government tried to restrict that further when Castro put into effect a law to try and bar unofficial Internet use. The measure limits Internet access to only those with telephone accounts payable in U.S. dollars, such as foreign businesses and government offices. Amnesty International immediately condemned the law as "yet another attempt to cut off Cubans' access to alternative views and a space for discussing them." But it is still unclear how many Cubans will be knocked off the Internet, since most use it through their workplaces.

The Cuban government says that, given its limited resources, it needs to ensure that the Internet is primarily used for the social good, according to a British Broadcasting Corporation (BBC) report on the measure. But dissident groups have expressed doubt that the authorities can control the Internet as much as they might wish, according to the BBC. Moreover, one need look no further than Cuesta's inventiveness to question whether *informáticos* (computer geeks) will be stymied long, or if they will simply find another way around this latest roadblock.

As Cuesta demonstrates, the Internet does not stop with what the government permits. A small but lively black market emerged after 2000. Sometimes legitimate account holders want to supplement their state wages by selling their access codes. Other times, people like Cuesta steal codes while repairing computers for company executives. Pirated codes go for thirty to fifty dollars a month for Internet access or ten to fifteen dollars for e-mail–only accounts. That is too steep for most Cubans, but affordable for some earning dollars from Havana's pulsing tourism. This new class of Internet users who circumvent government controls lend testament to Cuban ingenuity, says a U.S. diplomat in Havana who asks to remain anonymous. It also seems to indicate that the Cuban government cannot completely leash the teeming world of online information.

Cuesta should know. On the third try his modem hisses its familiar singsong, and this time a server elsewhere on the island squawks back. Cuesta doesn't look up from the monitor, but a sharp smile crosses his face. It's the smile of a child telling his friends he just got away with cheating on a test. "Look," he says, pointing as his Netscape browser opens. "Where do you want to go?" Soon Cuesta is on Hotmail checking his e-mail.

Cuesta says he was trained as a teenager to be a government hacker. Sitting in worn jeans and a knockoff Calvin Klein T-shirt, he hardly looks like a covert state operative. I could not verify his story beyond his stash of illegal access codes, but the respect he commanded from other *informáticos* was unassailable. His computer knowledge was likewise extensive, and, given the shortage of computers on the island until recent years, it seemed unlikely he could reach that skill level without formal training.

Cuesta describes excelling at science at an early age. When he was fourteen, he was selected to attend a specialized science boarding school. There, he was introduced to computers, and soon after he arrived, Cuesta says he started working on computer viruses for fun. While at school, he studied Trojan horses—hidden viruses—and had written one by the end of his first year. "I demonstrated it to the professors," he says and laughs. "They were a little bit jealous." Even at fourteen, Cuesta says, he had to look beyond his teachers for inspiration. He found it in his twenty-one-year-old girlfriend, who was studying cybernetics. "I would study with her," he says and pauses for a moment. The smile is back. "We would exchange ideas."

After graduating from the science high school, he sharpened his computer skills at an electronics institute in Havana. At twenty-one, Cuesta says he went to work for a state-run construction company that specialized in large projects like airports and hotels. His job: hacker. "The state trained me to circumvent passwords and access databases," he says. Most of this training came on the job at the construction company. "They would buy software, and then I'd be paid to break the dynamic code so we could load one copy on all the machines." An agent in the FBI's computer intrusion center and an executive for a computer and Internet security firm based in the United Kingdom both say the situations Cuesta describes are

University students, Havana, 2004. *Photo by Mimi Chakarova*

plausible, but neither had any firsthand information about hacker attacks by Cuban companies.

Cuesta says he left that job at the beginning of 2001 and began working as a freelancer. With two partners he does contract work designing software and Web sites. The work is not sponsored by the state, and therefore illegal. To minimize the danger for both the contractors and the programmers, the business relationship remains deliberately murky. Cuesta says he and his two associates are designing software for an Italian company. When asked, he says he doesn't know the name of the company, just the names of contact people he talks to weekly. And the Italian contacts don't know Cuesta's partners. "It's not convenient for them to know who we are," Cuesta says. When asked if he wanted to know more about his employers, he shakes his head. "It's better to know less." "They want cheap software," Cuesta says. "And we want dollars."

The quest for dollars does not stop at Cuesta's front door. From there one can look across stained rooftops sprouting TV antennas and makeshift satellite dishes to the Capitolio, the domed Cuban capitol modeled after its counterpart in Washington, DC. Inside is the Cibercafé—the first of its kind in Cuba when it opened in April 2000—which provides Internet access on seven computers for five dollars an hour. Pesos are not accepted, and the café's commercial license only allows foreigners and Cuban nationals married to foreigners to use the computers, says Rolando García, the café manager. Customers' passport numbers are written down before they can get online. García says the restrictions are simply a business decision, not a move to control access to information. He dismisses the notion that Internet access could facilitate social change in Cuba. "The revolution isn't afraid of this," says García. "The revolution is already committed to educating the population." He says he wants to apply to the Ministry of Science, Technology, and the Environment, which controls the café, for a license allowing Cubans to get online, but he has not yet started the process.

Most Cubans simply cannot afford to pay five dollars for an hour of surfing. If they could, García says, they would still be turned away. But one of the clerks, who asks to remain anonymous, says Cubans who can pay could get online. García declines to give specifics on how much revenue the café was bringing in, but he says he wanted to get permission from the ministry to reinvest some or all of the operational income. "Right now we'd like to finance ourselves," says García. "We're working on changing to a much bigger and more comfortable location."

The ministry, however, may be wary about the short-term loss of hard currency. Besides the initial investment in the computers and the cost of Internet service, the café has little overhead. García says his salary is about twelve dollars a month ($9 in 2004). The six other employees make less than he. The café looks to be a cash cow, and García says similar operations have been opened in the cities of Santiago and Santa Clara. The government is also not the only one getting dollars from Cibercafé Capitolio. The workers are too. "It's called *invento*," says James, a foreign national who has frequented the Internet café regularly during his four years in Cuba. "It's a creative way of stealing. Say you're online for two hours. You pay for that two hours, but they ring it up as one hour and pocket the rest." It didn't take long, he says, for an employee at the café to offer him a black-market Internet account for fifty dollars a month. When approached months later by a foreign national posing as a student living in Cuba, the same employee said he could arrange a black-market account. A meeting was scheduled with the employee's "friend" who supplied access codes.

Depending on the type of black-market account, service can be spotty. According to multiple sources, black-market accounts are usually created in one of three ways: the access code is stolen; the access code is sold by the legitimate owner; or an illicit account is created by a network administrator who oversees a server. "Let's say you work at CITMATEL [one of the government-run service providers], and you work for pesos," says Nelson Valdés, director of the Cuban Academic Research Program at the University of New Mexico. "During the day, you create a program to set up a proxy server on the commercial server. Now you have two servers effectively working on one. You're the only one who knows it's there, and you can sell accounts for dollars. . . . It happens all the time." Free software to set up a proxy server is readily available through online chat channels like Internet Relay Chat, or IRC. Valdés says that while doing research in Cuba, he paid fifteen dollars a month for an e-mail–only account set up illicitly on a proxy server. "Generally people who have Internet access are directors; they don't know anything about computers," says Cuesta. "We steal the accounts and just sell the codes. . . . Also, I have a lot of friends who give me connections anyway."

Some individuals with legal accounts sell their codes to make cash on the side. They then set up specific time periods for use. "My friend has an account that he can only use between eight at night and eight in the morning when the owner isn't using it," says Marelys Herrera, a young writer who shares a black-market Internet account with her mother. Her friend pays thirty dollars a month for the limited service. Herrera and her mother do a little better. "My mom works for a foreign firm," she says. "The firm hooks her up and pays the ten dollars for the account, but of course it's illegal."

The unregulated nature of the black market makes it impossible to tell how many Cubans are sneaking online or buying used computer parts to circumvent costly and restrictive government stores. Even more widespread is unofficial e-mail use. There are about 40,000 registered e-mail accounts in Cuba, but many account owners share their addresses with neighbors, friends, and colleagues. They print incoming messages for these other users and type in outgoing e-mails. Cuban students linger around the stairs to the central library at Havana University, where foreign students can open an account for five dollars and send e-mail on text-only computers running a Linux operating system. Cuban students are rigorously questioned and often denied an account, so they pass handwritten messages with an e-mail address scrawled on the top to any foreign exchange student willing to send it. "How many people have e-mail connectivity? We don't know," says Valdés. "One account can have eight people using it." Valdés says there are "easily 20,000" free Yahoo! e-mail accounts registered to Cubans. Many of these people do not have regular computer access, so they set their accounts up to forward e-mail to a friend who has regular access, he says.

Though more rare than surreptitious e-mail use, everyone from painters to diplomats say they know about the black market in computers and Internet accounts. "It's rare, yes," says Herrera, who asked that her name be changed. "But in my world, pretty much everybody has black-market access. We also share computer parts and things like that. In my world we're all *informáticos*."

Informáticos say they dodge the system for two main reasons: money and anonymity. If one can get government approval, an Internet account is prohibitively expensive unless a state agency subsidizes it. The National Center for Automated Data Exchange, known by its Spanish acronym CENIAI, oversees Cuba's four Internet service providers. The center charges 260 dollars a month–a lot more than the average annual salary of about half that–to Cubans and foreigners alike to register an Internet account. "You can go the official way through CENIAI, but that way they know everything," says Herrera. "They know exactly when you get on, exactly where you go, what numbers you call. The service is better, but we don't use it because of that—and it's expensive. So you just go through the black market. You find someone who has it and ask them how they got it. It's really easy to get Internet access."

The black market is also a primary source for computer hardware. "You pretty much have to use the black market to build a computer; it's a fortune to buy one in the store," said Herrera. Pedro Mendoza, a painter, turned to the black market to get a used desktop with a Pentium III processor for 900 dollars. "There's a black market for everything, but you need money," says Mendoza. "You find it. It's that easy. That's where you go if you want to get something done."

But not all Cubans have the money to shop the black market, or have Cuesta's ability to get online. These people have to go the official route, which is cumbersome and restrictive. At the National Library of Science and Technology, downstairs from the Capitolio, average Cubans can get online information, but they cannot get online. Instead, they submit requests to professional researchers who search the Web on one of seven computers. The fee is fifteen pesos per hour—about seventy cents. "We don't have sufficient technology to serve every Cuban," says Anierta Pereira, a researcher at the library. "There are limitations."

One of the limitations is that foreigners are given priority, says Pereira. "The only thing is they have to pay in dollars," she says. Foreigners are charged five dollars an hour for research, or they can get online themselves in the next room, where there are six computers with Internet connections for the same five-dollar-per-hour rate. According to Pereira, most of the information requests come from academics or students. Pereira says no Web sites are blocked at the library, but superiors can monitor researcher's movements. To demonstrate, Pereira opens the Web site for the Cuban American National Foundation, which is known for its militant anti-Castro stance. "You see?" she says. "We can access anything, but it's the time. We have to be productive. . . . The cost to use the Internet is very high, and we don't want to put the institution in a position where they have to pay more money."

The Internet is more expensive in Cuba than elsewhere. Pummeled by economic hardship as the West leaped into the information age, Cuba is now struggling to modernize an antiquated telecommunications system not built to handle electronic data traffic. There are no fiber-optic links off the island, and all digital data is relayed through two costly satellite links. In a bid to catch up, the government is overhauling its telephone network in a joint venture with Italy's Telecom Italia and Mexico's Grupo Domos, digitizing analog lines and laying new cables. When the project is completed—slated for 2004—there will be 1.1 million phone lines. That is less than one phone per ten Cubans. Until these improvements are made, there are about 623,000 phone lines, or one for every eighteen Cubans. More than half of these lines are analog and effectively useless for sending digital information. The improvements that the government expects to complete sometime in 2004 will make it considerably easier for more Cubans to log on—if the government allows it. By controlling the gateways, the government can still limit access to only the more skilled hacker.

For its part, the government frequently cites the lack of infrastructure and current Internet costs as the main hindrance to Cubans getting online. "Here, really the only restriction for getting on the Internet is technology," says Juan Fernández, head of Cuba's e-commerce commission.

"Cuba is not afraid of the challenge of the Internet." Fernández's assurances seem hollow, however, considering the post offices that are wired do not offer Internet access. Rather, they provide access to a national intranet, a closed network that only contains sites endorsed by the government. Cubans have to pay in dollars–$4.50 for three hours–to surf the domestic intranet or to send e-mail internationally. Web-hosted e-mail accounts like Yahoo! Mail or Hotmail are not accessible. Ostensibly, Cubans are allowed to send domestic e-mails for five pesos per hour, but at the main post office inside the new Ministry of Information and Communication, the clerk said even domestic e-mail had to be paid for in dollars. Later, a second clerk at the same post office said domestic e-mails could be paid for in pesos, but she did not know the rate. "Almost no one uses pesos," she says.

"We have to be realists," Sergio Pérez, head of the Cuban computer firm Teledatos, told the government-controlled newspaper *Granma* in April 2001. "Cuba, a poor country that is economically blocked by the biggest imperialist powerhouse in the world, has food rations and a shortage of medical supplies. How is it that we also wouldn't have Internet access limitations?" While Cuban officials frequently blame the U.S. trade embargo for the country's economic problems, the U.S. Treasury Department, which oversees U.S. financial dealings with Cuba, authorized U.S. companies in 1997 to negotiate with Cuban officials on opening a fiber-optic link between Florida and Cuba. The move came after the State Department issued a policy statement earlier that year indicating it supported a fiber-optic link to increase the flow of information and cut high phone rates between the two countries. The only condition was that no new technology could be given to Cuba. "Our end goal is that there would be a fiber-optic cable so that we could encourage a greater development of Internet between the United States and Cuba," says James Wolf, economic coordinator for Cuban affairs at the State Department. "To our knowledge there has not actually been an agreement between the Cuban phone company and any of the U.S. companies that have been looking into this."

A fiber-optic ring around the Caribbean was completed in December 2001, but it currently bypasses Cuba. Some observers have speculated that the network, known as Americas Region Caribbean Optical-Ring System, or ARCOS-1, could be linked to Cuba if the political and business factors fall into place. The ring passes within twelve miles of Havana, at which point a branching unit has been laid down. The international consortium funding the project includes twenty-five companies from fourteen countries, including AT&T, MCI, and Genuity (formerly GTE). Wolf would not comment on whether the consortium was negotiating with the Cuban side, but noted, "At this point there has not been a single application by any company to actually install such a cable." Martha Salas, a spokeswoman for New World Network, principal owner of the Americas Region Caribbean Optical-Ring System, said in 2004, "There are no pending discussions between us and Cuba."

Valdés, director of the Cuban Academic Research Program, framed the question facing the Cuban government in economic terms: "Do we bring in optical lines, or do we bring in pipes so we don't have to truck in water to Havana?" The U.S. diplomat in Cuba, however, viewed it differently. According to him, the Cuban government is making substantial revenue off high phone charges between the United States and Cuba. Operating an efficient fiber-optic network with a U.S. business partner would cut into its revenue stream. For U.S. government approval, the network would also have to allow for the free flow of information, undercutting the Cuban government's ability to filter or monitor where its citizens venture in cyberspace.

It is unclear how extensive government control over cyberspace is. In March 2004, the Cuban state blocked access to Web phone sites like dialpad.com and online conferencing services like Net Meeting. But both government-run computer centers and home computers had access to sites from anti-Castro groups and U.S. media outlets. "It is absolutely false that the government is controlling specific sites," Pérez was quoted in *Granma* as saying. "It is the companies or institutions connected to the Internet that decide where its workers and students browse. In what country in the world is a doctor allowed to use a hospital computer to visit porn sites or chat with a friend?"

In Cuba, though, all companies are owned by the state, and many computer users say they are certain the government monitors Internet activity. "Everyone knows it," says Santiago Ferrer, a young technician at CUPET (Cubapetróleo), the state petroleum company, and a friend of Cuesta's. "It's in the technology. Servers have the capacity to look and check where you were." But just the threat of monitoring may be an effective deterrent. "You don't have to check someone's urine everyday to see if they're taking drugs," said the U.S. diplomat.

Even someone like Armando Estévez, a well-placed state employee, is not entrusted with Internet access. Relaxing in the afternoon sun on the front steps of the Capitolio, he checks his IBM personal organizer and his cell phone, conveniences someone like Cuesta only reads about. The information services manager at CUPET, Estévez even has a laptop to work from home, where he can dial into a closed company intranet but not the Internet. Still, he plays down the idea that the government was worried online information could stir political change. "Undoubtedly there is an influence, but the political change is not very big," he says. "That information is coming into the country all the time—it has been for forty years. We can't blockade that kind of information. You hear it over the radio or by word of mouth. People know what's in the *Miami Herald* and compare it with *Granma*." Estévez suggests Cubans view the U.S. newspaper and the Cuban state-run daily with equal suspicion. "The problem is that the lies are very big on both sides," he says. "You can spot them immediately. That's what politics is."

Ferrer, both a colleague of Estévez's and an *informático* friend of Cuesta's, typifies a new generation of Cubans who get online to communicate. "It's very Cuban to cooperate through chatting," says Ferrer, who goes by "macdaddy" in chat rooms. "Usually when we're chatting, we get phone numbers. We meet at the beach and stuff. It's really weird and kinda funny. No one uses their real names when we meet. They say, 'Hey macdaddy,' and you don't know whether to use their real name or not." Despite the lack of home Internet access, Ferrer says chatting is "very common in Cuba now." He chats on the job. Monitoring the flow of petroleum during a twenty-four-hour shift has its downtimes, but Ferrer is friends with the network administrator in his division. Even though he is not authorized to have Internet access on his computer, Ferrer said the administrator lets him get online whenever he wants. "If you chat at lunch my boss won't do anything," he says. "It's not a problem. We shouldn't chat in front of him when we're supposed to be working, but we can surf the Web." Ferrer says surfing is actually part of his job responsibilities. "My boss knows. Everybody knows," he says. "My boss tells me to find stuff on the Internet."

As he talks, Ferrer leans against a glass display case in the electronics store at Havana's Plaza Carlos III shopping center. He is among a group of twenty-something males looking wistfully at a new shipment of modems, motherboards, and other computer gear, most without price tags. According to the store manager, the parts arrived three days ago, and the store headquarters had not yet decided how much to charge. The few items that did have prices were two to three times more expensive than in the United States. A Multi-Tech Systems 56K modem came to 230 dollars. The same modem is listed on buy.com for 115 dollars. Similar markups are found in the few other computer stores sprinkled around Havana.

Ferrer is building his computer piecemeal, cobbling together parts bought on the black market or loaned to him by friends like Cuesta. He still needs a monitor, a CD-ROM drive, and a modem to complete a creation he calls *Frankenstein*. "It's very expensive," he says, casting a sidelong glance at a modem. "Most of the parts I have I got from friends."

According to Ernesto Reyna, manager for the Plaza Carlos III store, anyone can come in and buy all the parts to build a complete computer system at one time. Although no hard drives, CD-ROM drives, or tower cases were on display, Reyna said the store had everything to put together a full system. Once the pieces are bought, Reyna says staff will assemble the machine if the customer requests. A Pentium III system with a CD-ROM, modem, and speakers would cost just over 2,000 dollars—more than double the price in the United States.

In the Cuban cyber realm—whether it's assembling computers bought in pieces or selling Internet codes—it comes down to ingenuity, connections, and money. Cuesta operates at one extreme, but the rules are the same even at the shiny state-run computer clubs he describes as "bullshit." The government started opening the clubs in the 1990s to help Cubans succeed in a technology-driven world. Affiliated with the Union of Young Communists, a government student organization, the clubs teach classes in Windows, Excel, and Word, as well as more advanced skills like Web design and multimedia presentations. They focus on youths, but you don't have to be a member of the union to use them, and they also offer classes for adults. There are some 174 of these clubs throughout the country, said Damián Barcaz, technical assistant director at the Central Palace of Computing, the flagship club. He said the government plans to have between two hundred and three hundred throughout Cuba's fifteen provinces. "There's really nowhere you don't need a computer," says Barcaz. "It's the way to the world." But many of these youth computer clubs, like the one in the Havana neighborhood of Vedado, lack Internet access. At the Central Palace of Computing in Old Havana, five of the ten computers available for students to do work outside of their classes have Internet access. Barcaz says no sites are blocked or filtered out, bringing up CNN's

A schoolgirl at a computer station, Central Palace of Computing, Havana, 2001. *Photo by Mimi Chakarova*

Web site when asked. "Staff walk around and can look where the students are going, but we don't block anything," says Barcaz.

Upstairs from the main hall, past a framed placard on which Castro wrote "Siento envidia!" or "I'm envious!" when he christened the center in 1991, a group of six- and seven-year-olds sit two to a computer in a modern classroom. They practice their spelling as brightly colored graphics of leopards and buses appear on their screens. Cuba, according to a World Bank report, has developed and donated game software to other Latin American countries. In addition, it uses the programs in its own elementary schools. In the next classroom, the mood is more serious. Groups of three or four adults huddle around each of the nine computers as they practice using Windows 2000 and Microsoft Excel. Many say they needed computer skills for their job. "At my bank, there's one computer, and I have to know how to use it," says Leticia Betancourt, twenty-three. "This is the only way we can learn how. Society demands that you know how to use a computer now, so we come here." Marta Baros, a fifty-year-old accountant, finds herself in a similar position. "I want to be able to use this," she says, gesturing at an Excel spreadsheet open on her screen. "If I can, my work will be much better."

And many say they will simply be more informed. "It's not like it used to be," says Ferrer. "Then we were in a bubble. We used to see the world through tinted lenses. It was very difficult." He is lounging against a Russian TV with a Marlboro in his hand, sunglasses on his head, and gold bracelets on his dark wrists. The shutters in the Central Havana apartment he shares with his mother are closed, and his mother is gone. "We don't have to see what they want us to see," he says. "The world is getting to know each other through the Internet. Everyone in the world is the same as in Cuba."

Cuesta, however, is more cautious in his assessment. "The state thinks the Internet can change society," he says. "Tourism is more abundant and is creating more of an effect, though. People compare their lives to the lives of outside people. That makes them think." He leans back in his chair against the closet door. Ferrer takes a drag of his cigarette, fiddling a bootleg Mariah Carey CD. He rests his eyes on *Frankenstein* for more than a few seconds. "You can't predict what's going to happen," he says.

Research assistance by Cyrus Farivar and Osvaldo Gómez

PART FOUR ~ *Searching*

The New Immigrants

Don't Hate Fidel

~ ARCHANA PYATI

They worked in an abandoned house at the edge of Guayabal, a dusty hamlet about an hour's drive from Havana. Slowly, they fit the wood and metal together to make a vessel sturdy enough to hold six passengers. When it was ready, a month and a half later, they packed water, food, and a few clothes for the long journey ahead of them. They kissed Hany, their five-year-old daughter good-bye and snapped a picture of her sleeping form, capturing the sheets and blankets tossed this way and that by her small legs. Four hours later, before the sun rose on August 21, 1994, Barbarita and Orlando sailed to Miami.

Orlando's sister, Miriam, remembers standing waist-deep in the black, tranquil water to push them off Playa Banes, a beach half an hour from Guayabal. The motor sounded strong, and the current was swift. She expected to hear from them in Miami in a day, but to ensure their safe journey, she left the beach that morning and walked six hours to pray at the church of Saint Lazarus in El Rincón. For twelve days, she heard nothing. Guayabal is a town where gossip and hearsay proliferate, so it wasn't long before rumors spread: Orlando and Barbarita had died at sea. "Those days were black," Miriam says, remembering one on which she waited for a public phone and overheard two women telling stories of people who had drowned in the Florida Straits. "I told them, do me a favor, and shut up," she says. And then the call came. Her brother and sister-in-law had been picked up at sea and taken to the U.S. Naval Base at Guantánamo Bay on the island's southeastern coast. Miriam, too, could have climbed aboard that August morning. Does she regret not getting on the boat? "Of course," she says. "But I saw the sea, and I panicked. I didn't have the heart to leave." After all, there was Hany, her five-year-old niece, to think about.

Overnight, Orlando and Barbarita became *balseros*, or rafters, the generation of Cuban migrants who preferred the risky venture across shark-infested waters to what they considered an intolerable life in Cuba. They were among 33,000 Cubans who left the coast in 1994—many of them that summer—with the intention of starting a new life in the United States. It would take the couple eighteen months to finally make it to south Florida. By the time they arrived, a radical shift in immigration policy between the United States and Cuba had taken place. That August, President Bill Clinton, concerned with south Florida's ability to absorb the new immigrants, announced the reversal of a thirty-five-year-old policy welcoming Cubans unconditionally. No longer would the Coast Guard invite Cubans aboard its boats to deliver them safely in the arms of Miami relatives.

Cubans had been leaving by sea for decades, but their desperation to do so reached new heights in 1994. The country found itself in the throes of the Special Period, a time of empty food pantries and a full-blown economic depression brought on by the demise of the Soviet Bloc. The long summer months proved especially difficult, and an increasing number of desperate souls started taking their chances at sea. When a policeman was shot trying to stop one of them, a riot broke out. Things were getting out of hand, so Castro threw up his hands in frustration and told Cubans that the Cuban Coast Guard would "not obstruct any boat from leaving Cuba."

Barbarita and Orlando decided to go. The couple had saved money to buy materials for a boat, and in that sense, they were among the lucky ones. Most *balseros'* departures were not that well planned. They often hastily cobbled rafts together from anything they could find: plywood, inner tubes, tires, Styrofoam, even doors. "They came in the most incredible contraptions," remembers one Miami social worker of that summer.

The *balseros* constituted the latest wave in an exodus as old as the revolution. Since Castro took power, each wave has come to Miami with a different set of hopes and fears. The first came to escape the political turmoil overtaking the island. As members of the bourgeoisie, they feared for their bank accounts as much as for their lives. The second wave began with a massive boatlift from the port of Camarioca, on the island's northeastern coast. Next came Operation Peter Pan, an airlift of thousands of children sent to the United States by their parents who didn't want their offspring to be taught in communist schools. For years after that, parents joined their children under the Freedom Flights program, a series of

A young man with a Miami T-shirt says that he wants to be free like a bird. For a small fee, one can buy a dove and set it free from the rooftop of an adjacent building. The birds are trained to return to their cages. Havana, 2004. *Photo by Mimi Chakarova*

chartered flights to the United States that ultimately transported around 250,000 Cubans. The next large group came during the Mariel boatlift in 1980, when thousands stormed the Peruvian embassy seeking asylum. Then, too, Castro permitted the exodus and thousands were picked up by their Miami relatives at sea.

As early as 1980, the U.S. government's attitude toward Cuban refugees began shifting from sympathy to tolerance. Socioeconomically, the Mariel Cubans were poorer than their predecessors. Some of them had criminal backgrounds, which eroded U.S. enthusiasm for Cuban migration even further. If economic necessity motivated those who came during Mariel, then such motivation was even stronger for the *balsero* generation. They represent, in a sense, the first generation of Cuban *immigrants*—a word that Cuban exiles consider an insult. To be an immigrant implies choice, which none in the earlier generation feels they had when they fled the island. In fact, many assumed they would return to Cuba when Castro fell.

The two terms *immigrant* and *exile* are not mutually exclusive for Barbarita and others belonging to the *balsero* generation. Unlike *el exilio*, this generation has grown weary of politics, having come of age in a political culture where signs posted in public places remind the country's citizens that "en cada barrio, la Revolución"—in every neighborhood, the Revolution. Unlike those who came before them, the *balseros* do not dream of dying in Cuba, nor have they packed their bags for an imminent return. They are not plotting Castro's downfall, nor are they trying to influence U.S. foreign policy to the detriment of those who remain on the island. Their attitude is more ambivalent, and less dismissive, toward life back in Cuba. They are trying to make a life for themselves in Miami or, like Barbarita, thinking about the child they left behind. Barbarita petitioned for Hany's visa on July 18, 1997, the day after she received her green card. In the spring of 2001, the child received a visa from the U.S. Interest Section in Havana, but had not received her exit from the Cuban authorities. Barbarita calls her situation a "reverse Elián" quandary, referring to the Cuban six-year-old whose separation and eventual reunification with his father, Juan Miguel González, in April 2000, inspired massive protests by the Cuban American community in Miami. Unlike Juan Miguel, Barbarita does not have the attorney general hastening her reunification with Hany. She waits in the world the exiles built.

In any culture, the older generation likes to set itself apart from those who follow. In the case of the Cuban exiles, this differentiation is based on age as much as ideology. It is not simply that the new arrivals are younger, poorer, and less educated than those who came forty years ago; it is that "they've been raised in a system where you don't have to fight," says Zoraida Hernández, a sixty-eight-year-old waitress. "It's a generation that doesn't have love for work. Our generation . . . we loved work."

Yet all around us at Versailles, a Little Havana institution on Calle Ocho, are young men and a few women, mostly under thirty and nearly all recent arrivals from Cuba, who are working as waiters, busboys, cooks, and managers. Hernández understands the rhythms of this restaurant—she has worked here since her own arrival more than three decades ago. Most of the employees, says the manager, work ten to twelve hours a day. A few have had trouble adjusting to the work schedule. As a member of *el exilio*, Zoraida has an understanding of modern-day Cubans frozen in time. Her stereotypes are creations of nostalgia for *la Cuba de ayer*, the Cuba of yesterday. Versailles, too, is filled with such sentiment, demonstrated in artifacts all around the restaurant. For twenty dollars, one can buy a Havana phone book from 1958, when the island's bourgeoisie was at the height of its decadence and revolutionary forces were still training in the jungles of the Sierra Maestra. Vintage issues of the influential literary and political magazine *Bohemia* decorate the walls with cover illustrations of the hero both communists and exiles can agree on: José Martí, one of the great Latin American writers and one who spent, and lost, his life fighting against colonial rule. Montecristos and Cohibas, brand-name cigars from the island, are for sale, while guava-filled empanadas and other sugary *pasteles*, pastries, sweat underneath display case lights. Zoraida says, "there is nothing like your homeland," and her words come to life on a walk down Calle Ocho, known to English-speakers in Miami as Southwest Eighth Street or the Tamiami Trail. I stroll past the faded poster of lounge singer Benny Moré, past the cross streets collapsing Cuban history into a few blocks: Afrocuban leader Antonio Maceo, another hero of Cuba's fight for independence from Spain; Brigade 2056 of the ill-fated Bay of Pigs invasion of 1961; and Brothers to the Rescue, the even more tragic rescue squad who flew humanitarian missions to rafters over the Florida Straits, and who were shot down by Cuban MiGs in 1996.

Defenders and critics can agree on one thing: the exile generation came to Miami and changed the city forever. What used to be a sleepy beach resort in the early twentieth century became Latin America's northernmost financial and cultural capital. More than forty years after the revolution, you can see the community's accomplishments. Over half of Miami businesses are owned by Cubans. The mayors of both the city of Miami and Miami–Dade County are Cuban, as is the chairman of *Miami Herald*, and its influential sister publication, *El Nuevo Herald*.

Maximo Gómez Park is an intimate corner of the exiles' world, tucked away near a busy intersection off Calle Ocho. Men gossip and sip sugary *café cubano* out of small, thimble-sized paper cups. Underneath a blue and red awning, the retirees play round after round of dominoes, and the chips clack against the table as cigar smoke fills the air. A "Summit of the Americas" mural frames the domino players. Deposed leaders —Alberto Fujimori, Jean-Bertrand Aristide—smile congenially under a cloudless blue sky alongside Ernesto Zedillo, Bill Clinton, and Vicente

Fox. Conspicuously absent from the painting, but ever present in the conversations of these men, is the man everyone loves to hate. Castro's name comes up when we talk of the city's latest Cuban residents. "What comes from over there was made by Fidel," says Amado Arregui, who arrived in Miami in 1948. With the milky blue eyes that come with age and dressed in a khaki windbreaker, Arregui leans on his cane and says he knows nothing about the revolution, except that "many of these kinds of people have a shot of communism in the arm," pointing an index finger toward his arm as if it were a make-believe syringe. "These people" means the *balseros*, and his analysis leaves little room for interpretation: "There are a few good ones. But more bad people came with the good."

It is easy for men like Arregui to draw such conclusions. Like many of the exile generation, he is insulated from the world of recent Cuban immigrants. He spends most of his day with other retirees, or with his children, who as Cuban Americans make up the most educated and wealthiest Hispanic minority group in the United States. His grasp of today's Cuba is tenuous. A "love-hate relationship," is how Francisca Vigaud-Walsh, a twenty-three-year-old Cuban American social worker describes the relationship between the exiles and the latest wave. "A lot of older Cuban Americans feel some kind of resentment toward them because they withstood the politics of Cuba for so long. There is a lot of suspicion about who they are," she says.

Another domino player, seventy-year-old Raúl Guarino, clutches a copy of *La Verdad*, one of countless newspapers written by and for the exile community. The headline reads, "El asesino Castro está en la mirilla" — the assassin Castro is in the rifle's scope. "They aren't like us," he says. "We came here because of the repression, because of the ideas the government supported. They have been educated in the system. They even think it's good." Guarino sees a fundamental difference between himself and the young Cubans working at gas stations or grocery store checkout lines. "They come here for economic reasons," he says with disdain. "They're looking for dollars."

They also don't carry the political grudges of the exiles. As one recent arrival, Iván Hernández, a thirty-five-year-old gas station attendant, says, "My generation wasn't raised in politics. What I got to experience was hunger, not politics," referring to the immediacy of need trumping the political culture. Hernández arrived with his wife and daughter in Miami via Spain in January 2000, just in time to experience the fury of Miami

Cubans over the seizure of little Elián González by agents from the Bureau of Alcohol, Tobacco, Firearms and Explosives in April. "I couldn't believe people would get on the television and say the boy couldn't join his family in Cuba," Iván says. "Family comes before anything else. Above politics."

Guarino had his own battles to wage against public perception when he came during the Mariel boatlift in 1980. These refugees earned a bad reputation in part because Castro allowed prisoners and the mentally ill to jump aboard boats leaving Mariel. They were often referred to by the pejorative name *Marielitos* by fellow Cubans in Miami. *The Miami Herald* issued this warning to its readers as refugees began occupying tent cities all over south Florida: "This is not the entrepreneurial class who came fifteen years ago. A Cuban ghetto might develop." To everyone's surprise, no ghetto emerged. The integrity of the Cuban enclave in Little Havana remained intact. The exiles complained about the *Marielitos* supposed delinquency and laziness, but in the end, no one suffered because of their arrival, though the city's African Americans felt their jobs had been taken away from them by the new arrivals from Cuba. Guarino recalls it was hard to find work. Then, like now, unemployment was high in Miami. A brother-in-law found him a job at Howard Johnson's, which led to other odd jobs in his twenty-one years in Miami. A few moments later in our conversation, Guarino's sharp take on the *balseros* softens: "A lot of people truly left [Cuba] because of the misery. There's nothing wrong with that, because it's the truth."

As soon as it appears, his sympathy for the new arrivals vanishes, and the conversation goes back to his favorite topic, espionage. He, too, is a journalist and has been hard at work on a commentary for the exile radio station Radio Mambí about how Cuban spies have even infiltrated Domino Park. And of course everyone knows that spies are running Miami's biggest Latin grocery stores, he says. "Sedano's, Presidente, La Mia," he whispers the names as he scribbles them in my notebook. How can he tell who are agents of Castro and who are not? "The Bible says, 'For their deeds, I will know who they are,'" he says.

Far away from the paranoia and political noise of Calle Ocho, Barbarita sits in the living room of her Hialeah condo, painted in the vanilla-colored stucco ubiquitous in south Florida. Hialeah has the look and feel of the suburbs with its wide streets, strip malls, and fast-food outlets. The town has always been known for horse racing, a sport which has attracted the likes of the Kennedy clan, Harry Truman, and Winston Churchill. It is now home to one of the largest Cuban communities in Miami–Dade County. The skeptics convinced that the *balseros* would fail in the United States need look no further than Barbarita and Orlando's home with its tasteful leather couches and sparkling white kitchen with its well-stocked pantry, or to the parking space outside, where a new, bright red pickup truck sits. The taste of success has been bittersweet. "Everything my husband and I do is thinking about her future," she says of Hany, her twelve-year-old daughter.

Barbarita works as a supervisor at a men's apparel factory where she oversees about thirty employees. Orlando owns his own auto repair and sales business named after the daughter he is unlikely to see anytime soon. He is considered a persona non grata in Cuba and is not allowed to return. Hany is the missing chapter from Barbarita's success story. Although she has seen her daughter twice since she left in 1994, these visits were both too short, and her daughter's absence looms over the Hialeah house. Even the kitchen is decorated with a sunflower motif because, Barbarita says, "Hany loves yellow."

Barbarita knew the trade-off when she stepped into the boat that August morning. Though members of the exile generation have long since claimed their relatives in family reunification programs sponsored by the U.S. government, the recent arrivals have not been so lucky. Christine Reis, a Miami immigration lawyer, says the wait is typically four to six years for permanent residents to successfully claim their children.

Meanwhile, Barbarita and Orlando work long hours to pass the time. The couple rarely goes out, except to visit friends from Guayabal who have also made it to south Florida. They have even decided against having another child, Barbarita says, because they don't want Hany to feel like a forgotten child. She contents herself with watching her daughter grow up through photographs. And they are everywhere.

Barbarita is trying to recall the lyrics of the song that gave her the idea for her daughter's name. It's a song by the Cuban music group Las Javaloyas in which the phrase "te quiero, Honey," "I love you, Honey," is repeated in the chorus. In the song, a man pines for a long lost love. *Honey* became Hany, and the girl cried with glee every time she heard the song on the radio. Orlando liked the name because he wanted it be something "short and sweet," Barbarita says. She and her husband have always been close, meeting each other as toddlers and growing up across the street from each other in Guayabal. Pretty soon, Barbarita was spending most of her time at the Azcuy house on Avenida 79. They married in 1988, and Hany was born a year later.

Neither Barbarita nor Orlando were outspoken critics of the socialist system, but they made it known they weren't true believers. They never went to communist youth group meetings and never hung a Cuban flag from their house, a symbol of revolutionary pride. In fact, their local branch of the Communist Party had been keeping its eyes on the Azcuy family for some time. At one point, the family owned a car, a motorcycle, and a television. The government initiated what it called the *plan maceta* in the mid-1990s to crack down on the noveau riche, the people who appeared to be acquiring material goods in the aftermath of the dollar's legalization in 1993. Literally, *maceta* means "flowerpot," and in this context, the word served as a metaphor for someone capable of flourishing in a society that discouraged the accumulation of wealth. In Guayabal, Orlando fixed cars, washing machines, or other outdated American appliances left over from the 1950s, an era when Cuba was flush with American consumer goods. It wasn't long before his own stash of dollars grew, setting him apart from his neighbors and drawing the attention of authorities. "Imagine it," Barbarita says of their departure. "We had no other choice."

The couple was at sea for less than forty-eight hours when a huge Coast Guard ship appeared. The battleship loomed before them, dwarfing their small boat. "When I saw that huge ship, I felt scared, and I thought, oh my God, what did we do?" Barbarita remembers. The Coast Guard ship stopped then, lifted them aboard, and spray-painted their boat to show that its passengers had already been picked up. The boat, which had taken them within thirty miles of the Florida Keys, floated away into the horizon. She remembers the boat as if it, too, was a family member. "We looked out on our boat, and all you saw was a little dot," she says. "It looked so small." During the next year and a half at Guantánamo Naval Base, the U.S. government embarked on a campaign to acculturate Cubans before they ever reached land. "Guantánamo was like a school," she says. "It taught us what life was like here." Her friends, fellow *balseros*, dispersed, some going to Virginia, others to California. She keeps in touch with many of them. "We were all like one big family," she says.

Once they got to Florida, Barbarita and Orlando began a work schedule familiar to many immigrants. Working two jobs, the couple slept four hours a night. Their day jobs at the same factory where Barbarita still works began at seven in the morning and ended at four in the afternoon. At five, their shift as janitors at a technical college in Broward County began, and they were in bed well after midnight. Relatives in Hollywood, a suburb of Fort Lauderdale, provided invaluable support in big and small ways, giving them a place to stay and fixing their lunches before they left for work in the morning. "We were so anxious to prosper," she says. "Here, at least you are working toward a goal. In Cuba, you're working toward nothing."

Barbarita has tried her best to be a good parent, in absentia. In the process, she has become a caretaker for the rest of her family in Cuba, a role commonly assumed by those who leave, says Antonio Aja, a sociologist at the University of Havana. "In the 1990s, the family solution was for people to designate a member of the family to leave," he says. "That relative would be sent to the U.S. . . . to establish himself and decide if he should bring family or send money. It's a decision of how to save your family. It's a question of how the family will float."

Hany isn't simply staying afloat with the money her mother sends her. Her life has become a lavish cruise filled with all the trappings of a preteen: dolls, toys, and clothes. She doesn't hesitate to tell her mother when she wants a new outfit. In fact, her mother entrusts me with a sleek, yellow pantsuit, the likes of which would be worn by twenty-something club girls, to deliver to her daughter, whom I am to interview in Cuba. Her daughter has been the locus of the dollars she sends home, but Barbarita has also helped plenty of people from her hometown once they reach Florida's shores. So many of them have settled in Hollywood, in particular, that everyone calls it "little Guayabal." She gives them a bed to sleep on and food to eat and expects not a penny in return. Her most recent guests have been her elder sister, Leopolda, who moved to Miami four months ago, and her family. She and her husband, Osvaldo, and their daughter, Juliet, share the spare bedroom in the Hialeah condo.

The joke in Cuba is to tell someone that you have *fe*, meaning not "hope" but "family in the exterior." Now, though, having *fe* has turned out to be a mixed blessing. For those who remain on the island, life becomes more complicated after family members leave. Remittances allow Cubans to survive, but at a social cost. The envy bred in those who do not receive

Cubans gather at El Malecón on a hot summer day, Havana, 2001.
Photo by Mimi Chakarova

money from family abroad toward those who do can tear a family apart. So, too, has Barbarita's family cleaved since her departure, and the fault line goes right through Avenida 79 in Guayabal. On one side is Rosario Pérez, Barbarita's elder sister, who lives in relative poverty compared to Miriam Azcuy, Orlando's sister, who is acting in loco parentis for Hany.

As I drive to Guayabal to meet Rosario, I am accompanied by her nephew Alain, who lives in Havana. He tells me "today, you will see what poverty is really like." Until that afternoon, Avenida 79 had been defined by the Azcuy house, an airy bungalow, smartly painted white with green trim, with a TV, VCR, and handsome furniture, consumer goods purchased on the black market with money Barbarita sends every month. But Rosario's house is constructed out of drab, unpainted concrete. She shares one bedroom with her daughter, a son, and a grandson. A few wall decorations made from cheap, golden lame adorn the gray walls. Both the TV and fan are broken, unable to provide relief from the boredom and heat of Guayabal. Flies from the pig and chicken coop out back invade the house. Rosario, a most gracious host, apologizes to everyone. Each time a fly falls into a guest's orange juice, she whisks it away and replaces it with a fresh one.

In March 2001, Rosario feels bad about Hany's predicament and says, "If only people were more humane, they would let her go." I assume the people Rosario is referring to are U.S. and Cuban officials. But no. It is Miriam who Rosario blames. Rosario goes on to explain that Hany has already received an immigrant visa from the U.S. government, but that the Azcuys have failed to follow up on the necessary paperwork. Hany also had a chance to go to the United States by boat. But, Rosario confides, Miriam called the authorities, and the boat trip was cancelled. Rosario's final barb is an accusation that Miriam fails to inform her of phone calls from family members in Miami.

Down the street, Miriam denies all of Rosario's claims, though it seems as if she has heard them before. No, she says defensively, Hany has not received a visa from the United States, but she does soon after our conversation. And, of course, if Hany had received one earlier, she would have gone right away because her other documents—passport and medical records—were in order. Miriam stands nervously when she talks, making it clear she wants us to leave. Her stress makes sense since she has, in fact, paid a price for being Hany's caretaker. In December 1999, she and her father were interrogated by state security in Havana about the girl's status and had to spend a day in jail. The Cuban authorities warned them that if they allowed Hany to leave illegally, they would be thrown in jail. State security even sends a representative to Guaybal every once in a while to check on them.

"If she got the visa tomorrow, she would go tomorrow," says Ofelia, Hany's grandmother. "It makes me laugh because they're lies," Miriam says about Rosario's statements, her voice indignant. "She lies because she's jealous of us. It's always something new with her. She should be embarrassed." Once warm, the relationship between the two sisters-in-law soured when Barbarita left in 1994. In the end, the fight was more about economic inequity than Hany. "They've been upset with us, and they've always had their own way," says Rosario about the Azcuys. "I don't know if it's because they have better living standards than we do."

In Hialeah, Barbarita cries when she finds out what Rosario said. She always thought of herself as an exceptional sister to Rosario, she says. She had always helped her sister in the past because as a single parent of five, Rosario needed all the assistance she could get. "I was like a mother to

them," recalls Barbarita. She says she doesn't send money to Rosario because "from the moment I started working, I had to send money to Hany
and my mother. I left all of my belongings to Miriam because she was
taking care of Hany. Rosario knew that. Everybody knew that." Barbarita found out there was tension between Rosario and Miriam through
a family friend. Yet she never brought up the issue to her sister on her
two visits to Guayabal. Ultimately, Barbarita corroborates what Miriam
tells me about Hany's visa and says she is forever indebted to her sister-
in-law. "What Miriam is doing is priceless," she says. "I could die, and I
still wouldn't have thanked her enough for taking care of Hany."

Immigration has been hardest on those left behind without access to
dollars. Rosario not only does not have such access but she is also dis-
connected from the siblings who are the closest to her. The four siblings
who remain in Guayabal "have their own families. They're not like the
others, who are more concerned," she tells me on a walk around Guayabal, past the lush orange groves that the government owns but that everyone in the town steals from. Rosario misses Leopolda the most and keeps
a passport-size photo of her underneath a piece of glass on her bedside
table. Leopolda has always given her good advice and has even lent her
money on occasion. The two of them have always been *comraditas*, best
friends, since they are only one year apart in age and share fond childhood
memories. "I didn't want to say good-bye to her when she left," Rosario
tells me, her eyes filling with tears.

Barbarita understands her sister's problems, but can do little to solve
them. Instead, she tries to be the best mother she can be ninety miles away.
She has left Hany with Miriam because she trusts her sister-in-law to give
her daughter as normal a childhood as possible. Hany does all the things
that a girl growing up in Guayabal would do: she goes to school, does her
homework, and watches Brazilian soap operas on TV. On weekends, she
has slumber parties with her friends, or goes out with them to the town
disco. She finds instant companionship in Miriam's own children, Sulesis
and Davier. She says she wants to be a model when she grows up. And
as she picks through her *arroz con pollo*, rice with chicken, one evening
at dinner, she exudes the aloofness and grace of someone who already
belongs on a runway.

Hany may, in fact, be having a better than normal childhood in com-
parison to Guayabal's other children, if happiness is measured by the size
of one's doll collection or wardrobe. After dinner, Miriam opens the ar-

moire Hany shares with her cousin to reveal a row of colorful dresses, fashionable pants with narrow waists and flared legs, and body-hugging Lycra tops. Dolls, ranging from miniature blond babies in nothing but diapers to a Barbie in full bridal wear, take up an entire wall. There are four shelves stacked with shoes, a Hello Kitty doll, a silvery purse, and teddy bears. Certainly, it is not material things Hany lacks. In their weekly phone conversations, she feels free to ask her mother for more clothes or shoes. But missing from her life are mother-and-daughter talks best held in person. "I miss her more now," Hany says. "If I want to confide in her, if I want to ask her advice, I can't. Supposing I had a boyfriend. I could ask her if she thinks he likes me."

The time right after her mother's departure proved difficult too. She had to face the stigma of classmates who teased her because her parents had left. One day, a girl pushed Hany too far. "I scratched her face and grabbed her hair," Hany recalls. "I started dragging her by the hair. The little girl was making fun of me because my parents had left. At the end of the day, I couldn't take it anymore." She lives with the memories of her mother's brief visits. They went to restaurants, to the beach, and they bought school supplies for Hany. They did all the things that Barbarita, on a tourist visa, could do. "At the airport, there is a rope to separate people who come and those who are waiting," Hany says, recalling her mother's arrival at José Martí International Airport. "I jumped the rope."

Six months after receiving her U.S. visa, Hany received her exit permit and arrived at her parents' home in Hilaeah, Florida, on September 9, 2001.

Research assistance by Eddy Ramírez

The Spanish Are Back

~ MEGAN LARDNER

*The old Spanish empire is no longer capable of dominating
the lands of young America.* — José Marti, 1890

Iván, a Cuban philosophy student, still remembers the scene vividly: It
was January 2001, and the Spaniards had descended on Central Havana,
draped in robes like royalty from the 1500s. In the lead, three men in a
horse-drawn carriage rolled leisurely along the tree-lined Paseo del Prado
to the clattering rhythm of hooves. Behind them, a troop of Spaniards
fanned out along the street, throwing candy to Cuban children. With the
kids in fast pursuit, the entourage glided past crumbling colonial homes
and emerged in front of the Spanish Cultural Center's newly refurbished
seafront mansion. There the crowd thickened, and the candy supply ran
low. People began to push and grab excitedly, trampling some children
in the midst of the confusion. One of the costumed Spaniards was especially rude. When the gifts ran out, he told the kids to get lost. Meanwhile,
Cuban television crews captured the images.

The Spaniards—modern-day diplomats and executives dressed up as
the biblical Wise Men for a traditional Spanish Epiphany parade—barely
made it back to their offices before the eruption. The local press called the
Spaniards "undignified clowns" and "imported monarchs" whose dangerous show encouraged Cuban children to fight over material objects. In
response to the affront, Cuban officials held a conference called "Neither
Kings nor Wise Men," and Fidel Castro warned: "We don't want to add
fuel to the fire in our relations with Spain, but let no one doubt that any
rudeness, provocation, or insult will receive an appropriate response."
His threat was no joke. The original Epiphany parade was banned after
Castro's revolution reinvented Cuba and emphasized national pride over
historical ties. By resurfacing, the Spanish-sponsored religious celebration
sparked resentment. Spain, for its part, pleaded innocence. "Our presence
is not some kind of recolonization of Cuba," said José María Coso, direc-

tor of the Spanish Cultural Center in Havana and the parade organizer. He lifted a Cuban cigar lovingly to his lips and gently exhaled smoke. "We're just trying to preserve our place here."

But by the summer of 2003, that place no longer existed—at least symbolically. Relations were strained even further by the European Union's condemnation of Castro's spring sweep that jailed seventy-five so-called dissidents. Castro retaliated by closing the Cultural Center, and for the first time in years, the number of joint ventures between Spain and Cuba declined to 98 from 105 in 2002, according to the Ministry of Foreign Investment and Economic Development. But if government relations have soured, Spain continues to reach out to Cuban citizens. In 2003, it relaxed the restrictions for getting a Spanish passport. Cubans of any age who have at least one Spanish grandparent can apply. And with the March 2004 election of a new socialist government in Spain, governmental relations between the two countries are likely to improve.

These are the ups and downs of a very old relationship. If most divorced couples married for twenty years complain about emotional baggage, imagine the unresolved issues shared by two countries with a five-hundred-year-old relationship. During many of those years, they fought. Then, in 1898, after a long, bloody war, Spain finally picked up its belongings and sailed home. But it left behind 50,000 soldiers who changed the face of the island; today their descendants populate Havana's boardwalk among the silhouetted fishermen and young couples stealing kisses at sunset. If the Cuban government has gone through several changes of heart toward Spain since 1898, developments in the past ten years also demonstrate the nations' enduring and difficult connections; how a former colonizer has become a necessary ally; how in the era of globalization, blood proves thicker than water and makes for some odd couples. Yet the emotional baggage remains, and the relationship continues to be tumultuous.

Unlike young love, the two nations are embroiled in a complicated affair. The Spanish lost the island a century ago, but now are returning to Cuba as business executives and benefactors. They began arriving in significant numbers in the early 1990s when Cuba hit an economic wall. Spain's socialist government, led by Felipe González, rushed to the rescue with millions of dollars in aid. González also encouraged Spaniards to invest. One of the early arrivals was Carlos Pereda, who opened Cuba's first tourist hotel in what used to be the sleepy coastal village of Varadero. The town—a two-hour ride from Havana along sleek highways—

A Spanish-built resort in Varadero, 2004. *Photo by Mimi Chakarova*

has thrived on the bittersweet fruits of tourism. Today, pricey Spanish and international hotels hug the coastline, shaded by thousands of perfectly cloned palm trees. From a windowless office just steps away from warm Caribbean waters, Pereda is working after hours on a steamy Saturday evening. His telephone rings constantly, and the grandfatherly Spaniard jokes amiably with the callers. Fluorescent ceiling lights glint off a dozen wall plaques that mark a decade of success. "It was like night and day when I came to Cuba," he says in an accent still thick with the lisping *zeta* of Spain. "Imagine arriving in a country where 75 percent of your work force is university educated and the other 25 percent is highly educated. Here, when it comes time to pitch in to help with a government project, everyone contributes."

Pereda is not the only one impressed by the Cuban workforce. Up until the decline in 2003, the tide of incoming Spanish investors flowed so swiftly that they founded the Association of Spanish Business Executives in Havana. Its president, Rafael García Arnal, is a friendly Barcelonan with a taste for Habanos cigars. His optimism is clear as he runs through the statistics: membership is up, with some one hundred Spaniards representing everything from banks to food services to hotels; there are nearly two hundred Spanish businesses on the island compared to just thirty-six in 1994; and Spanish firms make up 25 percent of total foreign investment and 40 percent of all European Union trade with the island. With the new troubles in 2003, this declined slightly, but with a new Socialist government in Spain in 2004, the numbers are likely to improve. "We're not just thinking about the distant future—we're making money now," García Arnal says, his affable face red from too much Caribbean sun. Like him, other Spaniards are beginning to call the lush island home. But the club president still looks forward to his yearly vacations in Spain. "I go there to refresh myself," he jokes, alluding to Cuba's harsh political and economic landscape.

Even with the challenges, Spaniards are reveling in their new connection with Cuba, and it seems that all they touch turns to gold. In 1995, the Cuban government relaxed strict guidelines and allowed foreigners to own more than a 50 percent share in a joint business venture. Spanish money poured in. By 1996, Spanish hotel chains had invested 75 million dollars in the island's tourism sector alone. But no matter how smoothly business deals unfold, Spanish executives have learned caution at the bargaining table. "Cubans complain of Spanish arrogance, something other countries don't have to worry about because they don't have the same historical baggage," says Mark Entwistle, Canada's ex-ambassador to Cuba and now a business consultant. And arrogance is just one stereotype the old colonizer must transcend in its evolving relationship with Cubans. Spanish hotel companies have also come under fire for discriminatory hiring practices. In 1995, the Spanish-owned Habana Libre hotel in downtown Havana was accused of trying to "whiten" its staff. "They were firing blacks to appeal to mostly light-skinned foreign tourists," says Alejandro de la Fuente, an associate professor at the University of Pittsburgh who writes about race in Cuba. "It became a scandal." The incident, he says, reinforced Cuban stereotypes about Spanish racism. More complaints have surfaced at other luxury hotels, yet de la Fuente says the conflict runs deeper than simple Spanish prejudice. "Cubans themselves also accept the false narrative of *buena presencia*, the idea that being white is more attractive."

As with any family linked by bloodlines, language, and a turbulent history, this ambiguity is par for the course in the Spanish-Cuban relationship. In the 1800s, when American colonies began to revolt against the mother country, Spain dubbed sugar-rich Cuba the "ever faithful island" and trusted she alone would never stray. Losing this favorite daughter to the United States in the 1898 independence war proved a psychological disaster for Spain. "Like losing a limb," explains Coso at the Spanish Cultural Center. Even today, Spaniards recognize the historical impact of Cuba's liberation. "Don't worry about it, more was lost in Cuba," they are likely to remark when something goes wrong. Cubans, who study Spain's violent war campaign in history class, enjoy their own humor about Spanish business people relocating to the island; they joke that Spaniards are back to get what they lost in 1898.

But today's Spaniards are arriving by airplane—not ocean vessel—and importing cash, new ideas, and high hopes of becoming Cuba's most trusted business partner. It wasn't always this way. In colonial days, Spaniards who emigrated to Cuba had little to offer. María del Carmen Molina, the Cuban granddaughter of Spanish immigrants, shakes with laughter remembering a television show she watched as a child during the early days of Cuba's revolution. The program poked fun at those early Spanish immigrants who—fleeing Spain's economic depression—arrived in Cuba penniless and had to prove themselves. But time has turned the tables, and today, all that is Spanish is the ticket to success. "Now everyone wants to be Spanish," Molina laughs.

There is more truth than irony to her remark. If Afrocuban dance and music have captivated the world in recent years, there are still more practical advantages to having Spanish heritage than African roots in today's Cuba. It all began in the early 1990s, when Spain's socialist government pledged generous humanitarian aid to the struggling island. In Cuba's most desperate hour, Spain also recalled its shared bloodlines with the island. Prime minister Felipe González made more Spanish passports available to Cubans of Spanish descent, and with that move, old bonds reawakened. Across the island, light-skinned Cubans rushed to sift through family documents, searching for birth certificates and letters—anything to prove a direct family connection to Spain. Ramona Álvarez, Molina's mother, was one of them. The Cuban-born daughter of Spaniards applied for a Spanish passport in 1994 when food was scarce and the future looked bleak. Little did she realize her quest would span five years and be overshadowed by another bitter fight between the two nations.

As Álvarez began her application procedure in Havana, Spain was undergoing a dramatic political shift that came to a head in 1996, when the

View of Old Havana and the Capitolio, 2004. *Photo by Mimi Chakarova*

conservative José María Aznar took power. With his election, Spain withdrew most of its financial assistance from Cuba and called for political reform on the island. Things heated up even more when Aznar named José Coderch as his new ambassador to Cuba. While still in Madrid, Coderch informed Spanish newspapers that the minute he arrived, he would "throw open the doors" of the Spanish embassy to Cuban political dissidents. Furious, the Cuban government refused to let him set foot on the island. But rumors spread quickly, and hundreds of Cubans stormed the Spanish embassy in hopes of getting a visa. Cuban officials had to send police-backed construction workers to cordon off the building. Political ties snapped.

For more than a year afterward, the Spanish ambassador's office in Havana stood empty. But ultimately, business sense prevailed. With millions of dollars already sunk into the Cuban economy, Spanish investors upped the pressure on Aznar and his conservative pro-business party, the Partido Popular. For their part, island officials maneuvered to protect the fragile economy by making overtures to Spanish executives. It worked. In 1998, a one hundred–member contingent of Spanish business executives arrived in Cuba. At the same time, Aznar announced Spain would loosen its purse strings and increase humanitarian aid. Meanwhile, Spanish-owned Iberia airline stepped up its weekly flights to Cuba in anticipation of increased tourism and business travel. Finally, Spain's new ambassador, Eduardo Junco, arrived on the island amid talk of "a new era in Spanish-Cuban relations."

This tentative reconciliation directly benefited Cubans like Álvarez. After five years of waiting, she finally received the cherished passport—and with it some perks. One of them is status. "Now she's *Doña* Álvarez, instead of *compañera*," the lively Molina says playfully. She shoots a glance at her mother, who obliges by lifting her head with a little nod. Already in her seventies, Álvarez has no illusions of actually setting foot in the land of her ancestors. "If I could travel to Spain I probably would, but it's unlikely now," she muses, settling back into her rocking chair after disappearing into the bedroom to retrieve her passport. "But I wanted this for sentimental reasons," she says, caressing the small yet valuable booklet.

Sentiment aside, the pocket-sized object also represents a better standard of living. In the past few years, Spain has begun offering pension money to its foreign citizens over age sixty-five in Cuba. "The announcement was like an explosion in Havana," says Molina, who waited—with about 1,000 other people—to apply for her mother's pension money last year. On average, the pensions are worth about two hundred dollars a month, which is equivalent to winning the lottery in a country where the average income is twelve dollars a month (nine dollars in 2004). As a direct result of the pension offer, the number of people applying for Spanish passports has nearly tripled since 1998, to 6,000 in 2000, and has steadily increased with the new relaxed rules in 2003. But while the money provides welcome financial relief, it only highlights the deep economic divide between Cubans and Spaniards. "It broke my heart to see doctors and teachers—educated people—waiting there for Spanish charity," Molina says, watching her mother's aged face, serene under a halo of white hair. Still, measured by the number of people who line up outside the embassy, Cubans are eager to accept Spain's offer.

Elvis Mendoza's eyes are glazed over by the time he reaches the shady gardens of the Spanish embassy. He is squeezed uncomfortably onto a narrow wooden bench next to a sunken old woman nodding off in the stifling heat. Nearly three hundred miles separate the capital from Mendoza's rural home in the tobacco-growing region of Sancti Spiritus. This time

A construction project funded by the Spanish, Havana, 2004.
Photo by Mimi Chakarova

his journey spanned twenty-four hours. The adventure included a delayed
train, a broken-down bus, and a communal taxi crammed to capacity.
Inside the gates of the elegant mansion—one of Havana's few restored
colonial buildings—the shy man is giddy with nervous energy and entirely
out of his element. Still, his mission lends him strength; Mendoza's aging
mother has a Spanish passport and needs money. The Spanish embassy's
humanitarian aid program is her last hope.

Mendoza is the living legacy of Spain's roots in Cuba. His Spanish-born
grandfather emigrated to Cuba in 1917, among the last wave of Spanish
immigrants destined for the island after Spain lost the war. Like him, one-
third of the 3.5 million Spaniards who left Spain between the late 1800s
and 1930 were destined for Cuba. "They were attracted to a place where
there are still family connections," explains Joaquín Roy, a professor of
Spanish-Cuban relations. On the island, Mendoza's grandfather raised his
family with Spain in his heart. He told stories to his grandson about peasants working the dry earth in Extremadura, of Arab palaces among olive
trees in the south, and of gruff fishermen in northern Galicia. Mendoza

has never been to Spain, but says he has imagined it all his life. "Because of my grandfather, I've always felt very Spanish." But this journey to the capital is for practical rather than nostalgic reasons. Mendoza's family has heard about the pension money, and he is in Havana to claim his mother's birthright.

Mendoza has a lot of company. In 2003 alone, more than 4,000 Cubans were registered to collect the Spanish pension money. Most days, long lines of people snake down the sidewalk outside the Spanish embassy a block from El Malecón, the waterfront boulevard. Some pace to break the monotony. Others animatedly compare family histories and commiserate about the wait. A young man named Fernando shows a generous smile as he reclines against the building, ducking out of the slant of mid-morning sun already threatening to boil the pavement. He says his family has been to the embassy several times in the past seven months. "Here we go again," he grins. Nearby, Fernando's mother holds their place in line, patient in her bright flowered dress that pulls a bit too tight in the arms. She clutches faded documents—a birth certificate and letters—that could pave the way to Spanish citizenship. For those around her, whose other option is the dangerous ninety-mile water passage to the United States, a Spanish passport offers a legitimate way out of Cuba—provided they can afford the airfare.

It's a legitimate path, but it often comes with long delays. Most business requires much bureaucratic paper pushing and shifting feet in line. Still, Cubans arrive and wait—something to which they are long accustomed. Just around the corner from where Fernando and his mother stand winds another line of people. This one is reserved for married couples trying to get a travel visa for the Cuban spouse. In line are all types; middle-aged couples who have been married for years in Cuba and simply want to visit family in Spain together; fresh-faced newlyweds; and older Spaniards with young, dark-skinned Cuban women, an increasingly common image in Havana's dollar-run tourist bars and nightclubs.

For Cubans like these with no Spanish bloodlines, the doorway out is often through marriage—a process that can be just as frustrating as applying for Spanish citizenship. Couples schedule numerous interviews at the embassy, often waiting for hours. Even with the hassles, Spain remains a popular destination for love matches these days, in part because of language and historical ties. Beginning in the early 1990s, when the economy plummeted, Cuban wives and lovers began turning up in Spain. Nowadays some 3,000 Cubans married to Spaniards apply for visas each year. A decade ago, there were just fifteen applicants a year, says María Cruz Arias of the Spanish consulate in Havana. The dramatic rise, Arias says, has coincided directly with the tourist boom. Some marry for love; some marry to escape the island. Still other Cubans find their way to Spain each year through study exchanges, training programs, and business connections. In 2000, nearly three hundred Cuban students were awarded study grants to travel to Spain. Once there, many never return to the island.

Beatriz Ávila is not going back any time soon. She arrived in Spain with a four-year study grant from the Spanish government and quickly found a well-paid job in a private clinic. Though she calls Spain home and has applied for residency, she admits frustration over Spanish stereotypes of Cubans. "Most Spaniards only think of Cuba for its famous sexual tourism," she says by phone from Madrid. "Sometimes when I meet people here in Spain, they make offensive comments about Cuban women." Still, Ávila says she doesn't see herself fitting back into the pattern of Cuban society after having been away so long. For her, Spain is the next best thing, given the two nations' intimate relationship.

Many Cubans apparently agree. The community grew quietly after the fall of the Soviet Bloc, and by 1996, there were 7,000 Cubans living in Spain. Today, there are about 16,000, making Spain home to the largest Cuban community outside the island after Miami. There is no doubt the European nation has a nostalgic pull. Castro himself is the son of Spanish immigrants, and in 1984, he made a historic visit to the remote northern region of Galicia where his father was born. Some of Castro's relatives live in Spain, as do an ever-increasing number of artists, writers, athletes, and political dissidents.

But leaving the island is not the only desire fueling the relationship between Cuba and Spain in recent years. There is no denying each has something the other wants. No one knows that better than Eusebio Leal, who as historian of the City of Havana is one of the most powerful men on the island. On a humid afternoon in his Old Havana office, he faces a dozen wide-eyed visiting student architects and poses the question: "Which is more important: food or beauty?" With no hesitation, he answers himself: Beauty. Yet Havana's beauty is ravaged by time; those early Spaniards would barely recognize the Caribbean gem they so loved. Its splendor is tarnished by peeling paint and gaping cracks. The ocean knocks relentlessly against El Malecón's rocky sea wall, its salty spray licking buildings and warping facades. If the sad image tugs on proud Cuban hearts, it has an equally strong effect on Spanish sensibilities. After all, Spain's history lives in the island's architecture. "For all our projects we need money, lots and lots of money," says the beige-clad Leal, his voice resonating through the corridor of a room. Spain is one of his biggest collaborators. Before the Spanish Cultural Center was closed in 2003, Spanish money restored the colonial building. And Spanish investors have restored seafront homes all along El Malecón. Cuban men and boys mix cement under the glaring sun at construction sites as vintage Plymouths speed by, pausing only to pick up pretty young women hitching rides. The projects are collaborative; Spain provides the funds and Cuba provides the workforce. But as in most joint ventures, there are bumps in the road. Leal says frictions occasionally arise when Spain tries to exert too much control. Still, Cubans know to tread lightly where cash is concerned. "We have to pursue money where we can get it," Leal states matter-of-factly.

Spanish generosity extends beyond architecture to restoring the century-old Alvear aqueduct in an effort to provide 16 percent of Havana's residents with purified drinking water. Spain is also Cuba's most enthusiastic partner in cinematography. The European nation funds half the films made each year on the island and finances extensive archival restoration. This new level of collaboration between the old colonizer and her dearest colony is sparking some unusual partnerships. In one of Havana's restored colonial jewels, Cuca Llagostera holds court. Wearing a stylish linen suit, the petite blond looks dressed for a chic downtown venue in Madrid rather than a quaint hole-in-the-wall in Old Havana. But then she throws on an apron, casually snuffs out the cigarette dangling from between her lips, and heads for the kitchen. There she whips up Spanish tortillas and fried garbanzos in one of two restaurants that she manages with a Spanish partner in the heart of Havana's tourist zone. At the Mesón de la Flota restaurant, Spanish wines are stacked along the wall: merlots from Barcelona, Solmayor from La Mancha, and the occasional local wine from Pinar del Río province. Two Cuban waitresses gossip at the bar, their curls twisted up inside identical flower wreaths.

Though she is one of an estimated 10,000 Spanish citizens who have recently immigrated to the island, Llagostera's story differs from that of the typical entrepreneur. She ended up in Cuba with her husband, who works in a joint business venture in shipping. That water theme is everywhere. A miniature ship model rests above the bar, and fishing nets drape grace-

Wearing a rented dress, a girl celebrates her *quinceañera*, a birthday celebration for fifteen-year-old Latino girls, with her family as her father proudly videotapes her posing in the streets of Old Havana, 2004.
Photo by Mimi Chakarova

fully next to filmy black and red flamenco shawls on the pale walls. A sign outside advertises the restaurant as "4,000 nautical miles from the point of departure," playing off the image of the Spanish conquistadores who reached Cuba by ship in the 1500s. "The sea here reminds me of Spain," says the Barcelona native, at home in her new surroundings. A slow smile creeps across her calm, sun-tanned face at the suggestion that she is setting a new trend for Spanish women in Cuba. "We're definitely pioneers of a sort, my partner and I. There are very few others doing what we've done here with the restaurants." Downtown regulars, businessmen, and tourists keep the kitchen staff busy, and Llagostera greets local patrons warmly, joking with her young, attractive Cuban staff. Still, Llagostera's point of reference is always Spain. "Most of my friends here are Spanish," she says. "We usually get together at each others' homes or at restaurants and form our own social groups." Many of her compatriots feel the same way. Pereda from the hotel in Varadero maintains his loyalty to Spain, even after eleven years in Cuba's tourist industry. He vacations in the cool green hills of his native land in northern Castille and León and prefers Spanish matadors to Cuban baseball stars. As part of a new generation of Spanish expats mainly focused on business activities, it benefits them all to remain connected to the powerful Spanish business community.

And their children follow suit. Even as Spaniards mingle with Cubans on a day-to-day basis, they maintain distinct separations. Across town from Llagostera's restaurant, in the peaceful, tree-lined Miramar neighborhood, is the Spanish School. "It's just as if the students were in Spain," explains Javier Rivera, the school's charismatic young Cuban director. Here, among foreign embassies and diplomats' homes, students study a strict Spanish curriculum. Exams are sent to Spain to be corrected, and students must wait weeks to get their results back by mail. "It's not the best system for the students," Rivera concedes, "but the instruction is excellent."

While the basics of math and science vary little, Rivera says Spanish and Cuban education systems part ways where philosophy and history are concerned. Greek philosophers like Aristotle and Plato reign in the Spanish School, while Cuban kids study Stalinist theory. And while Cuban students, in their tidy yellow and red school uniforms, memorize the island's history, the Spanish curriculum focuses on world history. "Unfortunately, they don't have time to study the history of Cuba, the country in which they reside," Rivera says. The majority of the Spanish students—who comprise nearly half of the entirely international student body—are the children of business executives. "If the business goes well, they don't leave," Rivera says. Things are going well. The school opened with 16 students in 1986; it now boasts 140. In a country where education is free, the Spanish School's price tag is far beyond the average Cuban family's reach. The two groups, for the most part, remain separate. "Spanish kids only integrate into Cuban society if their parents do," says Rivera, whose own daughter cannot afford to attend the Spanish School. Smiling through cigarette haze at her restaurant, Llagostera puts it more bluntly: "When you are very far from Spain, it's natural that you would want to spend time with other Spaniards."

Although that comment would make him flinch, Jesús Barros López, president of the Galician Association in Havana, also knows it's true. Part of the problem is economics, but part is that the Cubans who strongly identify with their Spanish roots are an older generation than the fast-paced *peninsulares*, as the newly arrived Spaniards call themselves. Only

a few miles across town from Llagostera's restaurant—but eons away—
is the Galician Cultural Center, one of more than a hundred Spanish cultural associations that still exist in Havana and are likely to survive the
ups and downs of government-to-government relations. But these are not
the groups that attract the newly arrived Spanish residents. "The Spanish business people in Cuba aren't interested in cultural associations," laments Barros López. "It's like we live in two separate worlds." And they
do. While Llagostera and her contemporaries enjoy going to clubs and so-
cializing at private parties, Barros López, in his eighties, spends his Saturday evenings at cultural presentations in the stately mansion that houses
the center on the corner of the Parque Central.

Up a sweeping stairway, in a cool, cavernous room far removed from
the bustle outside, a few older men are gathered at a table talking club
business; dues, music workshops, and the weekend event in the great
salon. Galician historians, poets, and politicians peer out from wall paintings. Two flags—one Galician, the other Spanish—stand at attention.
"Gallego!" one of the men suddenly shouts. From a raised platform at the
back of the room, a rumbling voice calls back, "Hold on, I'm busy." Barros López smiles. "They call me Gallego, but I'm Cuban-born, of course.
None of us is really from Spain anymore. We're just the sons of *gallegos*."

Wiry and gently bent with age, Barros López presides over a desk in
danger of collapse. His hand taps a pile of history books and board games,
punctuating each word: "There is less and less Spanish cultural presence
in Cuba." Not so in the old days. In its heyday, the thriving Galician
Center boasted 60,000 active members. But following the Cuban Revolution in 1959, cultural centers all but died out as the Cuban government
aggressively promoted unity through nationalism. The situation shifted
again during the financial crisis of the early 1990s. In the ensuing years,
Spanish associations resurfaced as important funnels for monetary aid to
Cubans. Consequently, association membership began to grow. "We've
been locating Spanish descendants all over the island," says Bruno Leyva
at the Andalusian Center, a short walk down the Paseo del Prado from the
Galician Center. "Many don't even know they have a right to be a member." And, members belong to a different generation with little direct connection to Spain. To maintain ties, a small number of older Cubans each
year travel to Galicia, funded by the Galician government. But people are
dying off. "Each year the assistance packages are a little smaller," Barros
López says, referring to the packages of soap, food, and presents that used

Flamenco dancer,
Havana, 2001.
*Photo by Mimi
Chakarova*

to arrive from Spain. In the midst of the Spanish investment boom on the island, Barros López confides, "I don't see a bright future for the cultural associations."

At least some Cuban schoolgirls, however, would be devastated if the centers closed. Of the many aspects of Spanish culture, traditional dance is thriving on the island. After-school flamenco class is the latest rage. Thirty ponytailed little girls whirl like dervishes on and off a narrow wooden stage at the Andalusian Cultural Center. The mad clacking of castanets combines with the feverish pounding of high-heel dance shoes and the swish-swoosh of multicolored ruffled skirts. A soloist steps to center stage, her face as proud and pained as any flamenco diva in Spain. The harried instructor, in her matching vest and mini skirt, barks, "Arms! Watch the arms!" The older girls imitate her, faces pinched in concentration, while the younger ones tickle each other in the wings. "Silence!" the teacher shouts. "Next time somebody bring me a microphone," she rasps.

No one is listening anyway; the Cuban mothers watching from the street through open windows are as swept up as their daughters in the haunting boleros and playful *sevillanas* crackling over the loudspeakers. Eleven-year old Johanna takes breaks every five minutes to pose and wave to her mom. "I've been taking classes since I was six," she says proudly during one of her visits to the window. But no Spanish girls are dancing with the Cubans on stage. "They don't go to flamenco dance classes," says principal Rivera from the Spanish School. "Their parents are more interested in practical activities—like English classes."

God, *Babalawos*, and Castro

~ **BRET SIGLER**

Oscar Leon Damién parts the faded floral sheet that serves as a bedroom door and steps into his blue shoe box of a living room. He sits in the wooden rocker, picks up his Bible, and runs through notes in his head, making mental checks to ensure that his sermon is in order.

A few blocks away, Mario Luís Ramos Madera rolls out of bed. He pulls an old but clean soccer jersey over his well-built shoulders. He slips past his son, careful not to wake him, and steps outside to have a smoke. He lights an unfiltered Popular—Cuba's national brand—and offers a bit of tobacco to Elegguá, the orisha of opportunity.

These routines seem ordinary enough, but Cuba's religious revival has sparked fervent debates absent for decades. As Cubans again begin to consider God—some for the first time—profound theological and social questions arise. Who is God? Who needs him? And whose God are Cubans likely to worship?

Pinar del Río is a small town in the interior of Cuba's most important tobacco-growing region. The coastal sea breeze that cools Havana never arrives here, leaving the dusty streets to bake in the Caribbean sun. Soviet-era water towers shaped like UFOs hover on the horizon, hoarding the province's lifeblood, as *pinareños* scurry along the shady side of Avenida José Martí, the town's only major thoroughfare. Locals are proud of their tobacco and their baseball, but in Pinar del Río, as in many other towns, religious possibilities are stirring the spiritual. Here Catholics, Evangelicals, and Santeros vie for souls on an island where most religious activity stopped when the revolution took hold.

When Fidel Castro's revolution triumphed in 1959, 80 percent of the population considered themselves Catholic. Many Catholics also practiced Santería, and Evangelical churches were just a blip on the holy radar. Before the revolution, many priests were anti-Batista and imprisoned and tortured for their political views. But church bishops supported the dictator until the end, and when Castro came to power, many of them fled to Miami with their rich congregations. Still, Castro initially indicated tolerance, if not support, of the church. In early 1959, he praised religious education in state schools. But as Castro began his social reforms, the church's support for the revolution faltered. By the end of the same year, many young Catholics had denounced Castro and the Catholic youth organization published an article that said reform could be carried out without communism.

This opposition made Castro take a second look at religion's role in his revolution. Santería was still tolerated, but the government decided Catholicism belonged to the conquistadores and the wealthy. Although Castro never outlawed religious practice outright, attending church became associated with antisocial behavior, and the government placed hurdles in front of the openly religious. They were barred from the Communist Party, the military, and the university. The Catholic Church kept up its pressure, and in August 1960, less than two years after Castro's victory march through Havana, those bishops who remained denounced Castro's government. "Whoever condemns a revolution such as ours," Castro responded to the criticism, "betrays Christ and would be capable of crucifying him again."

If Christ remained in the hearts of some, practicing religion became a clandestine affair. Religious education was banned from the school curriculum. Many churches shut down and fell into disrepair. Catholics and Evangelicals met in small groups behind closed doors where the pious erected makeshift altars in their living rooms. Most Cubans learned to live without religion and to love the revolution—religious believers dropped from more than 70 percent of the population to less than 30 percent according to official numbers.

But when the revolution lost the Soviet Bloc, things changed. Cubans were left to fend for themselves, and while much of the older generation persevered, the younger generation became disheartened and began to look for salvation elsewhere. Sunday attendance rose at the few remaining churches, and new ones opened. Evangelical groups expanded and university students formed religious groups. Religion exploded and Castro retreated. He admitted in 1990 that the religious had been treated unjustly, and in 1992, the once atheist government declared itself a secular state and banned religious discrimination with an amendment to its constitution. The official number of Evangelical churches almost doubled to 1,666 between 1992 and 2000 (although Protestant groups insist the

A prayer, Havana, 2004. *Photo by Mimi Chakarova*

number is much higher), and at least fifty-five denominations practice on the island. In 1998, 500,000 Cubans crowded into Havana's Plaza de la Revolución to attend Pope John Paul II's mass in Cuba. And a year later, a rally jointly organized by leaders of forty-nine different Protestant churches drew 100,000 people to the same plaza, with Castro himself seated in the first row.

But influences of the old religious policy remain. In more than three decades without organized religion, many Cubans have grown up with no notion of how it operates in other countries. Take Reinaldo Arenado, an angst-filled eighteen-year old, for example. He's a *pinareño* who has spent his whole life in Cuba's near spiritual void. He lives with his grandparents and his disabled father in the center of town. When Arenado was ten, his mother left the island suddenly, rowing for Florida. "She just kept telling me that she was going over the big water, but I didn't understand what she meant." He has not seen her since, and in her wake, Arenado has become an introspective soul-searcher. Although he is not religious, Arenado finds himself intrigued by religious mysticism. He sits hunched in front of a small, worn TV balanced on a rickety wooden bookshelf in

the open-air living room of his house—an old, colonial villa that the revolution has long since divided among several families—and pops a pirated
copy of the film *Stigmata* into the VCR. "This movie is pure fantasy. . . .
It's stupid," he says, but admits that he has never seen it. Arenado turns
off the lights forcing the dingy but ornately carved ceilings to fade into the
darkness. As the FBI warning flashes on the screen, the house falls silent,
interrupted only by the occasional dog barking in the distance.

He was right. The film is stupid. It's about a young American woman
who becomes mysteriously afflicted with the same wounds as the cruci-
fied Christ. The Vatican responds by deploying an envoy of priests, com-
parable to the CIA in their cunning and efficiency, to the woman's home
in Pittsburgh. Arenado was mesmerized. With his deadpan stare illumi-
nated by the rolling credits, he asked, "Is the Catholic Church really that
powerful?"

"Our North American friends want to know if there are any youth in
the church," Damién calls out to his congregation at a youth meeting at
his Assembly of God church on a Tuesday night in March. The crowd
erupts in affirmation. At sixty, Damién, the Evangelical minister, has aged
gracefully with a slight paunch and hair that is just starting to gray at the
temples. His face is dominated by a pair of thick, square glasses that constantly slide down the bridge of his round nose. As always, he dons a pair
of worn dress slacks and one of his multicolored *guayabera* shirts. The
church is a concrete box that sits on a long, dusty road on the outskirts
of town where the scent of burning tobacco fields often fills the air.

Tonight, young Christians from across the province have descended on
Damién's church to discuss the church's rural growth. Because Damién
has no car and little money to pay for other transportation, it's a rare opportunity to meet with members from outlying communities. The group
consists of mostly twenty-somethings, many with their young children
in tow. The churchgoers take special care to greet each other, one by
one, with a handshake or a hug. The music starts, and Damién times his
words to the beat of a salsa rendition of "May God Always Bless You." A
shabby three-piece band of drums, guitar, and synthesizer pounds out the
tune. "I need somebody who can ride a bike and who has enough faith
to carry him along," he implores the congregation—the microphone cord
coiled in his left hand in a style reminiscent of a fifties-era Vegas lounge
singer. There is new interest in the Assembly of God in San Cristóbal, a

nearby rural community, and Damién is looking for someone to spread the good word.

An Evangelical since his conversion at fourteen, Damién says that despite its limited resources, his religious community has exploded. In the nineties alone, the Assembly of God grew from 89 to more than 2,000 churches. But it isn't just Damién's group. Mario César Águilar, the pastor at Catedral San Rosendo, has also witnessed tremendous growth at his Catholic church on the other side of town. Águilar says when he came to Pinar del Río in 1984, the church had less than one hundred parishioners. Now he preaches to a filled chapel every Sunday. Rick Johnson, the Assembly of God's Caribbean area director in Florida, admits that he doesn't fully understand why religion is growing so fast on the island, but says that it is "fulfilling something in Cubans' lives that needs to be fulfilled." For Damién, it's simple. "Young people feel they are missing something," he said. "For many years, the government said there was no God. But God cannot be ignored or denied."

And apparently, neither can the pope. Religious attendance surged in Catholic and Evangelical churches alike after his visit to the island in 1998. As of 2000, 4 million Cubans—or 40 percent of the population—were baptized Catholic. Official Protestant membership is also up to 500,000, although many Evangelicals believe the true number to be much higher. "It's not enough just to believe in God. You have to be consumed by him," said Ramón, a nineteen-year-old Baptist youth group organizer. His reverend, Juan Carlos Rojas, agrees. Rojas is awed by the surge in young membership. "Cuban youth are an example to the world. They truly are inspired."

"You cannot be a man of faith if you're not obedient!" an assistant yells out to Damién's congregation. He is a tiny man leaning over a small, wood-paneled podium. He waves his arms to forcefully emphasize each word. The audience quickly turns their backs to the altar, kneels on the floor, and puts their heads face down on the rickety pews. Damién watches from behind a ramshackle piano. "Cast Satan out!" the man continues, his voice now becoming hoarse. The congregation begins to speak in tongues—some barely whispering, others nearly shouting in an almost rhythmic cadence. The smell of sweat fills the small temple. "Cleanse yourself of Satan. Accept Jehovah as your savior!"

But who is Satan? It's a slippery question for many *pinareños*. For Damién and other Evangelicals, he is embodied almost everywhere, especially in the Santería ceremonies that take place in their very neighbor-hoods. They say the worship of saints, or orishas as they are known in Santería, is a dangerous and powerful black magic not to be trifled with. And the use of money in its ceremonies compounds the evil. "Santería is the devil," Damién says plainly, his voice lowering as he pushes his bi-focals back up the bridge of his nose.

Damién's devil is just a few blocks away, locked up in Madera's closet. Here, behind a ramshackle wooden door in the corner of the house, Ma-dera, a Pinar del Río native and one of only three *babalawos* (priests) in town, guards his most powerful Santería ceremonial tools: a goat skull attached to a wooden stick, some bleached squirrel bones, and a long, white candle mounted on the skull of a cat. But Madera's tools are no anomaly. For centuries, Santería has been ingrained in Cuban culture and has transcended traditional religious boundaries as Catholics and non-Catholics alike have dabbled in the faith. "Santería isn't just a religion," says Dr. Margaret Crahan, a history professor at Hunter College in New York, who has studied religion on the island for more than thirty years. "It's part of the Cuban identity."

Santería is a mixture of Catholic and Yoruban traditions that evolved when Spanish fanaticism forced West African slaves to worship their orishas under the guise of Catholic saints. By 1840, the majority of Cu-bans were of African descent, and Santería had entered the mainstream. "People who lived in close proximity [to Santeros] began to adopt San-tería," Crahan says. "You can see how it permeated." And it continued to permeate as blacks moved from the plantations to the cities, taking their religion with them. In modern times, Madera says, Santería has been the darling faith of the Cuban people. According to some estimates, as much as 70 percent of the population practices some form of the tradition, many still blending it with the Catholic faith. Castro routinely refers to Santería as a point of pride in Cuba's Afro-Caribbean culture, and ceremonies are often broadcast on the national TV station. Some non-Santeros, however, are openly hostile.

"I have to turn off the television almost every night," said Rojas. "It disgusts me, with all the dancing. It's the work of the occult. It's noth-ing more than folklore." Rojas, the son of a minister, coordinates seven churches in the country's fourth-largest Baptist mission. He and his family live in a small apartment above the mission's largest church, located in Pinar del Río. He says that Santería is widely celebrated because so many people in the government practice the religion. But for religious leaders, popularity does not equate legitimacy. To this day, many Evangelical and Catholic authorities question whether Santería is a true religion. When the pope visited Cuba in 1998, he said that traditional Santero beliefs deserve respect but could not be considered a "specific religion." Yet it's unlikely to disappear. Santería was born out of resistance and survival. Cubans have always flocked to Santería priests, or *babalawos*, during hard times to ease their weary bodies, minds, and souls; and the current climate of economic instability proves no exception. Madera says demand for his services has grown noticeably in recent years. It's a popularity that frustrates many Evangelicals. "Santería and Christianity cannot exist together," said Ramón, a youth-group organizer at the Baptist church. He is standing in front of the temple and sweat gathers on his forehead as the Caribbean sun beats down. A medley of vehicles sputters by, spewing black exhaust into the church. "The Bible says there aren't any other gods but Him in the heavens or on the earth."

But for Madera, Santería is more than just a religion—it's his life. "The Evangelicals," Madera says from his living room, "have a tremendous struggle. They're very self-righteous. They think they have the answers to everything. Everyone keeps their religion like a son. But Santeros don't go out to criticize other religions." "Yeah," pipes in Madera's mother, an ancient woman with fiery red hair and gray stubble on her chin, "those Evangelicals think they know everything."

"Look," he adds, "if you feel bad—spiritually, psychologically, or physically—you come to me, we pray to the orishas, and you feel better. How can healing be diabolical?" But as vocal as Cubans can be about their beliefs, Madera says he usually keeps his opinions to himself. "I have many Christian and Catholic friends," he says, "but I don't talk about religion."

Madera, his mother, his wife, and their son live in a two-roomed hovel at the end of a long, narrow passageway that winds its way off the street. The spartan abode offers a cool refuge from Pinar's heat. Madera sees between seven and eight clients per day, but he says demand for his services has gradually increased in recent years. Sometimes he goes to a Santero's house to perform a *consulta* or a *limpieza*, the Santería counseling and cleansing ceremonies, but usually worshippers come to see him.

"Take off your shoes and place your feet on the mat," Madera says to a client as he prepares for a *consulta*. We are in the back room of his house. The sharp scent of urine fills the room—a reminder of the small pig the

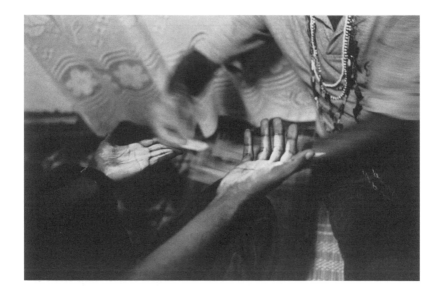

A *babalawo* begins the Santería ceremony by rubbing chalk on a man's hands, Havana, 2004. *Photo by Mimi Chakarova*

family is raising in the corner. "It only costs a few hundred pesos to buy one when they're young," Madera says, referring to the animal. After only a few months of eating whatever scraps of food the family can muster, the piglet will soon be fat enough to butcher and eat. While the young woman sits erect on a chair, her bare feet on the straw mat, Madera puts on a red and black velvet beret that he reserves for such ceremonies. "What do you call that hat?" I ask. "A hat," he replies, the corner of his mouth curling into a smile. But the cap is only a small part of the Madera's arsenal of religious paraphernalia. The dilapidated piano that juts out from the undersized kitchen is saddled with religious shrines, or *soperas*, dedicated to a motley array of orishas—Obbatalá, the god of power and health, Shangó, the god of morality, Yemayá the goddess of water.

Madera covers his and the woman's hands with white chalk and asks her to place a bill on the pile of shells and stones in the center of the mat. The monetary gift is a crucial element in Santería ceremonies–and one that Evangelicals criticize. "Money and religion don't mix," Damién says. "He can only say what he understands," Madera says, responding to the criticism. He insists Santería isn't a get rich quick scheme for *babalawos.* "Santería is for everyone," he adds. Most of the clients' money is used to buy the tobacco, rum, and sometimes animals that are offered to the orishas in various ceremonies. "It's not like in the United States," Madera says. "If I were living there, I'd be a millionaire from all the money Americans pay to those telephone psychics."

Madera repeatedly throws the stones, shells, and money onto the mat as he chants to the orishas. The shells speak. They say the numbers that combine in different ways spot the problem, lead to a story with a moral, or offer a piece of advice. He studies the patterns, and offers the woman his advice. "You are generally healthy, but if you feel a pain in your abdomen, go to the doctor—it could be your ovaries. . . . You are trustworthy and people are attracted to you. But be very careful with some of them, especially lesbians, homosexuals, and drunks."

Evangelicals' criticisms don't end with the Santeros. Relations with the Catholics have also been strained. They view Catholicism as a tired religion that relies on rehearsed prayers and arcane traditions to bring salvation—and they've taken their critique to the streets. In Havana, an Evangelical group passes out religious pamphlets after Sunday mass in front of Santa Rita, one of the largest churches in the country. "I don't mind if they're handing out pamphlets in front of the store or in front of military housing or wherever," said Jaoquín Bello, a layman volunteer for the church, his tight polo shirt straining to contain his round belly, "but after our masses? No."

"We don't just count numbers and say 'enough,'" Father Águilar says back in Pinar, adding that Evangelicals are too preoccupied with their official membership numbers. Águilar, a chubby patriarch of a man who begins most of his comments with "Well, my son," continues on. "You have to evangelize, but we try not to do it with fear or aggression. We try to educate with love and with God—and love demands respect."

But respect is often fleeting in Pinar's churches, and the town's religious leaders find themselves bickering over the particulars of faith. Águilar believes that communication is as imperative as boosting church memberships, but he says the Evangelicals have been stubborn. The Catholic Church, he says, has invited Damién and other Evangelical leaders to discuss the state of religion in Pinar del Río, as well as the possibility of coordinating small charity programs. The offer, he says, has been declined.

"Dialogue between the churches is very important," Águilar says, leaning back in his rocking chair. "But it takes two sides. We have demonstrated good faith . . . they have not. I hope that relations improve."

That's unlikely. "There is a famous Cuban saying," Rojas, the Baptist reverend says. "A good wall makes a good neighbor." Damién agrees. "I don't want to criticize. There are many Catholics that are very sincere in their religion—I was Catholic before I found the Evangelicals when I was fourteen. But you can't erase history. The Inquisition was brutal," he says, referring to the Catholic Church's purging of Jews and other minorities in fifteenth-century Europe. "They've invited us to these meetings, but we don't go," he adds, sipping on a glass of watered-down juice, a common beverage in these times of scarcity. Damién says the Catholics' history of global politicizing has damaged their relationship with God. "The Catholics are diplomats. Politics and religion shouldn't be mixed."

But the squabbling has not deterred locals from practicing religion. And for some *pinareños*, the particulars of each church are not important. "I go to the Baptist church often," says Mary Baez Íglesia, an elderly woman with dyed, jet black hair and pearly white dentures who lives around the corner from Rojas's church. When she hears that I'm investigating religion, she disappears into her bedroom to dig up her old Bible. It takes her several minutes to locate the worn, paperback volume that looks as old and dusty as her prerevolutionary house. Íglesia was raised Catholic, but stopped practicing during the revolution. In recent years, however, religion has beckoned once again. "The Baptist church is very beautiful," she says, as her nonreligious husband grunts under the worn bill of his baseball cap. "But I go to the Catholic Church a lot too. I just like it, with all the singing and the mass."

Still, switching churches isn't always so easy. And with many Cubans practicing religion for the first time, differing beliefs have created internal family strife. Jeremiah, a thirty-something Assembly of God member always flashing a broad smile, joined Damién's church four years ago along with his mother, two brothers, his wife, and his daughter. Damién introduced him as a convert: "He used to be a Santero . . . a drunk and a Santero." Jeremiah's face drops slightly behind his smile. "Yeah, I used to be a Santero, but that was all I knew. I didn't know Christ, and I didn't know it was diabolical." But he still has a brother and several friends who are practicing Santeros. He says their religious differences force them to have many discussions. "He talks and I listen, and then I talk and he listens," Jeremiah explained. "He hasn't converted yet, but I have faith in Jehovah." Ramón, a nineteen-year-old Baptist youth leader, says he joined the church two years ago after he accepted God into his heart. Ramón is having similar problems with his secular family. "It's difficult," he said with a nervous smile, "but now, God is my life. The church is my life. They don't understand, but I've had a complete conversion."

Crahan says Cubans, and especially Cuban youth, are joining churches in part because they are feeling increasingly disenchanted by the government's shortcomings and are looking for fulfillment outside of the revolution. "Young people feel particularly betrayed," she says. "In part, this is because the promises of the revolution and its certainties are obviously not seen to hold water with these individuals." Young Ramón does not speak so pointedly about the revolution, but in these times of scarcity, and with basic medical supplies at a premium, he admits that stories of God's healing powers helped pique his interest in the Baptist church. "There are many examples of God saving children," he said.

Many young Cubans are looking for promises and certainties in churches like Rojas's. On most Sundays, the faithful are forced to jockey for position outside his temple so they can peer in through the open-air windows that flank the building. One churchgoer said it was only a matter of time before more *pinareños* started practicing religion. "After the revolution, El Comandante said we couldn't practice anymore. But we kept pushing," he added, thrusting his elbow at an invisible enemy.

Still, there is a flip side to Evangelical growth. Despite the influx of young people, it has been difficult for the churches in Pinar del Río to recruit middle-aged members. Damién says attracting men of thirty-five years or older to the church has proven especially daunting. "They have work or they're in the armed forces," he explains. Crahan says the older generation is simply coming from a different place: "These are the people who participated in literacy campaigns, they received health care, and they do remember prerevolutionary Cuba." Their feelings are that "things have gone bad, but you can't blame the revolution."

Maybe not. But politics and religion are becoming inexorably intertwined. As Cubans continue to scramble for basic necessities, they have become increasingly dependent on churches to provide clothing, medicines, and even food to make up for the government's shortcomings. Religious leaders find themselves walking a precarious line between providing spiritual and physical fulfillment and angering Castro's government.

"Something has to change here," Damién continues, his brow knotted in concern. "Before, when the Soviets were around, we had everything, everyone was for socialism. But now we have very little. It's nothing for you to offer us aspirin, but you can't imagine how many people come to me every week asking for aspirin or some other medicine." And still, he says, it's not completely safe to be a Christian. "See that man over there?" Damién asks, pointing a gnarled finger at an elderly man at the back of the church. "He's in the police. . . . You don't know what it's like to live as a foreigner, as an enemy, in your own country."

And Damién is tired of being the enemy. He laments over simple things. "You know how difficult it is for me to go to Havana?" he asks, referring to the travel expenses and the financial inability for most Cubans to stay in a hotel. But even if he had the money, it wouldn't matter, he says. "You have to have relatives to stay with or the government is suspicious. Even going to our beaches for a visit is impossible. They're only for the tourists now."

But Damién, Madera, and the others stop short of saying that their churches are hotbeds of dissident organizing. "Santería is a religion of peace and healing," Madera says. "It can't be about rebellion." Rojas agrees, "There's no room for anything but the Bible in my church." He may be right, and many Evangelicals believe that's how the government wants to keep it. To accommodate their growing communities, Rojas and Damién have solicited construction permits from the government to build new temples for their respective churches. Both have been rejected. Many Evangelicals see these denials as a way for the government to control religious growth on the island.

"Look at us, we have to hold classes outside," Rojas says from the small vacant lot behind his church where he someday hopes to build a new temple. Space is even tighter at the Assembly of God. Damién lives with his wife in a tiny apartment above the church. The couple hopes to convert their small storage area into a much-needed temple addition. They're still waiting for a permit. To deal with space shortages, Damién says his church has opened "preaching points" in members' houses throughout the province. The Assembly of God has established 890 preaching points across the island. But still, Damién says officials will shut meetings down if more than fifteen people are present. The church constantly rotates the meetings between different living rooms. Johnson, its Caribbean director, says the government also tries to exert control over his church by grossly misrepresenting membership to downplay its impact on the island. Official numbers report 83,000 baptized Assembly of God members in Cuba, but Johnson says there are tens of thousands more practitioners.

Father Águilar also feels discrimination despite Cuba having become a lay state. "The method of oppression has just changed," Águilar says. "Now the government uses more psychological repression than physical," he adds, referring to government policies that still restrict complete religious freedom. The state routinely shuts down religious meetings in homes, for example, citing laws that limit the number of people allowed to congregate in private locations. "Perhaps it's changed in the sense that people can breathe easier, but it's still difficult." Although the majority of priests supported Castro's revolution, much of the hierarchy was in line with Batista and fled the island in 1959. And now, even though Pope John Paul II's 1998 visit opened up new possibilities for the religious communities, "the churches keep their distance from dissidents," Crahan says.

Apart from the Evangelicals, there are the Pastors for Peace, a group of progressive and activist U.S. church and community leaders that has been delivering so-called friend shipments to Cuba since 1992. In Havana, two American school buses from Pastors for Peace San Francisco were recently parked in front of a Baptist church. They were covered with sociopolitical statements painted in bright, multicolored letters written in English: "This bus is going to Cuba with medicine in defiance of the unjust U.S.-created embargo on Cuba." And on the back bumper, "Be a *real* revolutionary . . . practice your faith." This social justice group, however, focuses on humanitarian aid and highlights the embargo as unjust and immoral. It leaves the recruitment of souls to individual churches.

The Evangelicals have organized several events to spread God's word. Last year, the Assembly of God and other churches held an Evangelical religious rally in Pinar del Río's nearby baseball stadium. But the Catholics, Damién said, were not invited. The gathering came on the heels of a Protestant rally in Havana that drew more than 100,000 Cubans. "If the pope could do it, so could we," Damién says with a chuckle, referring to the 1998 papal mass that drew hundreds of thousands of Cubans. Despite prohibiting private gatherings of more than fifteen worshippers, the government has permitted the occasional release valves of religious fervor.

Many North American churches have shown their support by establishing relationships with their Cuban counterparts to help them cope

A family's dining room displays a framed drawing of Jesus Christ, Camagüey, 2001. *Photo by Mimi Chakarova*

with scarcity on the island. And these relationships have allowed many churches to provide much-needed clothing and medicine to some Cubans. In these times of scarcity, foreign donations can be a boon for local memberships. "If one minister has a car or a school, he'll be more popular," Crahan says. "Of course economics influence membership," says Rojas. "If you have a Bible to read and there are fans around to keep you cool, you will enjoy church more."

Even in Pinar, some religious leaders have traveled to the United States to foster these relationships and speak about conditions in Cuba. Rojas has visited several times and has been invited twice to First Baptist Church in Archdale, North Carolina, to preach and to receive "love offerings" of medicines, Bibles, and other necessities. Although Rojas still has several friends at First Baptist, he was shocked by the state of the Baptist faith in the United States. "They haven't lost their vision," he says, "but there is also great weakness. People work too much. They worry too much. Materialism has corrupted man." "He's just a whole lot more staunch in his beliefs," says Gary Green, a First Baptist Church member in Archdale, adding that he was a bit ashamed that his brethren drank and smoked in Rojas's presence.

Damién has also fostered relationships abroad. He has visited Assembly of God Churches in Los Angeles and Las Vegas ("People aren't meant to live in those conditions," he said, commenting on the desert heat), and Father Águilar has spent many months in Miami—most of them while recovering from knee surgery. But despite religion's ever changing role in Cuba—and it's ability to provide for some where the government cannot—it is difficult to know if churches will prove to be a major point of resistance against Castro. "I'm not going to predict what is going to happen," Crahan says. "Churches are stepping in to fill that void within their means. Their overseas connections and access to money make them prime candidates to do so."

In Cuba politics are life, but for Damién there are alternatives. "People think there are only two options," he says, holding up his small and index fingers. "To be for the revolution or against the revolution. But there's a third way," he adds while extending his thumb: "to be a *Christian.*"

Research assistance by Kelly Jackson Richardson

Son de Camagüey

∼ ÁNGEL GONZÁLEZ

Y morir por la patria es vivir.—*Cuban National Anthem*

From my airplane window I look down to the coast. There lies an island known by many names—the Bulwark of the Indies, the Faithful Isle, the Pearl of the Antilles, the Lady of the Mexican Gulf. "Cuando salí de Cuba," says a popular 1960s tune, "When I left Cuba, I left my life, I left my love . . . when I left Cuba I left my heart buried in there."

I have never left Cuba. Instead, I am visiting the country my father fled in 1961, returning to the cities and landscapes I have imagined since childhood. This is the land my ancestors discovered, populated, and built. Looking at it bathing in the Caribbean, I struggle to hold back tears. It must have been difficult to leave this land. Maybe that's why my uncle, Carmelo González del Castillo, chose to stay when my father left.

Who was Carmelo González? From what I know, he was an idealist, deeply involved in one of the most important events in the history of the Western hemisphere—the Cuban Revolution. Carmelo was a revolutionary, but also a counterrevolutionary. Some say he despised Castro, but despite his aristocratic background and his serving time in prison for fighting against the revolution, he lived out his life working for it. So who was Carmelo González? And how does he fit in our long familial tradition of warmongering, rebellion, and political involvement? That is what I have come to find out.

"Hay sol bueno, mar de espuma," there's good sun and a sea of foam, reads an advertisement at the airport, promising paradise-like beaches. To me, those words say much more: they come from a poem written in 1889 by José Martí when he lived in exile in the United States, a poem that, line by line, my grandmother asked me to memorize when I was a child. I, too, lived in a kind of exile, born as I was in Venezuela, but brought up in the Cuba of my grandmother's memory. From her I learned Martí's poem, the names of Cuba's first seven cities, the order in which they were founded, and the sweet Caribbean accent of Camagüey.

My grandmother Elba del Castillo is an aristocratic woman, a descendant of the liberal Cuban planters who rose against Spain in the wars of 1868 and 1895. She was born in the early years of the republic. Her father, Ángel Castillo y Quesada, commanded a regiment of the Cuban cavalry in 1895, following in the tradition of his father, General Ángel del Castillo Agramonte, who was one of the original conspirators behind the birth of the first Cuban republic in 1868. My great-great-grandfather was killed, according to the Cuban history books I used to read as a child, by a Spanish bullet, crying out, "See how a Cuban general dies!" Their battles became my childhood fantasies, and in my grandmother's room, full of books of Martí and maps of Cuba, I forgot entirely about Caracas and the limited life of a five-year-old. The endless stories about pirates, elegant ballrooms, revolutions, and the strange Marquis of Santa Lucía — a distant relative who had lived in England and ate canaries and mocking-birds — proved far more interesting, far more real.

My little brother and I commuted between kindergarten lessons about Bolívar's liberation of South America and my grandmother's Cuba. In both worlds, we indulged in the cult of independence heroes, but in my grandmother's country, we had heroes that bore our name. On the same shelf where my grandmother placed a glass of water to our ancestors — a magical custom inherited from her black nanny — there was an album that contained a picture of her family: my grandmother, my grandfather, Carmelo González de Ara, a dark, elegant Spanish accountant, Rose-crucian, and their two sons, Ángel and Carmelo. Ángel, my father, a student at the University of Havana when the photograph was taken, had inherited his mother's fair skin and ironic smile. Carmelo, my uncle, was a revolutionary student leader still in high school at the Liceo de Segunda Enseñanza of Camagüey. He bore his father's dark skin and fiery, Arab eyes.

That picture was taken in 1960, barely a year after the fall of Fulgencio Batista and the triumph of the Cuban Revolution. In the following months, that family, like many others of the time, would be divided between those who supported Castro and those who chose to leave. Like many members of the middle class, my grandfather had supported the revolution, but bridled at the executions and opposed Castro's embrace of communism. "Even the music is sad," he used to say of the socialist hymns of the era. In 1961, he arranged for my father and Carmelo to take a ship to Venezuela. My father left, but his brother stayed. By this time, Carmelo had turned from revolutionary to counterrevolutionary, and he was determined to oust Fidel.

"Your father was very smart, but Carmelo was always surrounded by women. And he was a *guapo*," my grandmother says using the Spanish word for "handsome." In its Cuban inflection, it also means "reckless" and "brave." Carmelo was a *guapo* like our grandfathers, the legendary fighters for the Cuban independence, had been.

It's an early, fresh Cuban morning, and I wake up to the sound of Fidel's voice on TV. I am staying at a splendid 1950s apartment in El Vedado. Sunlight fills the room, the smell of the sea, mixed with gasoline, is everywhere, just like the chirping of canaries. The caged bird is a Cuban obsession. This is the center of Havana which has the great hotels like the Nacional, the Capri, and the Habana Libre. Amid the ruined high-rises, crowds wait for the *camellos*, the huge Hungarian-made buses that can transport up to four hundred people. I try to picture Carmelo as an eight-year-old, at the time when my grandparents lived in this city, taking a different, American-made bus to school.

"Habana, quien no la ve no la ama," Havana, who hasn't seen it, cannot love it, goes the saying. And it is true: even though I was brought up with stories about its splendor, I never imagined it could be like this, the most beautiful city I have ever seen. Its late-nineteenth-century architecture reminds me of the monumental constructions of Madrid and Barcelona. Its warm climate and houses with verandas remind me of Sevilla. A huge Cuban flag flies from the Nacional, its lone star waving in defiance. Only in the presence of this flag have I felt something resembling pride, nationalism—sentiments I usually disregard. It's the symbol my grandfathers fought for.

I try to picture how it must have been before the revolution. Some things must look the same: the art deco buildings, the incredible abundance of 1950s cars. But many things that my father talked about are missing: the street vendors who used to sell mussels in lemon juice, the advertisements, the elegantly clad people, the bourgeoisie that built these modern houses and apartments that are now crumbling. Other things are here, however. The Yara movie theater that shows films by Tomás Gutiérrez Alea, and Coppelia, the ice cream parlor where Cubans stand in line to satisfy a national obsession with ice cream. My father would not recognize the Soviet-made Ladas and the East German Trabbis, symbols of an alliance with socialist countries; and he would be surprised at the Toyotas and the Nissans driven by the European, Canadian, and Mexican managers of the new economic regime.

I feel vaguely at home, for the weather, the colors, and the sounds of the street are remarkably like those of Caracas. These high-rises are part of a city that used to be American: they would not be out of place in Miami's South Beach. While Havana feels frozen in time, dynamism, energy, and wealth are slowly returning. Hundreds of foreigners walk the streets amid thousands of Cubans. Everyone is hustling. I can barely walk a couple of blocks without an *habanero* coming up to peddle cigars, a tour of the city, or a fine woman. Bicycle taxis swarm around tourist hot spots. The bar at the rooftop of the Hotel Inglaterra is as alive with music as it was during its heyday in the 1930s. Life is coming back to the frivolous city the revolution changed.

From the steps of the imposing University of Havana, founded in 1737, you can see the ocean, and I imagine my father and Carmelo meeting there, by El Malecón. My father, the practical twenty-two-year-old engineering student on his way to Venezuela, tried to talk his little brother into abandoning the fight against Castro, a fight that was not Cuban anymore. It was in the hands of the United States and the Soviet Union, the cold war superpowers. But Carmelo insisted on staying, and so my father left him standing by El Malecón. That was the last time they saw each other.

Carmelo Héctor Antonio González del Castillo was born in the city of Puerto Príncipe de Camagüey in 1942, at a time when the world was at war and Hemingway was chasing Nazi submarines off the coasts of Cuba. He belonged to an increasingly Americanized middle class that profited from the prosperity brought by the war.

From the air, I see the red tiles of his city, so different from the Bourbon-inspired glitz of Havana and so reminiscent of the early days of Spanish colonization. I can picture our great-grandparents riding on horseback through the surrounding plains, amid sugarcane factories on fire.

"What a joy. The city of Ignacio Agramonte, Ángel Castillo . . . this is the birthplace of immortal feats, and the immense dust of the streets seemed luminous to me." These lines were written in the late 1880s by Enrique Loynaz del Castillo, a distant relative of mine and Carmelo's cousin, who eventually became one of the main figures of the war of 1898. Loynaz was born in exile, and the Camagüey he returned to was the Cuban city that kept the traditions inherited from the Conquest in their purest form. Many families, like the Castillos, kept a strict record of their genealogy, tracing it back to the conquistador Vasco Porcallo de Figueroa.

As I descend from the Soviet-made Antonov whose safety signs are still imprinted in Cyrillic letters, I wonder if forty years of communism will have erased all traces of my family's past.

It's dusk already, and churches and royal palms dominate the skyline. It's hot and humid, and there are very few electric lights on—it looks so sinister and impoverished, this city of my ancestors. But in the central plaza, as if to assuage my fears, there's a statue of a man closely related to Carmelo and our family: Ignacio Agramonte, Camagüey's most prominent warrior in the struggle for independence against Spain.

Yolanda del Castillo is my grandmother Elba's sister, the youngest of the thirteen children of Colonel Ángel Castillo Quesada. She is eighty-six years old, and I am meeting her for the first time. I had talked to her by telephone, and when I call her from the Gran Hotel, she recognizes my voice. "Family is a strong tie," she says, adding that I talk just like my father, who lost his Cuban accent a long time ago and speaks like a *caraqueño*.

Yolanda lives on Calle Jaime, behind the Iglesia de la Soledad, Camagüey's impressive Romanesque church. In the entrance a young woman waits. She has pale skin and looks exactly like my grandmother, but sixty years younger. "Hola. I am Livia. We are family," says Livia del Castillo, Yolanda's niece, embracing me cautiously.

A lone oil painting of my great-great-grandfather dominates the wall— General Ángel del Castillo Agramonte, with his pointy mustache and beard and his sober military uniform. That portrait was painted in 1868, and a copy of it is present in every house of every branch of our family. We were taught to venerate it, and I always carry a copy with me. But I never imagined the original to be in color—all the copies my family has, which come from a photograph taken in a hurry before leaving in 1960, are in black and white. Our *abuelito*, as Livia refers to our ancestor, captured the first canon used by the Cuban Liberation Army during the first independence war.

"Ángel del Castillo had created the best-trained and most brilliant nu-

The original 1868
oil painting of Gen-
eral Ángel del Castillo
Agramonte, Camagüey,
2001. *Photo by Mimi
Chakarova*

cleus of the Liberation Army at the time," writes Jorge Juárez Cano in his
book *Apuntes de Camagüey* (Notes from Camagüey). His exploits ended
in 1869, when he was killed trying to defeat a Spanish garrison. He is described by historians as an impulsive, violent man with endless courage.
La tempestad a caballo, the storm riding on horseback, as he was called
by his followers. Carmelo and my father grew up in the shadow of this
portrait, surrounded by war memorabilia and the past glory of a patri-
otic family. "When Carmelo was a child, he wanted to be as brave as
abuelito," says Yolanda. Yolanda reminds me of my grandmother—aristocratic, headstrong, orderly. She and her husband were like parents to
Carmelo and my father when they were children. At times, they spent as
much as six months a year living at their home and their hacienda. "We
never had any children, so they were like ours," she says. The Carmelo of
Yolanda's stories is a brave, impulsive, and intelligent little kid. "We gave

a horse to your father and Carmelo when they were little," Yolanda says. "We kept it at our ranch. One morning, on hearing that the animal had fallen inside a hole in the field, Carmelo woke up and ran outside, screaming 'I am going to save my horse.' " The horse could be saved, but it was eventually sold. With the money, Yolanda bought my father and Carmelo their first suits.

I walk by the Casablanca movie theater, a whitewashed remainder of the times when the Cubans, the most avid moviegoers of the Western hemisphere, came to watch Humphrey Bogart and Ingrid Bergman. In 1959, Castro's revolutionaries put a bomb in this place. My uncle was involved in the affair.

Carmelo had grown up to be a popular high school student. At seventeen, he was elected president of the school's student federation. He identified with the family's independence heroes, and the building revolution against Batista offered an irresistible draw. He prepared Molotovs, distributed political fliers, and sold revolutionary bonds, which Yolanda bought in great quantities. The revolution triumphed in January 1959. Fidel entered the city, and my grandmother, like many other middle-class housewives, offered shelter to the long-haired, olive-clad *barbudos* (revolutionary fighters) on their march to Havana. The students expressed their sympathy toward the new government by wearing red and black armbands with the colors of the M-26 movement. Many thought democracy would follow. But the revolution proved to be "olive green on the outside, red on the inside," as many Cuban exiles would say. When Fidel embraced Marx, Carmelo, like many others who had cheered the revolution, objected.

Huber Matos, the revolutionary commander of the province of Camagüey, wrote a letter to Fidel in October 1959, resigning from his post and warning him of communist infiltration. Fidel answered by sending the legendary commander Camilo Cienfuegos to Camagüey to arrest Matos, who was then charged with plotting an uprising and sentenced to twenty years in prison. Others were unhappy as well. When Soviet foreign minister Anastas Mikoyan visited Cuba in April 1960, he placed a wreath in the shape of a hammer and sickle on the grave of José Martí. A group of students led by Alberto Muller protested by placing a wreath in the shape of a Cuban flag on it the following day. The students carried banners that read "Long live Fidel" and "Down with communism." The police broke the march and threw many of the students, including Muller, who knew my uncle, in jail. "It was there that we realized that Castro had the intention of establishing a totalitarian regime," says Muller, who lives in exile in Miami.

In the next couple of months, my uncle and others created the Directorio Revolucionario Estudiantil (Revolutionary Student Directorate) to overthrow Fidel. Muller said the members came from the student organizations that had led the fight against Batista. Carmelo was among those ready to form the counterrevolutionary *directorio*. "We are going to do to Castro the same thing we did to Batista," he told a cousin back then, and it wasn't long before he became the *directorio*'s provincial leader in Camagüey.

"Cuba has a very violent history. We have always been under attack. Even our ancestors came here attacking," says my great-uncle Laines as we enter his beautiful but run-down house on Calle Tomás Betancourt. He hugs me frequently, not quite believing that I am here. Laines was a baseball player, an adventurer. "I was the black sheep. There is always one in every generation," he says, referring to his favorite nephew who lived in this house after he got out of jail. Laines points to his brown and white square shirt. "This was a gift from your uncle," says the tall ninety-year old. "What a great man he was. What strength, what character!"

And the time he lived in called for it. After the arrest of Matos, the acts of violence multiplied, and most Cubans unable to live with a regime that had turned communist left. When the revolutionary governor of Camagüey heard that my father and his family were leaving, he summoned my father to his office, asking him to convince Carmelo to leave as well. Carmelo refused.

During that year of 1961, a strong guerrilla force composed of anticommunist students and peasants operated in the mountains of Escambray. Bombs exploded in the cities. Electricity plants were sabotaged. Insurgent expeditions disembarked every month, and the government detained more than 100,000 people to prevent an uprising on the eve of the Bay of Pigs. Sometimes it seemed as if the revolution would fail, but its opponents, who counted on American aid to counter Soviet support to the regime, were crushed.

In a dark room, full of portraits of old baseball legends and newspaper clippings, Laines keeps an archive of our family's history. "Look at this," he says, handing me a huge packet of newspaper clippings containing the history of the Castillos. "Our genealogical tree." Among the papers I find a yellow typewritten sheet, dated June 1962. Carmelo, it states, was part of "a group of counterrevolutionaries that had been operating in our country under the political direction of the State Department of the United States, and its organization of betrayal and espionage denominated CIA." The transcript says Carmelo and others were caught unloading a weapons shipment in Santa Cruz, in the northern province of Pinar del Río. They intended to set out for south Florida to join "mercenary forces" there. They were carrying weapons and fired them against security forces when they were discovered. "Carmelo González y del Castillo was captured with an olive green uniform and a pistol caliber .975," says the report.

Yolanda and her husband got news of the ambush through the Voice of America. The first radio report announced that Carmelo González had been killed. "That very same afternoon I had had an intuition," she says. "I told my husband to prepare luggage, for we would have to make a trip." Her husband and my grandfather took Yolanda's car and went out to ask about Carmelo's whereabouts. State security said that he had been captured alive. Three months later, he was transferred to Camagüey, unrecognizable behind his prisoner's beard. According to Yolanda, young communists drove their cars around the prison screaming "paredón para Carmelo" (execute Carmelo). But Carmelo wasn't shot. At twenty, he was sentenced to thirty years in prison. That was the end of his counterrevolution.

A bicycle taxi takes me to the Children's Hospital. "This used to be known as La Colonia Española, a clinic for rich people," says my taxi driver, pedaling furiously. I step down off the cab, pay my fare, and start taking pictures of the yellow, formerly luxurious 1920s building. A middle-aged man in a *guayabera*—the Cuban white plaid shirt that is still a symbol of tropical elegance—comes toward me. He is a state security agent, I'm sure—a journalist friend who lived in Cuba told me once that the *guayabera* is the uniform of state security. He asks me what am I doing. "My grandfather died here," I answer.

In April 1964 Carmelo was allowed a short visit to my grandfather on his deathbed. He arrived at the hospital escorted by state security guards. "Your grandfather could barely recognize Carmelo," says Laines, who witnessed the encounter. Carmelo was eventually transferred to prison at Isla de Pinos, rebaptized Isle of Youth. My grandmother had to traverse across the island to see him. His rebelliousness earned him long periods of time in the *gaveta*, literally a "drawer," a small cell with no light, which damaged his eyesight. While he was in prison, he married the daughter of a prominent official of the regime. Soon after, his sentence was commuted to seven years, but even before he left prison, his marriage failed.

"Carmelo lived here right after his liberation," says Laines, showing me Carmelo's shoes and college textbooks. "He slept on that very same sofa you're sitting on." When Carmelo was set free in 1969, he found work as an electrician at a local factory. The next year he began studying agronomy at the University of Havana. And in 1974, the same year that he married Josefina de Quesada, a cousin of his and a Communist Party militant, he started to work at Triangle 3, Camagüey's biggest ranch. Eventually, he became the director. "Even after he left, he used to come here all the time in his jeep. 'Uncle! Uncle!' he used to yell," Laines says, "and drove me all around the city."

"Your uncle was a great man," says Jesús Rodríguez, one of Carmelo's best friends and the director of Triangle 3, Camagüey's biggest state-owned ranch. Camagüey differs from the other provinces of Cuba in the fact that its wealth is based on cattle, not sugarcane. Rodríguez reminds me of a Venezuelan hacendado, with his macho manners, straw hat, and an assurance that comes from years of experience. He is a man in his late fifties, the same age my uncle would be if he were alive. "He saved me more than once from being fired," Rodríguez remembers. I imagine Carmelo as his friend describes him, sitting at his desk, going through two packs of cigarettes a day, smoking the butts when he ran out. "He didn't want to interrupt his work to look for more cigarettes," Rodríguez says.

That discipline enabled Carmelo to become a leader in the Triangle. I have a picture of him in a white *guayabera*, giving a solemn speech in front of an audience, maybe talking about the wonders of the plan, defending the achievements of the revolution. I ask Rodríguez about Carmelo's revolutionary involvement. In Miami, the font of all Cuban gossip, I had heard that Carmelo might have been a double agent—a circumstance that would explain the commuted sentence, the decision to stay. Rodríguez doubts it. Carmelo failed when he was young," Rodríguez explains. "He was a revolutionary, but became involved with some people in this province that betrayed the ideals they had been fighting for, and he paid for it. But this is a great revolution, and it knows how to recognize a leader."

Josefina de Quesada is a handsome woman in her fifties. Even though she works as chief nurse in one of Camagüey's hospitals and teaches at the local university, she lives in a cramped apartment in a modest neighborhood close to the train station. She was a nursing student when she started dating Carmelo. Josefina, who is accompanied by her sister Elita, brings out a folder of pictures. And there he is, larger than life. In one taken in Angola in 1978, he is standing in front of a truck, shirtless, smiling, looking at the horizon while one of his comrades aims a Kalashnikov at some unknown target. "He was an agricultural advisor," says Josefina, who remains a Communist Party militant. When I ask again, specifically about what he was doing in Africa during a two-year stint that ended in 1980, Josefina insists he was an agricultural advisor. The picture suggests more, but I don't bother to press. Instead, I can't help but feel proud to see my uncle there, looking at the horizon, carrying the family's martial tradition to other lands, other continents. I can picture him in the swamps of Kuanza, giving instructions to Angolese farmers, or, who knows, soldiers. "In Angola they used to mistake Carmelo for a Moor," says Josefina.

Cuba's involvement in Angola reached its height in 1975, when the Portuguese colonial government retreated from the country. Cuban volunteers helped the Movement for the Liberation of Angola, a Marxist guerrilla group, gain control of the situation. And during the next decade, more than 50,000 Cuban troops helped the newly established government control insurgency and repel a South African military invasion. The fight became, in Cuba's eyes, a war against apartheid. And Cuba's victory over South African troops is regarded as one of the most important feats in Cuban military history, celebrated both in Cuba and in Miami. Its victor, General Arnaldo Ochoa, was regarded by many as Fidel's potential successor. But he fell into disgrace in 1989 and was judged, demoted, and shot under drug-trafficking charges by the same revolution that he defended.

Josefina dispels the notion that Carmelo was a counterrevolutionary. "He failed when he was very young," continues Josefina, echoing what I heard from Rodríguez. "He got involved with some people he shouldn't have been, with that traitor Huber Matos. But when he was in prison they saw that he was a good man, brave and stubborn, and they gave him the opportunity to join the revolution." "Carmelo could have left, but he didn't," she says, "because he convinced himself of the mistake he made when he was young." Josefina said that Carmelo never became a communist militant himself, but his honesty and character were such that he

Resting child, Camagüey, 2001.
Photo by Mimi Chakarova

was allowed to join the ranks of the revolution abroad and was given a top responsibility at the state ranch. "He always had a car," she adds, to underline the sign of his privileged status. "But the guilt of having failed at such a young age haunted him for the rest of his life," she continues. His life demonstrated it. He worked hard in keeping up production at the state-owned ranch, collaborated with state security, and participated in the revolution's exotic adventures abroad.

Carmelo's heavy smoking developed into cancer in 1984. The disease was detected in September, and three months later he died. More than three hundred people attended his funeral. According to several accounts, it resembled an official funeral. The entourage included representatives from the Ministry of the Interior, who said that Carmelo had worked for state security and that his efforts had been greatly appreciated by the revolution.

Back in Havana I sit on a terrace overlooking the Paseo del Prado, the city's equivalent to the Champs-Elysées. From here I see the Capitol, a perfect imitation of the one in Washington, DC. I also see the Teatro del Tacón, the Madrilene buildings, and the art deco skyscrapers built by American banks, silent monuments to a Cuba that might have been. I wish Carmelo were here, sharing a drink with me and telling me if it was worth it, if the country he inherited is better off now than it was in 1959. I would ask him if there are not different ways to establish justice and to satisfy nationalist pride than give away most freedoms and submit, even symbollically, to the voice of a caudillo. I wonder if my uncle imagined that the voice would last for so long. What would he think of his nephew, a student at an American university, sitting on this terrace full of European tourists, watching his revolution come to an end?

Suggested Reading

Ackerman, Holly. "Searching for Middle Ground: Cuba's Chronic Dilemma." *Peace News*, January 1997.

Ackerman, Holly, and Juan M. Clark. *The Cuban Balseros: Voyage of Uncertainty*. Miami: The Policy Center for the Cuban American National Council, 1995.

Adams, David. "Cuban-Americans Support Repatriation," *St. Petersburg Times*, May 21, 1995.

Anderson, Jon Lee. "Letter from Havana." *New Yorker*, February 21, 2000.

"Approved Cuban Migrants." Bureau of Western Hemisphere Affairs, U.S. Department of State, August 28, 2000.

Arnold, Michael, "Tourists Flock to Cuba's Version of Paradise." *Pacific*, December 1991–January 1992.

Barberia, Lorena. "Remittances to Cuba: An Evaluation of Cuban and U.S. Government Policy Measures." Working paper, MIT, 2002.

Bethell, Leslie, ed. *Cuba: A Short History*. New York: Cambridge University Press, 1993.

Bragg, Rick. "Cuba's New Refugees: Rafts Are Out, Hiring Smugglers Is Back In." *New York Times*, July 21, 1999.

Brent, William Lee. *Long Time Gone*. New York: Times Books, 1996.

Brinkley-Rogers, Paul. "People on Run Finding Selves at Home Abroad with Castro." *Miami Herald*, March 10, 2001.

Castañeda, Jorge G. *Compañero: The Life and Death of Che Guevara*. New York: Knopf, 1999.

———. *Utopia Unarmed: The Latin American Left after the Cold War*. New York: Knopf, 1993.

Castro, Fidel. Interview (in Spanish) by Havana Tele Rebelde and Cuba Vision Networks, August 6, 1994.

———. *Women and the Cuban Revolution: Speeches and Documents*. Ed. Elizabeth Stone. New York: Pathfinder, 1981.

Catasús, S., et al. *Cuban Women: Changing Roles and Population Trends*. Geneva: International Labour Organisation, 1988.

"Chronology of U.S.-Cuban Relations, 1958–1999." U.S. Department of State, 2000.

Church, George. "Cubans Go Home." *Time*, September 5, 1994.

Colomer, Joseph. "Exit, Voice, and Hostility in Cuba." *International Migration Review* 34, no. 2 (2000).

Colon, Yves. "Weather Hard Times Embolden Immigrants." *Miami Herald*, January 20, 1999.

Corti, Egon Caesar. *A History of Smoking*. Trans. Paul England. London: Harrap, 1931.

"Cuba Country Report." The Economist Intelligence Unit, United Kingdom, February 2003. Available at usinfo.state.gov/regional/ar/us_cuba/cubach .html.

"Cuba: CPJ's Mission Confirms Dire Situation for Imprisoned Journalists and Their Families." July 18, 2003. Available at www.cpi.org.

"Cuba Party Central Committee Says Time Is Ripe for Political and Institutional 'Improvement,'" BBC *Summary of World Broadcasts*, February 19, 1990.

"Cuba's Agricultural Revolution: A Return to Oxen and Organics." World Resources 2000–2001. People and Ecosystems: The Fraying Web of Life. United Nations Development Programme. World Bank, World Resource Institute. Available at www.sustag.wri.org/pubs.

DeGeorge, Gail, and Gail Reed. "Private Farming: Ten Acres and a Loan." *Business Week*, March 17, 1997.

Deleplace, Ghislain. "A Model of the Dollarized Cuban Economy. Working paper, delivered at the 20th Symposium on Banking and Monetary Economics, University of Birmingham, England, June 5–6, 2003.

De Young, Karen. "Cuba Climbs Economic Ladder." *Washington Post*, July 24, 2000.

Diaz-Briquets, Sergio. "Emigrant Remittances in the Cuban Economy: Their Significance during and after the Castro Regime." In *Proceedings of the Fourth Annual Meeting of the Association for the Study of the Cuban Economy (ASCE)*, vol. 4.

Dominguez, Jorge I. "The Country Castro Will Leave Behind." *New York Times*, July 25, 2003.

Emling, Shelly. "Five Years after Mass Exodus, Smuggling of Cubans Rises." *Palm Beach Post*, June 18, 1999.

Espín Guillois, Vilma. *Cuban Women Confront the Future: Three Decades after the Revolution*. Melbourne: Ocean, 1991.

———. *La mujer en Cuba: Familia y sociedad; Discursos, entrevistas, documentos*. Havana: La Habana Federación de Mujeres Cubanas, 1990.

Espino, María Dolores. "International Tourism in Cuba: An Economic Development Strategy?" Available at *lanic.utexas.edu/la/cb/cuba/asce/cuba1/ espino.html*.

"Exclusive Cigar to Light Up Havana." *Miami Herald*, February 9, 1998.

"Exit Controls and GOC [Government of Cuba]–Imposed Barriers to Travel." Bureau of Western Hemisphere Affairs, U.S. Department of State, 2000. Available at usembassu.state.gov/Havana/wwwhexit.html.

"Fact Sheet: The Cuban Adjustment Act." Office of Cuban Affairs, Bureau of Western Hemisphere Affairs, U.S. Department of State, March 16, 2000.

Faiola, Anthony. "Spanish Firms Revive Latin American Conquest." *Washington Post*, February 14, 2000.

García, María Cristina. *Havana, USA: Cuban Exiles and Cuban Americans in South Florida, 1959-1994*. Berkeley: University of California Press, 1996.

García Márquez, Sandra, Marika Lynch, and Eunice Ponce. "Crash Survivors Can Stay in U.S." *Miami Herald*, September 22, 2000.

Geyer, Georgie Anne. *Guerrilla Prince: The Untold Story of Fidel Castro*. Kansas City, Mo.: Andrews McMeel, 2001.

Golden, Tim. "Just Another Cuban Family Saga." *New York Times*, April 23, 2000.

González, David. "At Edges of Elian's Spotlight Are Other Divided Families." *New York Times*, February 14, 2000.

"Gorbachev and Castro at Havana News Conference," BBC *Summary of World Broadcasts*, April 6, 1989.

Grogg, Patricia. "Population: Migration from Cuba Is Mainly Economic, Study Says." Inter Press Service, September 18, 1998.

Gunn, Gillian. "The Sociological Impact of Rising Foreign Investment." Georgetown University Cuba Briefing Paper Series, January 1993. Available at www.trinitydc.edu/academics/depts/Interdisc/International/Caribbean%20Briefing%20Papers.htm.

Gunn-Clissold, Gillian. "Can the Windward Islands Survive Globalization?" Georgetown University Caribbean Briefing Paper Series, March 2001.

———. "Reaching Out To, But Not Touching, Cubans." *San José Mercury News*, January 12, 1999.

———. "U.S. Policy Changes Won't Help Most Cubans." *San José Mercury News*, January 12, 1999.

Hernández-Catá, Ernesto. "The Fall and Recovery of the Cuban Economy in the 1990s: Mirage or Reality?" IMF working paper, April 2001. Available at www.eldis.org/static/DOC8613.htm.

"The Hispanic Population in the United States." U.S. Department of Commerce, Economics, and Statistics Administration, U.S. Census Bureau, March 2000.

Holt-Seeland, Inger. *Women of Cuba*. Trans. Elizabeth Hamilton Lacoste with Mirtha Quintanales and José Vigo. Westport, Conn.: L. Hill, 1982.

"The Information Age," 2003 World Development Indicators, World Bank. Available at www.worldbank.org/data/wdi2004/pdfs/Tables_4.pdf.

"INS Fact Sheet: Third Special Cuban Migration Program." U.S. Department of State, June 5, 1998.

"Jet Taken to Cuba from Coast in Longest Hijacking in U.S." *New York Times*, June 18, 1969.

Kaufman Purcell, Susan. "Collapsing Cuba." *Foreign Affairs* 71, no. 1 (1991–92).

Klepak, Hal. "Cuba's Foreign and Defense Policies in the 'Special Period.'" Canadian Foundation for the Americas. February 25, 2000. Available at www.focal.ca.

"Latin America/Caribbean Admissions Program." Bureau of Population, Refugees, and Migration, U.S. Department of State, March 1, 2001.

Lederer, Edith M. "U.S. Urges Cuba to Support Family Reunification." Associated Press, September 22, 2000.

LeoGrande, William M. *Our Own Backyard: The United States in Central America, 1977–1992*. Chapel Hill: University of North Carolina Press, 1998.

Lewis, Oscar, Ruth M. Lewis, and Susan M. Rigdon. *Living the Revolution: An Oral History of Contemporary Cuba*. 3 vols. Urbana: University of Illinois Press, ca. 1977–78.

Lynch, Marika. "New Country Proves Vastly Different Than Cuban Rafters' Dreams." *Miami Herald*, July 5, 2000.

Mabry, Marcus. "Putting the Squeeze on Fidel." *Newsweek*, September 14, 1992.

Martin, Lionel. *The Early Fidel: Roots of Castro's Communism*. Secaucus, N.J.: L. Stuart, 1978.

Martínez, Sandra. "Cuban Refugees Flood onto Keys." *Miami Herald*, November 6, 2000.

Martínez McNaught, Hugo. "The Black Market Flourishes." *Pacific*, spring/summer 1992.

Masud-Piloto, Felix Roberto. *From Welcomed Exiles to Illegal Immigrants: Cuban Migration to the U.S., 1959–1995*. Lanham, Md.: Rowman and Littlefield, 1996.

McManus, Jane. *Cuba's Island of Dreams: Voices from the Isle of Pines and Youth*. Gainesville: University Press of Florida, 2000.

Mead, Walter Russell. "Castro's Successor?" *New Yorker*, January 26, 1998.

Miller, Tom. *Trading with the Enemy: A Yankee Travels through Castro's Cuba*. New York: Basic Books, 1996.

Moody, John. "Splits in the Family." *Time*, September 5, 1994.

Moore, Marjorie, and Adrienne Hunter. *Seven Women and the Cuban Revolution*. Toronto: Lugus, 1997.

Nieves, Gail Epstein. "Cuba's Spy Network Revealed." *Miami Herald*, January 12, 2001.

Nollinger, Mark. "Cuba Returns to the Caribbean." *Pacific*, spring/summer 1992.

"No More Socialist Camp, Castro Says." TASS Agency, March 19, 1990.

Nuccio, Richard A. "Unmaking Cuba Policy: The Clinton Years." *Foreign Service Journal* 75, no. 10 (1998).

Ojito, Mirta. "Fleeing Cuba, Hoping to Soar on New Stag." *New York Times*, December 5, 2003.

Ondetti, Gabriel. "Western European and Canadian Relations with Cuba after the Cold War." Programs in International Affairs, Trinity College, Caribbean Project. 1995. Available at www.trinitydc.edu/academics/depts/Interdisc/International/Caribbean%20Briefing%20Papers.htm.

Padula, Alfred. "Cuba Comes Home." *Times of the Americas*. February 21, 1990.

Pérez, Jesus Guanche. *Espano en la Savia de Cuba: Los hispánicos en el etnos cubano*. Havana: Editorial de Ciencias Sociales, 1999.

Pérez, Lisandro. "Saving Elián." *Frontline*, PBS, February 6, 2001. Available at www.pbs.org/wgbh/pages/frontline/shows/elian/interviews/perez.html.

Pérez, Louis A., Jr., ed. *Slaves, Sugar, and Colonial Society: Travel Accounts of Cuba, 1801–1899*. Wilmington, Del.: Scholarly Resources, 1992.

Portes, Alejandro, and Alex Stepick. *City on the Edge: The Transformation of Miami*. Berkeley: University of California Press, 1993.

Randall, Margaret. *Women in Cuba: Twenty Years Later*. New York: Smyrna, 1981.

Rice, John. "Castro Details Woes as Cuba Marks Its Fortieth."*Chicago Sun-Times*, July 27, 1993.

Robinson, Linda. "Is a New Exodus in the Cards?" *U.S. News and World Report*, August 22, 1994.

Robinson, Linda, Kenneth T. Walsh, and Tim Zimmermann. "Storm Clouds over Havana." *U.S. News and World Report*, September 12, 1994.

Roman, Mar. "Spanish Visitor to Cuba Find New Family in Havana; Cubans Rediscover Spanish Roots Too." Associated Press, February 3, 2003.

Romney, Lee. "Castro's Capitalism." *Pacific*, spring/summer 1992.

Ross, James E., and María Antonia Fernández Mayo. "Cuba's Dollar Food Market and U.S. Exports." Cuba in Transition, volume 13. Washington, D.C.: Association for the Study of the Cuban Economy, 2003.

Scarpaci, Joseph L. "The Emerging Food and Paladar Market in Havana." Cuba in Transition, volume 5. Washington, D.C.: Association for the Study of the Cuban Economy, 1995.

Sierra, Jerry. "The Spanish-Cuban-American War: Also Known as the Sec-

ond War for Cuban Independence." Available at www.historyofcuba.com/
history/scaw/spawar.htm.

Smith, Lois M., and Alfred Padula. *Sex and Revolution: Women in Socialist Cuba*. New York: Oxford University Press, 1996.

Smith, Wayne S. "Castro's Cuba: Soviet Partner or Nonaligned?" Latin American Program, Woodrow Wilson International Center for Scholars, Washington, D.C., 1984.

———.*The Closest of Enemies: A Personal and Diplomatic Account of U.S-Cuban Relations*. New York: Norton, 1987.

Stubbs, Jean. *Tobacco on the Periphery: A Case Study in Cuban Labour History, 1860-1958*. London, Cambridge University Press, 1985.

Sullivan, Mark P. "Cuba: Background and Current Issues for Congress." Congressional Research Service, Library of Congress, January 17, 2001.

Suro, Roberto. *Strangers among Us: How Latino Immigration Is Transforming America*. New York: Knopf, 1998.

Szulc, Tad. *Fidel: A Critical Portrait*. New York: Morrow, 1986.

Thomas, Hugh S. *Cuba: The Pursuit of Freedom*. New York: Harper and Row, 1971.

Thomas, Hugh S., Georges A. Fauriol, and Juan Carlos Weiss. *The Cuban Revolution, Twenty-Five Years Later*. Boulder, Colo.: Westview, 1984.

Thomas, Jo. "The Last Days of Castro's Cuba." *New York Times*, March 14, 1993.

Timerman, Jacobo. *Cuba: A Journey*. Trans. Toby Talbot. New York: Knopf, 1990.

Verdon, Lexie. "Thousands in Cuba Ask Peruvian Refuge." *Washington Post*, April 7, 1980.

Walsh, Kenneth T. "Following in Kennedy's Footsteps." *U.S. News and World Report*, September 12, 1994.

Wong, Edward. "Cuban Boat Immigrants Have Benefited from Cold-War Era Legislation." *New York Times*, April 20, 2000.

Notes on Contributors

JULIANA BARBASSA, a native of Brazil, is covering immigration issues, the environment, and agriculture for the Associated Press in California.

ANA CAMPOY, a native of Mexico, is a reporter with Dow Jones Newswires in Frankfurt/Main, Germany. She covers macroeconomics and economic integration in Germany and the Euro Zone.

MIMI CHAKAROVA is a lecturer in photography at the Graduate School of Journalism at the University of California, Berkeley.

LYDIA CHÁVEZ is a former reporter in Latin America for the *New York Times* and currently serves as chair of the executive committee at the Center for Latin American Studies and associate professor at the Graduate School of Journalism at the University of California, Berkeley. She is the author of *The Color Bind: California's Battle to End Affirmative Action* (1998).

JOHN COTÉ is a reporter for the *Modesto Bee*.

JULIAN FOLEY works as a freelance writer in Berkeley, California.

ÁNGEL GONZÁLEZ, a native of Venezuela, is a reporter for *Al Día*, the Spanish-language daily published by the *Dallas Morning News*.

MEGAN LARDNER is a producer for public television and a freelance writer.

EZEQUIEL MINAYA works as a reporter for the *Los Angeles Times*.

DANIELA MOHOR, who has dual citizenship in Chile and France, is a freelance reporter based in Santiago, Chile. She writes on social and international issues for different magazines including *El Sábado*, the Saturday supplement of Chile's leading newspaper *El Mercurio*.

ARCHANA PYATI is living in Colorado Springs.

ALICIA ROCA lives in the Bay Area and is working on a memoir.

OLGA R. RODRÍGUEZ, a native of Mexico, is a correspondent with the Associated Press in Mexico, where she covers the U.S.-Mexican border.

BRET SIGLER is a documentary filmmaker and freelance writer living in Brooklyn, New York.

ANNELISE WUNDERLICH is a documentary filmmaker living in San Francisco. Her work has a strong focus on Latin America and Latino communities in the United States.

Index

Page numbers in italics indicate photographs.

Library of Congress Cataloging-in-Publication Data

Capitalism, God, and a good cigar : Cuba enters the twenty-first
century / edited by Lydia Chávez ; with photographs by
Mimi Chakarova.
p. cm.
Includes bibliographical references and index.
ISBN 0-8223-3482-8 (cloth : alk. paper)
ISBN 0-8223-3494-1 (pbk. : alk. paper)
1. Cuba—Civilization—21st century. 2. Cuba—Economic
conditions—21st century. 3. Cuba—Social conditions—21st
century. 4. Cuba—Civilization—21st century—Pictorial
works. 5. Interviews—Cuba. I. Chávez, Lydia.
II. Chakarova, Mimi.
F1788.C25643 2005
972.9106′4—dc22   2004027165